Database-Driven Web Sites

Database-Driven Web Sites

Jesse Feiler

Morgan Kaufmann Publishers, Inc.
San Francisco, California

MORGAN KAUFMANN PUBLISHERS, INC.
340 Pine Street
San Francisco, CA 94104
www.mkp.com

Library of Congress Catalog Card Number: 98-48692
International Standard Book Number: 0-12-251336-3

Printed in the United States of America
99 00 01 02 03 IP 9 8 7 6 5 4 3 2 1

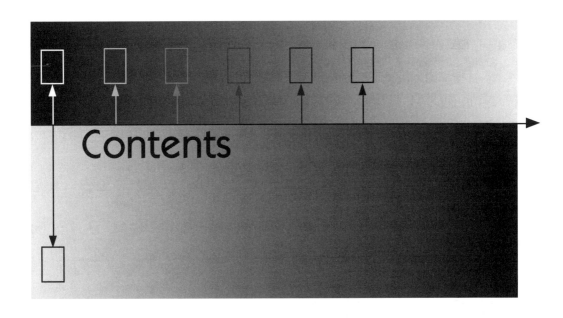

Contents

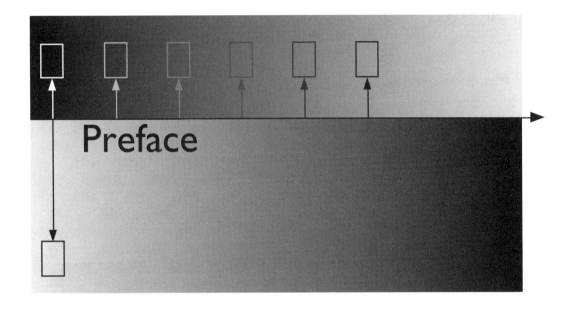

Preface

This book helps database developers add Web capabilities to their databases; it also is designed for Web masters who want to add database functionalities to their Web sites…and it also is designed for people who are new to both databases and Web development. It covers the general issues in the first part and then goes on to more detail in the sections that follow.

Depending on your background, you may want to skim (or even skip) certain detailed chapters—or to jump ahead for more thorough discussions of issues with which you are somewhat familiar. Database-driven Web sites are so powerful in large part because you need to know a little—and only a little—about several major technologies. Nonetheless, the fact that several technologies are involved does *mean that there are a number of different sets of terminology to learn (sometimes including different terms for the same concepts in the worlds of databases, the Web, and networks).*

For More Information...

You can find further information on this topic (together with errata for the book) on the author's Web site at http://www.philmontmill.com.

Application Servers

Application servers are discussed in "Application Servers and Development Tools" starting on page 169. They are a critical part of database-driven Web sites. In the case of large sites, application servers can be a very large part of the site's design and functionality. An entire book could be written about application servers—and it has: *Application Servers: Powering the Web-Based Enterprise* by Jesse Feiler (Morgan Kaufmann, 1999).

Acknowledgements

Database-driven Web site developers, owners, and designers from around the world have graciously provided information about their sites. This book would not have been possible without the help of Enrico di Cesare, Glenna Giveans, Cindy Miller, Jonathan Paull, Corey Redlien, Mike Senechal, Daniel Starr, Marie Verdun, and Mark Wickens.

Internet service providers TNet (Taconic Technology) and Digital Forest have provided answers to key questions at critical moments. In particular, Holly Bogenholm (Digital Forest) and Mike Brooks (TNet) deserve to be thanked for their quick answers to sometimes obscure questions.

Ken Morton and Julie Champagne of Morgan Kaufmann once again have provided the skills and expertise that contribute mightily to the successful development of a book like this. Mary Prescott's copy editing is patient and thorough—and a tremendous help to an author. Finally, Gary Ragaglia of Metro Design deserves credit for an elegant and striking cover.

Carole McClendon of Waterside Productions has made this project—like so many others—go smoothly.

This book was written and produced on Macintosh computers using Adobe FrameMaker. Other products used include Adobe Photoshop, FileMaker Pro, Flash-It, FreeHand, Microsoft Word, Microsoft Windows, SoftWindows, Microsoft Access, and AppleWorks.

Despite the help and assistance from so many people, any errors remain the author's.

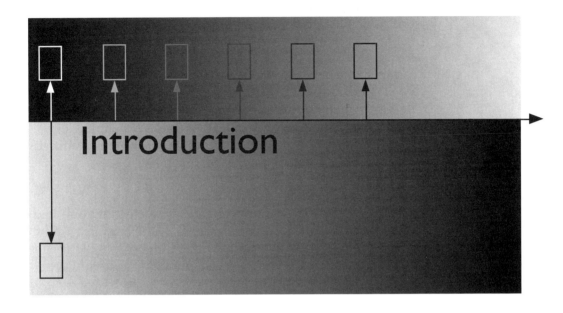

Introduction

In the 1980s, many of the world's largest computer users—governments and corporations alike—faced a looming crisis: a programming backlog. At the rate that computer programs were being requested and then being written and debugged, one organization after another calculated that a decade or more would elapse before the backlog could be erased. And that did not take into account new requests that would inevitably be made.

It also did not take into account the proliferation of personal computers; the rise of end-user productivity tools such as word processors, spreadsheets, and personal database; and the telcommunications revolution of the last two decades which make instantaneous communications (in all media) a way of life. (Some old timers can remember "booking" an intercontinental telephone call—usually the day before they wanted to actually talk to someone overseas.)

Today, the Internet provides a tool that enables a large number of people (but still a very small fraction of the earth's population) to communicate with one another and to find all sorts of information remarkably quickly. Yet many people are surprised to find out how much information is not on the Internet—and how much of it is out of date or wrong.

The Internet—or at least the World Wide Web—is still largely a highly labor-intensive and manual project. If anyone had time to calculate a "Web page backlog"—the amount of time it would take to actually produce all the Web pages requested by people around the world, the amount of time would probably be measured in centuries.

The Web functions most efficiently when it presents information from a primary source—the owner or originator of the information. Every time a Web page is designed that relies on a designer copying data from another location (whether by typing, scanning, or cutting and pasting), the backlog lengthens—as does the chance of error. On the other hand, every time a Web page is designed that automatically retrieves information from a data source that is maintained by someone else, that backlog is cut down, and the margin for error is reduced.

Databases are an ideal tool to do this: they have been designed over decades to provide high performance in storing, retrieving, and indexing data; they also all come with a host of parameters and settings that let the database designer control the quality of the data. Fields can be specified as being required, or of having a certain range of values; the integrity of the database can be maintained by specifying that given relationships among certain data elements must be maintained (for example, a sum must equal its components).

New technology embodied in application servers and rapid application development tools let data from databases be merged automatically with templates to produce changing HTML pages. Some leaders in this field produce Web sites with hundreds of pages, only a handful of which have been designed by hand. The others are all generated automatically as needed.

For some organizations, this technology means a drastic reduction in cost; for many, many others, however, it means the difference between being able to have a Web site (and a good one, at that) and not being able to afford the ongoing maintenance. The examples in this book are mostly drawn from the ranks of small organizations. It would not be surprising to find the largest companies in the world doing this; what may surprise—and even inspire—you is finding the small enterprises taking advantage of these tools. In fact, technologies such as these give a proportionately greater benefit to small rather than large organizations.

Who Can Do It?

Database-driven Web sites are within the reach of almost every Web user. This book describes the processes involved in setting up such a site. Programmers, database administrators, Web page designers, and interested Web users will not find their abilities unduly taxed by the tasks needed to create a database-driven Web site such as the one shown in Figure I-1.

This is the home page for a database-driven Web site; it comprises two frames (separate Web pages). The one on the left is a standard HTML page; it is located on a Web server in upstate New York. The larger frame (on the right) contains information retrieved from a database; the database and its Web server are located in Seattle. Users rarely if ever notice that this page has such geographically varied sources.

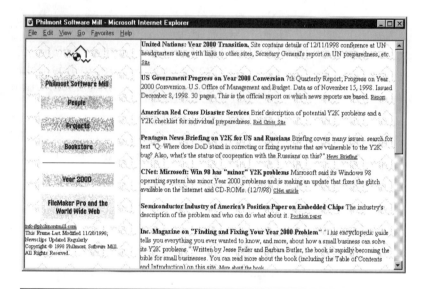

FIGURE I-1. A Database-Driven Web Site

Once a page such as this has been designed, its maintenance requires very little expertise. In the case of this page, the items shown in the frame at the right are selected automatically from a database. The rule—established when the page was designed—is that the frame at the right contains the ten most recent entries in a database that have been identified as "News Clippings." (Other pages on the site retrieve entries from the database that have other categories assigned to them.)

The formatting of this page is done once—for generic entries. Thus, the maintenance of this page involves no Web coding, no uploading of files, and no expertise beyond that necessary to complete the data entry form shown in Figure I-2. (You may note that the fields "Time" and "Duration" are not applicable to this data; however, this same database has other categories that are used to display calendar information on the Web.)

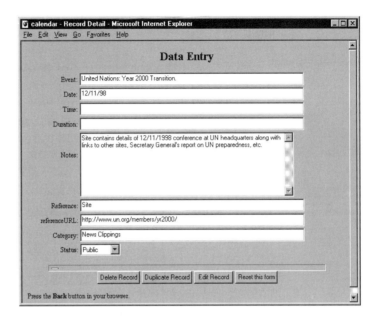

FIGURE I-2. Updating the Database-Driven Web Site

You may be comfortable setting up your own database-driven Web site using the techniques described in this book. On the other hand, you may be more comfortable having no more involvement than filling in a Web-based form such as the one shown in Figure I-2. In that case, this book can serve as an overview of what is going on behind the scenes.

What Can You Do?

The technology used in this site can be used to drive all types of database-driven Web sites—sites that support e-commerce, those that provide Internet publication of information, sites that form virtual communities that share information and materials, and other purposes that people have yet to think of.

The same techniques and technologies are used in all of these sites—and they are really quite simple.

For example, from the standpoint of Web site and database design, the example shown in the previous figures is virtually indistinguishable from an e-commerce site. With a few rearrangements to the form shown in Figure I-2, you can create a form that lets people enter their name and address, the product they want to order, and their credit card number.

Costs

This book shows you how you can create a database-driven Web site for well under a thousand dollars. The variables are many, and for large organizations that amount will clearly be larger, but for smaller organizations, the amount will be less.

The ongoing cost of maintaining a database-driven Web site is remarkably low. The site shown in this chapter, for example, costs $70 a month for the Web site and database support at the two Internet service providers that are used to generate the composite page shown in Figure I-1. (That price is neither the highest nor lowest price currently available for such a site.)

There is also an ongoing cost involved in maintaining the site. When a site is planned to use a database, the updating involves relatively untaxing skills such as filling in the form shown in Figure I-2. That major skill involved in the updating of the site is determining what information to place on it—and that is a skill that falls squarely in the realm of the site owners' expertise rather than in the realm of technology and computerese. Other skills are needed to maintain specific types of sites, but these skills are always more related to the purpose of the site (commerce, information presentation, etc.) than to the technology that supports the site.

Opportunities

Opportunities in this area abound for everyone. For database designers, this is a flourishing market for your skills; for Web site designers, this is a chance to design sites for customers who can afford the initial investment but are hesitant about ongoing costs of maintenance.

It has frequently been said that the Internet breaks down barriers of time and space, allowing people around the world to interact with one another almost instantaneously. Database-driven Web sites go further: they can break down the barrier of complexity that has made creating Web sites the province of a select few.

Overview:
Databases on
the Web

Databases on the Web

When you start to talk about databases on the Web, you will quickly find that everyone has a different idea of what you are talking about. To some people, databases on the Web mean access to vast stores of data; others see databases on the Web as the key to electronic commerce (e-commerce); still others see them as a way to form a virtual organization, free from the traditional paper-based transactions.

All of these points of view are valid, and each is a way in which the Web can be integrated with databases. This chapter describes the basic models of integrating databases with the Web:

- *Publishing data on the Web. Here, you use the Web as a publication tool; browsers interact with dynamic hypertext markup language (HTML), application servers, and database queries to present the information as requested. The data flow is one way: from the database to the user.*

- *Sharing data on the Web. In this scenario you use databases and the Web to share data among people; the data flow is bidirectional—some people enter data, other people look it up.*

- *E-commerce. This area includes all online commercial transactions. Although the data flow is bidirectional, it typically consists of a relatively large amount of data that flows from the database to the customer (during the shopping and evaluation steps); that is followed by a relatively small amount of data that flows from the customer to the database as the sale is consummated.*

- *Totally database-driven Web sites. You can use databases to generate Web pages and keep them up to date. In this case, the database is usually invisible to the user; it is a behind-the-scenes assistant to a Web site.*

Using a Database to Publish Data on the Web

This is one of the most basic applications of database-driven Web sites; it is also one of the oldest and most familiar. Database data takes many forms. In Figure 1-1, you see a table of data that is generated dynamically from a Microsoft Access database using Open Database Connectivity (ODBC).

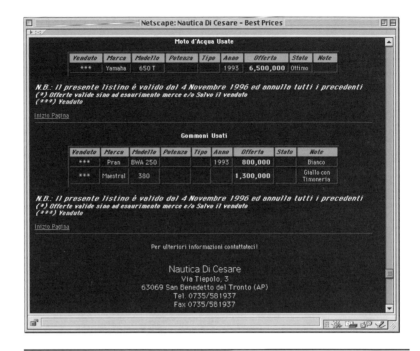

FIGURE 1-1. Nautica Di Cesare Price List

In Figure 1-2 you see the database of the library at the Museum of Modern Art (the "DADABASE"—see a history of early twentieth century art for a discussion of the Dada movement).

It is quite clear that this is a traditional database. It is identified as such by name, and users are invited to search it just as they would search a traditional database (or card catalog in a library).

This site uses Voyager software from Endeavor Information Systems to manage the site and display the pages; the underlying database is Oracle. It is discussed further in Chapter 17, "Publishing Data on the Web" starting on page 393.

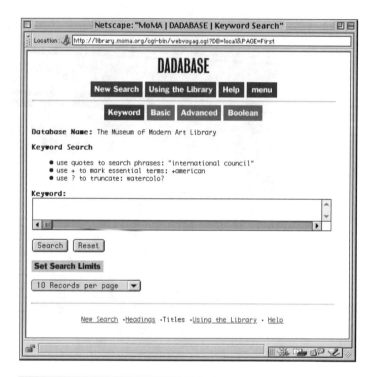

FIGURE 1-2. Museum of Modern Art Library Dadabase

Figure 1-3 shows another database on the Web and yet another approach to the database. In this case, it is not at all clear that a database is involved. Although the data is in fact presented in a table, the absence of borders makes it difficult for the untutored eye to know that it is not simply formatted text. Furthermore, the presence of underlined hypertext links can mislead people who do not realize that the results of a database query can be links that lead users from the database data to other data on the Web.

This database is FileMaker Pro, which handles the Web interface through its FileMaker Web Companion.

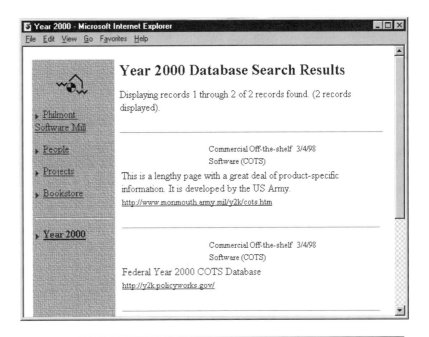

FIGURE 1-3. Database Data Presented as Text

Using a Database to Share Data

You can use databases on the Web to share data. This section describes two such cases: a message database and a mailing list database. In Chapter 18, "Sharing Data on the Web" starting on page 407, you will find another example of data sharing: the Upper Valley Materials Exchange uses a database to share surplus supplies with nonprofit organizations.

Sharing Messages

Figure 1-4 shows a database of messages on the Web (or on an intranet); it lets people enter and retrieve their messages no matter where they are in the world.

This site uses FileMaker Pro software to run the database and to create and display the Web pages.

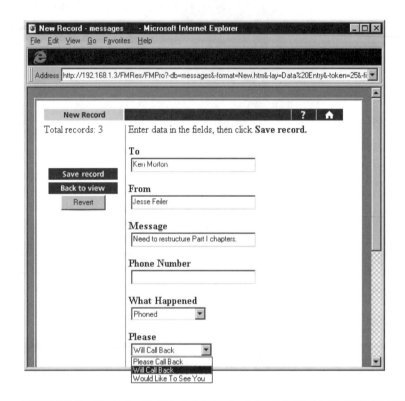

FIGURE 1-4. A Message Database on the Web

Sharing a Mailing List

The structuring of data that a database provides can be applied to other types of shared data. For example, mailing lists were very popular in the early days of public access to the Internet. (Listserv and Majordomo are typical mailing list programs; mailing lists are also often implemented with manual and scripted semiautomated processes.) With a mailing list, interested parties can subscribe to the list; thereafter, any message sent to the mailing list address is automatically sent via e-mail to each of the subscribers. The programs that support mailing lists are widely available and take advantage of the existing e-mail software running on the Internet server.

The disadvantage of a mailing list is its simplicity: all messages go to all subscribers, and they go at the convenience of the sender. An improvement over mailing lists is the Internet newsgroup protocol; in that case (as with a bulletin board), you post a message to the newsgroup and subscribers retrieve it at their convenience. Furthermore, the postings can be threaded—related to specific other postings. That lets discussions within the newsgroup continue on their own; you can follow a thread and retrieve the messages of that thread while ignoring others. Unfortunately, there is also a disadvantage to newsgroups: they require special software to be run on the Internet server. Unlike mailing list software, this is fairly complex software that requires the Internet service provider to implement the Internet news protocol—sometimes a significant effort, particularly considering the volume of messages that may be involved.

You can get the best of both worlds by using a database to support a mailing list rather than a mailing list program or the Usenet news protocol. Figure 1-5 shows how you can query the database of mailing list messages using standard database searches. Figure 1-6 shows the results of such a search.

It is worthwhile to note that this mailing list uses the Listserv software and combines both a traditional mailing list and a Web-based database (this is a proprietary database inside the L-Soft product). Subscribers to the mailing list post—and receive—messages as in a traditional e-mail–based system. People who do not wish to subscribe or who wish to search for old messages can use the database-driven Web site to handle their requests.

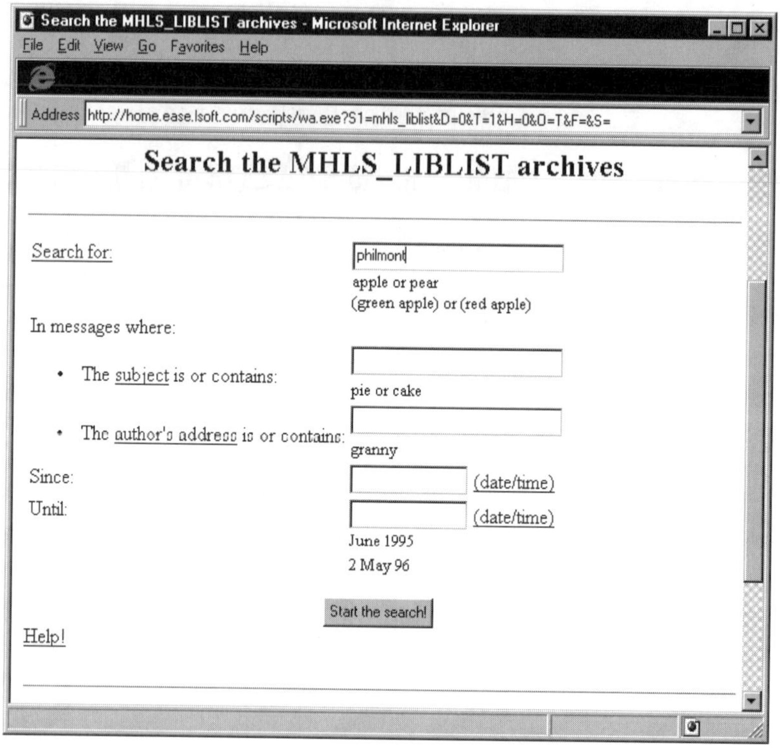

FIGURE 1-5. L-Soft (Listserv) Search Screen

Notice in Figure 1-6 that the hypertext links (underlined) let you move from the summary information about each item to the full item (as in the start of the full item shown at the bottom of the screen). If you compare Figure 1-6 with Figure 1-5, you will soon realize that whereas Figure 1-5 can be designed as a standard and static Web page, Figure 1-6 needs to be constructed automatically based on the results of the query. This book explores how to do that.

FIGURE 1-6. Listserv Search Results

Using a Database for E-Commerce

One of the hottest areas of Internet activity today is electronic commerce. A virtual showcase on the Web can let large numbers of people see products that heretofore could have been displayed only in a large chain of stores or in expensive advertisements. Furthermore, as people become accustomed to purchasing items over the Web, companies are seeing large savings in their operations.

These opportunities are available to companies large and small. In the case of small organizations, the ability to sell their products over the Internet represents a vast new market; for large companies, e-commerce represents an opportunity to streamline their operations and reduce their overhead.

E-Commerce on a Grand Scale—the Apple Store

For example, Figure 1-7 shows part of the Apple Store, where you can configure and purchase computers.

FIGURE 1-7. Apple Store: Build to Order

The buyer can see the choices available and read a description of the specifications of each model. So far, this is much like shopping in a traditional store.

In Figure 1-8, however, you can see where a Web site can take off from the traditional sales channel. Each part of the computer (processor, memory, hard drive, removable storage, video memory, modem, and display) is configurable by the user, who constructs a machine that may be unlike any other in existence.

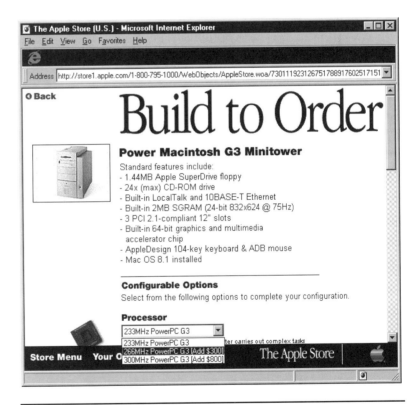

FIGURE 1-8. Apple Store—Select a Configuration

The software that runs the site (WebObjects) keeps track of the components selected and can verify that they will work together properly. Furthermore, the site is able to notice omissions and opportunities for additional sales—such as a printer to go with the computer.

It has been widely noted that what would be obnoxious in a human salesclerk may be accepted and even welcome in a computer-driven sales site. The clerk who is constantly pestering you to buy a printer, dust cover, or personalized mousepad may be an annoyance; the computer—which can be dismissed with a mouseclick—is not so annoying to most people.

The Apple Store is covered in more detail in Chapter 19, "E-Commerce" starting on page 419.

E-Commerce on a Small Scale— International Motor Parts

International Motor Parts in Belgium sells automobile parts—replacements for body parts, mirrors, and light units. Their Web-based business combines aspects of Web publishing with e-commerce. Figure 1-9 shows how you can query the IMP database.

FIGURE 1-9. Querying the IMP Database for a Front Fender (in German)

The response to the query entered in Figure 1-9 is shown in Figure 1-10.

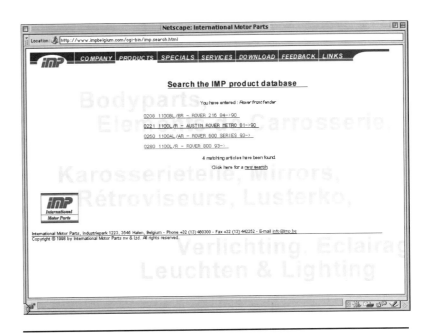

FIGURE 1-10. Rover Radiators from IMP Database

You click on the car model in which you are interested, and get the full details of the part as shown in Figure 1-11.

Note that the site supports queries in a variety of languages such as English, French, German, Dutch, Polish, Czech, and Rumanian. Databases do not have any inherent knowledge of the language that they are using: the string of characters "front fender" serves as a database key just as easily as the character string "kotfluegel vorne" (front fender in German). (In view of the fact that the U.S. front fender is the U.K. front wing, this is particularly useful.)

For a small business in the heart of Europe, providing trained staff that is fluent in eight languages is a daunting prospect: maintaining a multilingual database is simplicity itself.

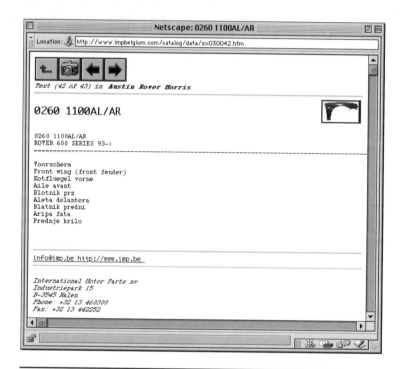

FIGURE 1-11. Details on Fenders, Wings, Etc.

(Remember that in maintaining a database, a clerk can easily take half an hour to search up the official translations of "fuel tank," "rear view mirror," or "right headlight"—and once it has been done, it is done for all users of the database. When the potential customer is on the telephone, that amount of time is generally unacceptable.)

Once a site like this has been created, new areas of business can open easily. For example, Figure 1-12 shows some of the private areas of the IMP site: dealers can download information, newsletters, and other support information that is not available to ordinary customers.

Adding new lines of business is simple when the infrastructure of a Web site exists; furthermore, when those new areas involve the collection and marketing of existing information, the entire transaction can be consummated from your database. (For a fuller example, see Chapter 21, "Reinventing Your Organization" starting on page 457.)

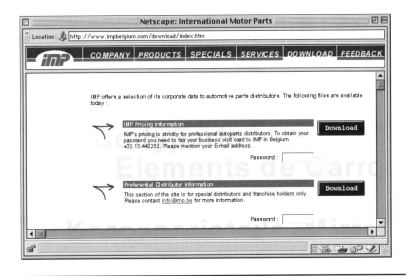

FIGURE 1-12. Dealer Information (Password Protected)

Using a Database to Keep Web Pages up to Date

The last basic paradigm of database-driven Web sites is the case of databases that are used to keep Web pages up to date. Figure 1-12 shows a television station's Web site that contains current weather information.

There is nothing on the page to indicate that a database lies behind it; the clue is the shortcut shown at the bottom of the window (indicated with the arrow). URLs (uniform resource locators) identify an Internet scheme (such as mail, the Web, file transfer, or news), a machine, and a resource on that machine. In the case of a resource that is located on the same machine as the current resource, a relative URL is used, assuming the current scheme and machine. Thus the URL at the bottom of Figure 1-12

```
weather.qry?function=getfive
```

is a relative URL to

```
http://www.rnntv.com/
```

which is the address of the page shown. The full URL is

```
http://www.rnntv.com/weather.qry?function=getfive
```

The question mark is a sign to the cognoscenti that a database is likely to be involved here (Tango is used extensively elsewhere on this site; it is discussed in detail in Chapter 8, "Application Servers and Development Tools" starting on page 169). In a URL, a question mark introduces what is called either a searchpart or a query. Within that section (function=getfive, in this case), information is entered that is passed to the resource for processing. Typically, the Web resource described in the URL is not an actual page but a program that processes the query and produces a dynamic HTML page.

FIGURE 1-13. RNNTV Weather

This site is described more fully in Chapter 20, "Totally Database-Driven Web Sites" starting on page 435.

Summary

The simplest way to look at the opportunities is to start from either end. If you have a database, you can add Web access to it. Note that this means adding access using the *technology* of the Web—your database can be on the Internet, an intranet, or a local area network (LAN).

Likewise, if you already have a Web site, you can add database features to it. Instead of preparing 100 pages of product information for a Web-based product catalog, you can prepare a single template page and then use a database to fill in whatever product information a customer wants to see.

All of this—and much more—is discussed in the pages that follow.

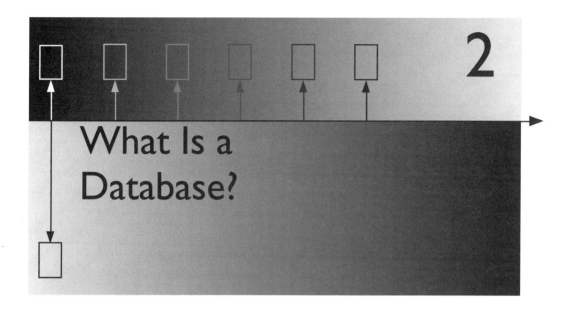

What Is a Database?

"Database" is one of those terms that is widely used without having a precise definition that is shared by all its users. (In this way it is like "multimedia" and even "computer.")

This chapter presents the terminology used in this book. It is an introduction to databases of the sort that occupies many hundreds of pages in textbooks. If it is more than you want to know about databases now, come back to it as you read the book.

"Database" Defined

At various times, "database" can refer to any, several, or all of the following:

- A database may be a body of data—often a large body of information—usually stored and indexed on a computer or other electronic device.

- A database may be the software (and sometimes hardware) that is used to store, retrieve, and manipulate data.

- A database may be a combination of data, software, and custom-written code and procedures that address a given problem. The database for a doctor's office can consist of patient records (data); a database manager such as Access, DB2, or Oracle (software); and custom-written layouts, reports, and procedures that provide operational and management guidance.

In this book, those concepts are expressed with three different terms:

- **Database** is used in the first sense: a collection of data.

- **Database management system (DBMS)** is the term used for the second sense.

- **Database project** is used for the final sense—the combination of data, software, and the reports, layouts, and procedures that make everything work together for a given purpose.

If you want to make a further distinction among these three concepts, you can consider who owns or creates them:

- Databases are owned or created by users.

- Database management systems are created by software developers—Microsoft, FileMaker, Oracle, IBM, etc.

- Database projects are created by consultants, end-users, or others familiar with both the data in the database and the capabilities of the database management system.

However you define them, certain characteristics of databases (and their associated database management system and database projects) are commonly recognized. From a practical, real-life point of view, here are some of the generally accepted characteristics of databases.

Databases Handle Large Amounts of Structured Data	Individual values are not databases—your name is a value, not a database, and its relationship to your address is not a database. A collection of names, however, can be a database. It makes sense to think of a database of the children in a class (or a school) or of a database of the securities that are in an individual's portfolio. Similarly, the aisle in which you have parked your car at the shopping mall is scarcely a database, but the collection of license plate tags and aisle numbers that a valet parking clerk maintains does sound like a database.

In each of these cases, the database is a collection not only of a relatively large amount of data but also of data that has certain similarities within itself. A database consisting of the names of children in a class as well as the destinations to which an airline flies sounds—and would be—strange. (See "The Structure of Database Data" on page 28.)

| Database Data Can Change Quickly (Often Unpredictably) | The databases suggested in the previous section contain different types of data. Although each could be large, given sufficient resources it is possible to present the data from the database in a nondatabase form, such as a printed list. In the case of the children in a class, a class list could be—and normally is—produced once a semester. The relatively few enrollments and dropouts can be marked in pencil on the printed list. Likewise, an airline's destinations can be presented in a printed schedule that is updated a few times a year. |

In the case of a database of parked cars, however, the situation is likely to be impossible to handle with a printed list. Each time a car is parked or removed, the list needs to be updated. The line of patrons waiting to park or retrieve their cars would quickly grow to unmanageable dimensions if a new list had to be prepared each time.

What is important to note is that while databases may contain relatively static data (such as the class list), their nature allows for rapidly changing data (such as the parked car directory).

| Database Data Needs to Be Selected and Displayed in Different Ways (Sometimes Unpredictable) | Whether or not data changes, databases allow it to be selected and displayed in various ways. Whereas a printed list of the students in a class will always be presented in one way—alphabetically by last name, in rows and columns corresponding to classroom seats, by birth date, or by address—the fact that databases can present data on an ad hoc basis means that the way in which data is stored has little to do with the way in which it is retrieved. |

These first three points—the fact that databases normally contain large amounts of data, that they can manage changes to the data, and that they can select and display the data (and parts of it) in different ways—are the most important characteristics of databases. The other characteristics follow from these.

Databases Have Tools to Manipulate Their Data

Database management systems are designed to perform the manipulations needed in storing, retrieving, updating, selecting, and displaying data. They are usually highly optimized for these purposes.

Data stored in standard computer files ("flat files") must be manipulated by custom-written software that manipulates the data directly. This is usually less efficient and much more expensive than using database management systems. Much of traditional programming is incorporated into database management systems. (Although the cost of coding nondatabase projects is sometimes less than that of coding database-driven projects, over time the cost of maintenance of nondatabase projects almost always exceeds that of database-driven projects.)

Databases Contain Meta-Data

In order to manipulate database data, database management systems store **meta-data** in addition to the data. Meta-data (data about data) describes the data. Aspects of meta-data that are stored include:

- A name for each data field ("birth date," "customer name," etc.). The name of the data field is distinct from the **value**s in the database ("Rajiv," "Jan," "Carmen," "Joussef," etc.).

- A type for each data field—whether it is text, an integer, a date, etc.

- Additional information that can optimize storage and retrieval.

Databases Contain Data Validation and Integrity Features

Database management systems contain routines that can be invoked to edit data as it is entered. Following are some typical types of validation and integrity features:

- Values must be unique (for example, ID numbers).

- Values must correspond to other databases (if you enter an invoice, the account number must be valid).

- Values can be generated automatically (such as serial numbers).

- Values must be within a certain range (earlier than today, greater than 124, etc.).

- Values can be calculated automatically (total price = quantity × unit price).

You can often specify error messages to be displayed if these edits fail. Note that this is another example of the database management system containing routines that otherwise would be programmed manually. You specify the validation rule and the message that is to be displayed if it fails. You do not write code such as

```
if (validation ≠ good) then
        display (error message)
```

The processing is handled for you by the database management system based on the conditions that it finds.

There is a very important distinction between procedural programming, in which the sequence of events is paramount, and database programming, in which the state of data is paramount. An overly simplified rule of thumb is that in the procedural world, time is important—this happens, then that happens, then the other thing happens. In the database world, you do not know in which order things happen, but once they have happened (for example, once an entry has passed validation checks), you know that all of the rules have been satisfied.

Databases Are Often Shared across Time and Space

If you consider the facts that databases usually have large amounts of data in them, that the data can change, and that the data can be excerpted and displayed in various ways, it is obvious that the database can appear—and be—different at various times. In fact, one way of thinking of a database is not as a static body of data but as a static *structure* for the storage, retrieval, and manipulation of a body of dynamic data. This means that the data in the database may be different today (or may be presented differently today) than it was yesterday.

Although the technological underpinnings are quite sophisticated, there is little difference between one person accessing a database on two different occasions and two people accessing a database from two different locations. The sharing of data across time and space is an integral part of what people think of when they think of databases.

Databases and Their Data Can Be Related to One Another

Often, databases contain data that they share with one another. A customer database may contain a list of a firm's customers; an invoice database may contain current invoices—including references to customers in the customer database. Further, an inventory database may contain references to items in inventory that are referred to in the invoice database.

There are a number of ways to link databases together formally; many databases today use the relational model—the ability to specify that a certain data field in one database matches a data field in another. Thus, the customer-name data field in the customer database may match the name-of-customer field in the invoice database. This is part of the meta-data for both databases.

Other models exist that allow databases to be linked together. These can be implemented in database management systems or they can be implemented using manual procedures. (Your "customer database" might be a drawer of file cards while your "invoice database" is an Oracle database.)

At this point, "database" is used in its broadest and least technical sense. In relational databases—the most prevalent type in use today—data is stored in tables within databases; in such cases, the relationships described in this section are most often among tables within a database rather than among databases themselves. In this chapter, no distinction is made between tables and databases—as is the case for very simple databases that contain only one table each. This is discussed more fully in "The Relational Model" on page 197.

The Structure of Database Data

Database data is more than just a large body of data that can be stored, retrieved, and manipulated easily by database management systems. Database data has certain structural characteristics that make those processes possible.

| Databases Contain Multiple Instances of Similarly Structured Data | Databases are used to organize data (just as physical filing cabinets and bookshelves are). As in the physical world, the storage structures are often customized for what they will contain. Thus, the shelves on which you place books are likely to be different from the hooks from which you hang garden tools, and the freezer in which you store ice cubes and daiquiris is a far cry from the drawer in which you keep your socks. |

In general, the more similar the data instances are, the more efficient a database can be. You can create a database into which you place the names and addresses of people, but if you know that the database will be used to store names and addresses of students rather than of clients, you can often construct a more efficient and logical database.

The following terms are used to describe the data in a database:

- A **record** is a given data instance—one student, client, inventory record, appointment, message, etc. Other terms that are sometimes used synonymously are instance, observation, row, and case. Each record within a database has the same structure as every other record.

- A **field** is a single piece of data within each record— the date of an appointment, the time of an appointment, the location of an appointment, etc. Other terms that are sometimes used synonymously are data point, column, and variable. All fields are present in each record of a database, but they need not have data within them. Furthermore, a record cannot have any data that is not part of a field.

- A **key** is a field that is used to retrieve data. Often keys are unique (identification numbers, for example); it is sometimes necessary to construct such a field when the real-world data may not be unique (names are not unique). In many databases, any field can be used to retrieve data; however, in designing a database project, you normally distinguish between keys of retrieval and nonkey fields as you develop your project.

- A **value** is the contents of a field in a specific record— the name John in a student record or the name Sari in another student record.

Databases Can Be Normalized

As noted previously, the structural aspects of databases— multiple instances of similarly structured data objects—are not new. People have been categorizing and storing objects and information for millennia. There are many theories and techniques that have been developed to make information storage and retrieval more efficient; the methods of enumeration and identification that were used in ancient Egypt and Greece are far from out of date.

Some specific methods for structuring databases have been developed and are categorized under the general term **normalization**. Your database does not have to be normalized— many are not. However, normalized databases function more efficiently than others, in large part because database management systems are optimized to handle data that is structured in this way.

With the issue of normalization, one of the most important aspects of database design is raised: it is not a mechanical process or even a science. Developing an efficient and useful database is a matter of experience as well as of trial and error. It requires a knowledge of databases in general as well as of the data that is to be used and of the uses to which it will be put. No database designer can properly create a database without an understanding of the people who will use the database.

Summary

This chapter has provided a very high-level overview of databases. If you are new to the entire area, it may be quite daunting—never fear: the rest of this book is devoted to making the processes described in this chapter possible.

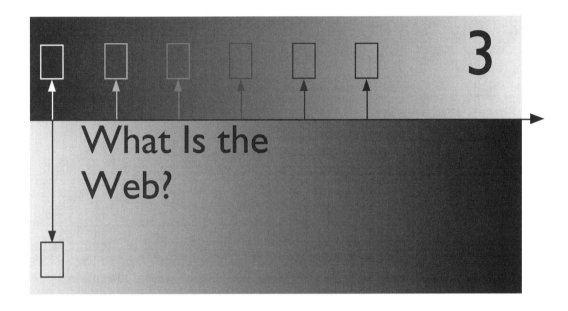

What Is the Web?

It is less than a decade since the World Wide Web was first proposed and implemented. Just as spreadsheets (particularly VisiCalc) made the first personal computers a mainstream tool, the Web has made the Internet an essential part of late twentieth century life. (It is unlikely that the extraordinary spread and use of the Internet would have occurred if people still relied on file transfer protocol (FTP) and Gopher for information search and retrieval.)

Many books have been written about the Web, and you probably have a browser installed on your computer and have used the Web yourself. (If you haven't, you should take some time out very soon to install a browser and get used to using it: this book assumes a basic familiarity with the Web from a user's point of view.)

This section of the book examines the World Wide Web from a high level—much as the previous section examined databases from a similar high level. When you look at databases and the World Wide Web from such a high level, you find a remarkable degree of similarity.

The Web Described

The Web can be described in terms very similar to those used for databases.

The Web Can Manage Large Amounts of Data	From its inception, the Web was designed to manage large amounts of data. You can manage a day's appointments on the back of an envelope; you can probably even manage a week's appointments on both sides of a big envelope. A year's appointments, however, require a different technology.

An important point to note in dealing with large amounts of data is that the issues involved in storage, retrieval, and manipulation do not scale simply from one size to another: there are discontinuities (as in the difference in managing a year's appointments versus those of a day or week). The Web addresses the issues of large-scale data management. |

See "Databases Handle Large Amounts of Structured Data" on page 23.

Web Data Changes Quickly (Often Unpredictably)	Because the Web is decentralized, its data is subject to constant change. When you place a link on a Web page, there is no guarantee that the destination link is valid (although if the destination is on a page that you also control, that is your

responsibility). Anyone who has used search engines such as Yahoo or Alta Vista has encountered dead links and loose ends—links that go nowhere or that go to peculiar places.

See "Database Data Can Change Quickly (Often Unpredictably)" on page 24

Web Data Needs to Be Selected and Displayed in Different Ways (Sometimes Unpredictable)

One of the reasons for the quick adoption of the Web by corporations is that they have discovered that customers (and potential customers) are very happy to spend a lot of time browsing—as long as the browsing is under their control. A 300-page printed catalog can easily be a nuisance to a customer who is only interested in the 2 pages it contains about horse blankets; on the Web, however, that customer can very happily spend half an hour comparing horse blankets of various kinds. The selection of information—dynamic and under the control of the information user rather than the information provider—constantly changes.

See "Database Data Needs to Be Selected and Displayed in Different Ways (Sometimes Unpredictable)" on page 24.

The Web Has Tools to Manipulate Its Data

The Web is a collection of data and links to data. Its specifications and standards allow for the possibility of various search engines (such as Yahoo, Excite, and AltaVista), but they are not part of the official Web definition. In practical terms, however, most people consider these tools—selection and manipulation tools—part of the Web.

See "Databases Have Tools to Manipulate Their Data" on page 25.

Web Pages Contain Meta-Data

Web pages are constructed using hypertext markup language (HTML), which contains all sorts of formatting and descriptive information that is enclosed in brackets <such as these>.

Figure 3-1 shows a typical Web page.

The beginning of the HTML code used to generate that page is shown here:

```
<HTML>
<!--DESCRIPTION: For use with the Standard Site Assistant-->
<!--This file created 1/13/1998 6:17 PM by Home Page
    version 3.0-->
<HEAD>
   <TITLE>Philmont Software Mill</TITLE>
   <META NAME=GENERATOR CONTENT="Home Page 3.0">
   <X-CLARIS-WINDOW TOP=52 BOTTOM=525 LEFT=68 RIGHT=656>
   <X-CLARIS-TAGVIEW MODE=minimal>
</HEAD>
```

Most of the code consists of bracketed formatting instructions, which many people would consider a form of meta-data. The italicized code is clearly information about the information contained on the page and is meta-data by anyone's definition.

Note that only the boldfaced text in this code sample is actually shown in Figure 3-1: everything else is formatting or descriptive information. Also note that the italics and boldface type are used for illustrative purposes here and elsewhere in the book: HTML itself does not rely on any such formatting styles.

See "Databases Contain Meta-Data" on page 25.

FIGURE 3-1. Philmont Software Mill Web Page

Web Pages Are Often Shared across Time and Space

Finally, it should go without saying that Web pages are often shared across time and space: that is the primary reason for the World Wide Web.

See "Databases Are Often Shared across Time and Space" on page 27.

In short, databases and the World Wide Web represent two different and complementary approaches to the problems of managing large amounts of information and manipulating it effectively—often across the normal boundaries of time and space. The similarities between databases and the Web are not obvious to many people because they have been developed by different sorts of people with different backgrounds, but the fundamental similarities are striking.

Summary

The parallels between databases and the Web itself are striking. There are many obvious differences—perhaps most important the fact that databases have a much more rigid and identifiable structure than does the Web. Nevertheless, these important similarities have meant that many people try to do similar things with databases and with the Web. In the next chapter, you will see how they can be used together.

How Databases Work on the Web

4

To understand how databases work on the Web, it is helpful to look back at the evolution of contemporary software architecture. This path led from the earliest days of mainframe computers and dumb terminals (originally teletype machines) to the modern architecture that may incorporate mainframes, personal computers, and a variety of networking technologies.

This chapter examines the major steps along this road; it then deals with the contemporary design of systems.

This history is an oversimplification. Furthermore, it has the benefit of hindsight: at the time, it was not always clear where the road would lead.

The Story So Far...

Several common threads run through the evolution of contemporary system architecture. Among them are:

- The rapid increase in the power of computers

- The equally rapid decrease in their costs

- Similarly rapid increases in communications media (high-speed modems, fiber optics, etc.)

- Corresponding decreases in communications costs

- An increasing market for computers and software applications

- A growing backlog of unfinished software projects

- Persistent questions about the apparent lack of productivity improvements with many computerized operations

- An apparently disproportionately high cost for custom-written and vertical market application software

- Complaints about the difficulty of using computers

There are four significant steps in the evolution of the systems that are being developed today:

1. Mainframes and dumb terminals (from the earliest years of the computer age—the 1950s)

2. The rise of operating systems and structured programming (starting in the 1960s)

3. The development of the personal computer (in the late 1970s)

4. The growth of the Internet and the World Wide Web (early 1990s)

Dumb Terminals and Mainframes

From the beginning of the computer age until well into the 1970s, the architecture shown in Figure 4-1 was the standard design of computer systems. The left side of the figure represents the physical (hardware) aspects of a system; the right side represents the logical (software) portions.

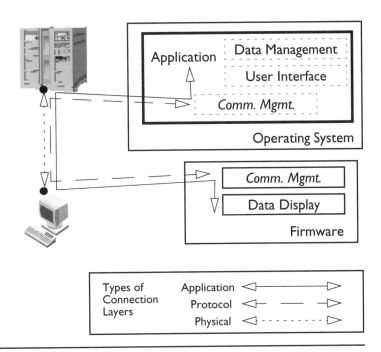

FIGURE 4-1. Mainframe/Dumb Terminal Application Design

Applications

An application ("program" or "system") runs on a mainframe computer. That application is responsible for managing its data and for presenting its results to the user. The application is shown in a box with a heavy outline in Figure 4-1. This is what needed to be written—and rewritten—for each software development effort.

The application is responsible for its own data management, user interface, and communications management. Thus, in Figure 4-1, these features are shown in dashed boxes: they were integrated with the application. This means that they needed to be implemented anew for each application: anew— and usually differently.

Communications   Communications involve a number of layers of connectivity; in a simplification of the seven-layer international standard, you can think of three primary layers:

1. Physical layer

2. Protocol layer

3. Application layer

These three links are shown in Figure 4-1.

Physical Layer   The physical layer between the user's device and the computer is usually some form of telephone connection—often over telephone lines, with a modem (the circles in the figure) at each end. For high-speed or secure connections, dedicated phone lines are used to connect terminals to computers; for short distances, direct connections from computer to terminal are possible, as are direct connections for the devices on a local area network within a single office or building.

The physical layer between the two modems requires agreement on physical characteristics such as line speed and parity bits.

Protocol Layer   The protocol layer between the mainframe and the user's terminal is transported over the physical layer, but its standards are set by the communications management protocols of the mainframe's operating system and the communications management protocols of the terminal: they had to agree to talk to one another.

When this architecture was in widespread use, the protocols of the protocol layer were often specific to the operating system and the terminal: terminals connected to Burroughs mainframes required some reconfiguration to be attached to IBM mainframes or to VAX/PDP minicomputers.

Digital Equipment's VT100 terminal was one of the most popular of these dumb terminals; its communications protocols are in use today.

Application Layer A final level of communication is between the application itself and the terminal's data entry screen. This communication is conducted over the link established between the mainframe and the terminal, which in turn is carried over the physical connection between the two modems or other communications devices.

The link between the data entry terminal and the application is specific to that application: a clerk who knows how to enter data to an airline reservation system usually needs to be retrained to use a bank teller's system when this architecture is used.

User Interface The user interface software depended on the devices that would be available to users; typically, input was via punched cards or magnetic tape, and output was produced on high-speed printers. For applications in which users would interact directly with the computer, both input and output were via dumb terminals—teletypes or CRT screens. (Thus, in Figure 4-1, the dumb terminal in the lower left stands not only for itself but also for these other devices—printers, magnetic tape, etc.)

Operating Systems and Structured Programming	By the end of the 1950s, it was clear that the incorporation of communications management, user interface software, and database management functionality in each application was tremendously wasteful. People began to search for ways to eliminate these redundant programming efforts.

Three developments made this possible:

1. Operating systems—the software that controls computers—were becoming more complex and more powerful. More powerful computers were able to spare precious machine cycles for the "unproductive" work of the operating system. At the same time, the rise of time sharing required sophisticated manipulation of multiple computer jobs as well as elaborate bookkeeping. As operating systems grew, some of the functionality that had been written into each application was incorporated in the operating system. An early case in point was communications management (as shown in Figure 4-2). This allowed an application to use the operating system's communications tools without reinventing the wheel. It meant, however, that that application was tied to that operating system, because each operating system had its own idiosyncrasies with regard to communications management.

2. Structured and reusable code became popular in the 1970s. Many aspects of the user interface lent themselves to reusable code (scanning text for a blank, logging error messages, etc.). With the development of a number of methods for reusing code, programmers were able to avoid recoding many repeated functions. The reusability of this code was limited by the standards of the developers who had written it. It was not necessarily tied to an operating system, but it was often tied to an individual programmer's way of think-

ing and coding. Programmers tend to reuse their own code—not someone else's.

3. In addition to the user interface, data management was clearly an area in which reusable code libraries could be applied: after all, storing and retrieving data are not particularly dependent on the nature of the data. The first data management systems were indeed reusable code libraries; gradually, however, a new feature emerged: a standard way of communicating with the database. The most widely used standard was SQL—the Structured Query Language, developed in the 1970s by IBM and adopted as an international standard in 1986.

These three developments—the growth of operating systems, the ability to reuse code, and the adoption of standards for communicating with databases—helped to tame the complexity of software development by the early 1980s. The architecture shown in Figure 4-2 began to come into play.

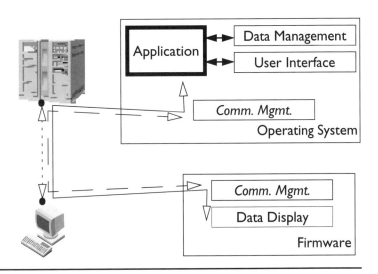

FIGURE 4-2. Second Stage of Mainframe/Dumb Terminal Architecture

Note that once again the heavy line outlines the application that must be rewritten for each project. In this case, it is much smaller, because the operating system, database, and reusable code libraries contribute to the effort.

In practice, however, there were serious problems. So many pieces contributed to this puzzle that there was always something being rewritten or replaced on almost every mainframe system. Shared code was fine—but if one application that was sharing the code needed a change, all of them needed to adapt. In a similar vein, relying on the operating system for shared services (such as communications management) tied applications to a single vendor and a specific version of an operating system. The complexity of this environment began to outweigh the benefits. By the mid-1980s, analysts were talking of decades-long programming backlogs.

Personal Computers and Client/Server Architecture

With the development of the personal computer in the 1980s, a new architecture called client/server came into vogue. It is shown schematically in Figure 4-3.

What is significant is that the dumb terminal has been replaced by a personal computer. Although the diagram becomes more complex, there was hope at the time that the added complexity would be offset by ease of use and a significantly easier development effort.

The dumb terminal's firmware is replaced by the personal computer's operating system. It can do much more; in fact, it can run programs. The user interface software, which previously ran on the mainframe, was now able to run on the personal computer. This reduced the load on the mainframe and improved performance: the time it takes to process keystrokes and mouseclicks is much less when all of this is done on the personal computer and the system does not need to communicate with the mainframe for every user action.

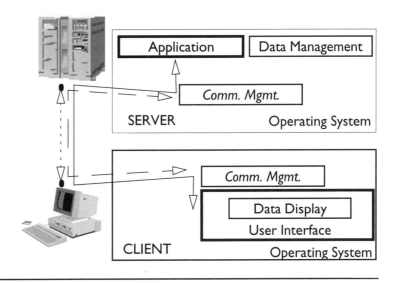

FIGURE 4-3. Client/Server Architecture

Programming the user interface (on the personal computer) can be very different from programming the application on the mainframe. In fact, different people and different programming languages are often employed. In many cases, the server software on the personal computer can be written as ad hoc programs by end users (that, at least, is the theory).

Through the early and mid-1990s, the client/server architecture became increasingly popular. As personal computers proliferated on desks and in other work environments, the cost of deploying a client became less and less: the personal computer and its operating system were often in place, and it was only a matter of installing the user interface program.

Still, in the client/server architecture the communication between the mainframe (server) and the client is often idiosyncratic or proprietary: the communications management software on the client has to be in synch with the communications management software on the mainframe. In the late 1980s and early 1990s, many people who used client/server software found themselves switching among a number of different communications management tools such as 3270 emulation, VT100 emulation, and others too embarrassing to mention.

It is important to note that by the early 1990s, servers built from personal computers replaced mainframes in many of these configurations.

The Internet Arrives

The Internet was developed in the mid-1960s to allow computers to communicate with one another. Its early users were in the defense, research, and education areas. In the late 1980s, it was opened to public and commercial users: the response was phenomenal.

TCP/IP

With the advent of the Internet, international standards for communications became more widespread than ever. Most important, the protocol layer (shown with the dashed line in the previous figures) became a single protocol: TCP/IP. Thus, the constraints involved in connecting a particular personal computer with its communications management software to a particular mainframe with its communications management software were largely removed: everyone speaks TCP/IP. (Figure 4-4 shows the previous client/server architecture with TCP/IP replacing idiosyncratic communications managers on both the client and the server.)

Of course, a very large number of old (legacy) systems remain; they use older protocols and many still use dumb terminals—or personal computers pretending to be dumb terminals. The savings in Internet connectivity are mitigated in an environment that preserves such devices.

HTTP and the Web

In Figure 4-3, the communications between the user interface software on the personal computer and the application on the client used whatever protocol or standard they had agreed on for the application layer. An Internet standard—the Web and the accompanying HTTP protocol—made it possible to further simplify the picture.

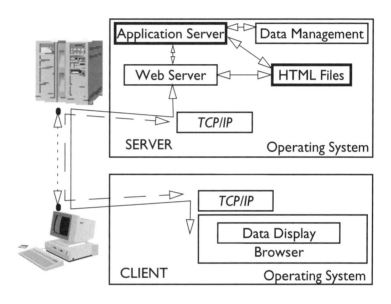

FIGURE 4-4. Client/Server Architecture

Instead of custom-written user interface software on the client, you can use a Web browser to access Web sites. If one of those Web sites happens to contain the data that previously resided on a server, you have reconstructed the traditional client/server architecture using a standard communications protocol (TCP/IP (transmission control protocol/Internet protocol) and a standard high-level protocol (HTTP (hypertext transfer protocol)) and the Web). The use of a standard piece of software on the client—a Web browser—reduces development time and the time it takes for users to learn new applications. In this scenario, the only custom-written software is the application server (outlined with a heavy line in Figure 4-4).

This is the old application from the previous figures, renamed in accordance with late 1990s parlance. The transformation of the name is legitimate: this is a far less functional piece of computer code than the full-fledged application shown previously in Figure 4-1, but the entire system—encompassing Web browser, TCP/IP, and database manager—is just as powerful if not more so.

Client/Server Architecture on the Web

The evolution is complete at this point. The TCP/IP protocol contains addressing information: the message that is sent from the client to the server need not be destined for that computer. If the server is not the correct recipient, it can forward the TCP/IP message on to another computer, which in turn can continue the process if necessary. (This process can span the globe.) This is shown schematically in Figure 4-5 with specific Internet protocols identified.

The physical connections among the computers together with the TCP/IP protocol can transfer standard messages—like those of the Web's HTTP protocol—all over the Internet. Each of the servers in Figure 4-5 contains all of the paraphernalia shown in Figure 4-4: the TCP/IP protocol, one or more application servers, perhaps a database…the list varies from server to server.

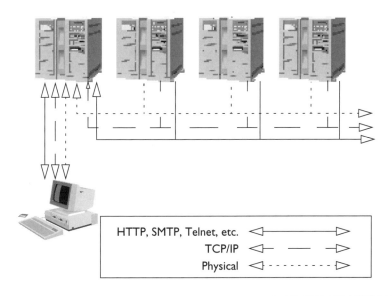

FIGURE 4-5. Client/Server Architecture on the Internet

How the Internet Works

Each server may support a number of Internet protocols such as HTTP (for the Web); News (for newsgroups); SMTP (simple mail transfer protocol), POP (post office protocol—for reading mail), and IMAP (Internet message access protocol—a more sophisticated mail reading protocol); Telnet (for terminal emulation); Gopher (for text searching); and other public and private protocols that travel over TCP/IP. A server that supports the mail protocols may be called a mail server; one that support HTTP may be called a Web server.

The Web itself is based on the Internet protocols and transport mechanism. This section provides an overview of what you need to know. Even if you are an experienced Web user, you may find this section useful, since it presents some issues that are normally not important but will become crucial when you publish databases on the Web.

Connecting to the Internet

The most basic step is connecting to the Internet. For most people, this involves using a modem attached to their computer to connect to another modem at their Internet service provider (ISP). This is the physical connection shown with a dotted line in the figures in this chapter. Over this physical connection the protocol and application connections are transmitted.

Your ISP is your gateway to the Internet. In Figure 4-6, the client/server architecture of Figure 4-5 is shown again: it is the typical architecture that you use when you use the Internet. The ISP is identified as provider.net—it could be a local company or a large company such as AT&T WorldNet, America Online, or CompuServe. You have an account with the ISP and you typically pay for the service—either at a flat monthly rate or on a per-hour basis. The service for which you pay is the physical connection between your computer and the ISP as well as the use of services on the ISP such as e-mail.

Normally, you have one modem attached to your computer; your ISP typically has scores (sometimes thousands) of modems connected to its computer for its customers to use because each connected customer requires the use of a modem at the ISP. Standard telephone switching systems are used to place the call.

Variations on this theme are common. For high-volume users, the connection may be a leased telephone line rather than a dial-up connection. In addition, one modem can be shared by several users—often over a LAN. (Devices called routers are often used to accomplish this.) Furthermore, rather than the telephone network, cable television lines can be used for connectivity. Lastly, remember that some organizations function as their own ISP.

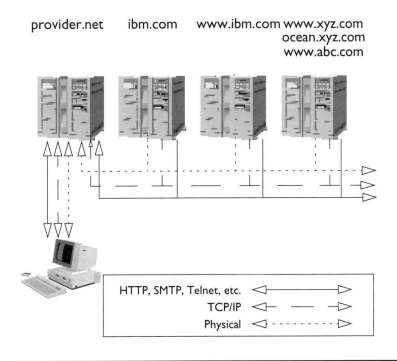

FIGURE 4-6. Access to ISP and Internet Sites

Once the connection to your ISP is made, you are on the Internet and ready to function. You can assume a direct link between yourself and your ISP (at the left of the diagram), but the telephonic connection is an integral part of the connection.

Connecting to an Internet Address

You request a Web page by typing in an address—such as http://www.*ibm.com*/index.html. Your ISP connects to the ISP that serves that domain—the part of the address italicized here. Conceptually, that ISP is a **domain**—such as ibm.com. A domain usually corresponds to a single organization such as Yale University (yale.edu), FileMaker (filemaker.com), Apple (apple.com), Microsoft (microsoft.com), or the British royal family (royal.gov.uk).

Inside a Domain

Within a domain, there may be many different computers: in the diagram, the computer ibm.com is shown communicating with a separate computer that is named www.ibm.com; presumably this is the Web server for that domain. (A domain can have multiple Web servers.)

The figure illustrates some of the variations in configuration that are possible. Whereas www.ibm.com, ibm.com, and provider.net are shown as separate computers, the computer at the right is shown to host several different domains. In real life, Internet service providers that provide database hosting to many clients appear like the computer at the right.

Internet routing tables are used to map these names to specific Internet addresses, but none of that is the responsibility either of the user or of the content provider.

What happens beyond the connection—inside ibm.com or provider.net—is only its business. In fact, you will sometimes connect to an Internet site such as www.apple.com and notice that the actual address you have reached is something like www3.apple.com. In order to handle large numbers of users, some Internet sites use mirrors—duplicate computers with duplicate data; they route users to www1, www2, www3, or whatever their mirror computers are called so that the load is spread evenly.

Connecting to a Web Page

Once you have connected to the Internet and then to a specific site, you download a Web page and view it in your browser. Following the address of the computer in your http request is a file name—index.html in the example used previously.

What Is a Web Page?

What your browser actually receives is a string of text characters—the text on the Web page as well as the HTML formatting information. There may be nontextual elements on the page—images, sound, or even executable code (such as Java applets)—but they are wrapped in the stream of text characters.

In many cases, Web pages are simply text files: on request, the file is read by the ISP's Web software, and it is transmitted character by character to the receiving ISP and thence to the user's browser. This need not be the case, however. Remember that what happens within the domain to which you connect is its business: all that is required is for the ISP to return that string of text characters (with possibly some embedded images, sound, or applets) to the user.

So a computer can generate a Web page programmatically on request rather than reading it from a file. Of course, this means that the computer needs software to format the Web page, but such software is available. In real life, such dynamically created Web pages often combine template or format information from a file with dynamic information from a database.

| Sessions and Transactions | The architecture described here has two different types of connections. The connection between the user and the ISP—often over a telephone line using modems as shown at the left in Figure 4-6—is a **session**. It is a relationship between two individual modems, and it is usually billed to a single account. The session may last for some time—it may even be kept open at all times—and it may include all sorts of transactions such as e-mail, Web browsing, and file transfers. |

The request for a Web page described in the previous section is a **transaction**: a request from the user is sent to the appropriate domain, and a response is provided in the form of a Web page consisting of text and possibly embedded nontextual information. The transaction is not designed to be lengthy, and it consists only of the request and the response.

(If no response is received, the user's browser presents an error message.) There is normally no relationship between any transaction and any other.

You will notice when you use a search engine that sometimes the address that you go to will contain more information than the name of a file. It may contain one or more search terms, which are preceded by a question mark. Thus, if you search for "http rfc" in Yahoo, you will see that you are connected to http://search.yahoo.com/bin/search?p=http+rfc. This is the primary mechanism by which additional information is passed to the destination. It will be discussed extensively later.

When using a shared resource such as a database, people usually think that they have established a connection that is like a session: you often need a password to access a database, and you may initiate many queries. In fact, the normal implementation of database access on the Web is transactional, not session based. Each request contains all of the information needed to let the database accomplish its work. In order to do this, many hidden fields of data are sent back and forth both in the requests and in the responses. (A common such field is the record number of a database record.) This issue will come up many times in this book; it is good to start thinking about the distinction between sessions and transactions now.

You may see the term **state-less** used to describe systems that do not keep track of information about users between requests. The system—in this case the Web server—does not keep track of the state of any individual user, and each transaction or request is completely self-contained. Because many transactions do require state information, there are a number of ways to work around this issue.

Servers, Sites, and ISPs

A **site** is a registered location on the Internet (or on an intranet). It is associated with an ISP through address tables (DNS (domain name system) tables) with addresses assigned by Internet organizations. A site can use whatever ISP services are available on the ISP, although the relationship between the organization running the site and the ISP may specify limits and fees for that use. The relationship between the site and its host ISP is maintained through the DNS tables. You can move a site from one ISP to another by applying to the Internet organization that manages addresses in your country (in the United States it is InterNic—http://www.internic.net).

Summary

This chapter has delved into how the current database environment on the Web has evolved. The structure that may seem complicated and daunting is actually a structure that is quite familiar to old-time programmers. This is a critical point, because it means that many legacy systems (those designed for mainframes decades ago) are relatively easily transported to database-driven Web sites.

This part of the book has covered the basic concepts that you need to be familiar with to work with database-driven Web sites. In the next part, you will find details of the components that you need to use: Internet service providers, databases, and application server software.

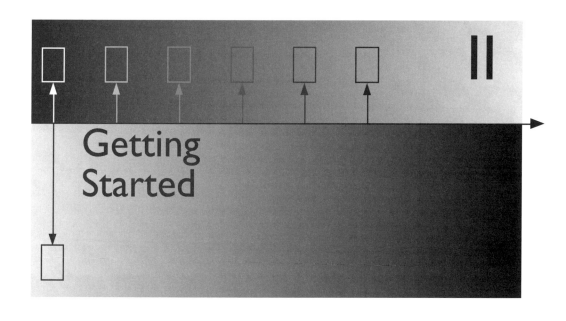

Getting
Started

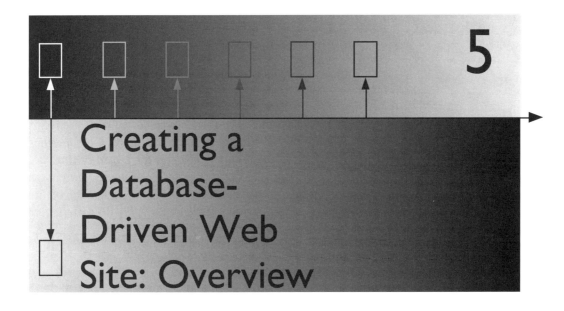

5

Creating a Database-Driven Web Site: Overview

This chapter provides a roadmap to the other chapters in this part of the book. It places them in perspective with one another as well as with the environment with which you may currently be working.

If there is one theme that runs through this part of the book, it is that these parts are interchangeable. The architectures described in the first part of the book (databases, the Web, and the Internet) are fixed. For the most part, they are several decades old. What is new is the widespread availability of the Internet and these services as well as the drastic reduction in cost that has been made possible not only by this availability but also by the deployment of easier to use and much more reliable computers.

Experienced computer users almost all would offer the same advice to newcomers: do not let yourself be locked into a particular vendor's products. It is your data, your Web site, and your development cost. You have every reason to expect that those investments are yours and that you can reorganize your database and Web assets just as you would the chairs in your office. When you are evaluating a new product or service, you will often be shown how easy it is to convert your existing data or Web site to the new product. Keep your eyes open: ask how easy it will be to convert your data or Web site from that new product to yet another new product (possibly from another vendor). Nothing is forever—particularly in the world of computers. The people who have had the most success in developing database-driven Web sites have often changed many if not all of the components of their sites several times before settling on a particular combination that works for them.

Internet Service Provider/Database Service Provider

Your first step is to find an Internet service provider. Today, ISPs are often providing an array of services unheard of only a year ago. Your ISP may offer a bundle of services that includes all of the other components mentioned in this chapter. Often, such a bundle is very convenient and relatively inexpensive. In other cases, such a bundle is also convenient but the ISP may consider that the convenience should carry a premium. One-stop shopping is no guarantee of a bargain.

Your ISP together with a telephone company (sometimes a cable company or wireless company) provides you with your physical connection to the Internet. Because the total cost of your Internet access depends on the ISP charges as well as the telecommunications charges, it is usually best to select the ISP closest to the location from which you will be connecting to the Internet. This is true even if that ISP does not provide the database services that you need.

As shown in the diagrams in the previous chapter, it is easy for ISPs to communicate with one another; a Web site may actually be spread over a number of different ISPs, with users being none the wiser. It is very common to select a second ISP to host your Web site and to provide your database services. Such an ISP is a database service provider (DSP). It may also provide ISP services to people who are physically close to it, but its expertise is in the database services that you need. Your DSP may also be your ISP, but in this book, DSP is used to identify the services that are distinct from the basic Internet connectivity services of an ISP.

For more information, see "Other Internet/Database Service Provider Services" on page 88.

Database Software

The heart of your database-driven Web site is your database software. Usually, this is one product, but remember that the same architecture that lets you combine multiple computers into one virtual Web site lets you integrate a number of database software products.

Your choice of database software must be supported by your database service provider and the application server that you choose—not to mention the fact that it must be satisfactory to perform the work that you need to do. Database software comes in many varieties; the major categories are:

- Software designed originally for desktop applications. This includes products such as Microsoft Access, FileMaker Pro, and the XBase (FoxBase, etc.) products. Over the years, these products have been expanded and strengthened to be able to support network and multiuser configurations.

- In the middle, a new breed of object-oriented database software products—some written in Java—are starting to emerge. Many of these have been designed specifically for use on the Internet.

- At the high end, enterprise database products such as DB2, Oracle, Informix, SQL Server, and Sybase have been the workhorses of databases for years. These have recently been equipped with interfaces to application servers, and some have application server functionality built into their suite of services.

- Beyond the high end, new concepts such as data warehousing are being developed that tie together far-flung databases (often using a variety of products) into very large repositories of data. Data warehouses typically do not drive Web sites: on the contrary, the sheer magnitude of a data warehouse usually dictates that it drives the system and that Web pages serve it (rather than the reverse design, which is common with traditional databases).

For more information, see "Database Software" on page 93.

Application Servers and Other Intermediaries

As shown in the diagrams in Chapter 4, an application server will pass queries to your database and generate HTML in return. Application servers are often described as **middleware**.

Application servers may be part of a Web server product or they may be part of a database. In a third scenario, they may be totally independent products. Because the application server may be part of another product, you may have trouble isolating it in a vendor's proposal. Never fear: it is there, and it is your right to ask where it is. Even if it is bundled as part of the DSP's service, you should know what product provides the service. In almost every case, standard products are used—even if they are marketed as part of XYZ's Dynamic Database Service, Inc. (or some other marketing jargon).

Since the application server must interface with the DSP's Web server software and with the database software that you use, be careful that the products you select will work together.

For more information, see "Application Servers and Development Tools" starting on page 169.

CGI Scripts and Perl

Your database, application server, and Web server may be all that you need to construct a database-driven Web site. Together, they can deliver the data, the dynamic HTML, and the static HTML that provide the user interface. In some cases, however, you may need more: scripts and commands that interact with other applications on your Web server or other computers.

CGI (common gateway interface) scripts are a standard means of implementing such "glue" routines. CGI scripts may be written in any of a number of programming languages; Perl is one of the most common, along with heavy-duty programming languages such as C and C++. These scripts typically take data from HTML pages (often from form data entered by users) and send it to other routines—such as e-mail servers, databases, and flat files.

For more information see "Programmer-Centric Tools" on page 173.

Transitions

Although the chapters in this section describe how to set up and maintain database-driven Web sites, the reality is that you often are not starting from scratch. This can pose yet another constraint in the design and implementation of your Web site and in the tools that you use.

There are transitions possible at every step of the way. You may have an environment that is based largely on CGI scripts written in Perl; converting them to a more sophisticated application server may not be feasible. On the other hand, living with old designs can be very expensive. A Telnet-based database access system may well have worked for years—or decades—with dumb terminals being used to access mainframe-based systems. The people who design, develop, support, and use such systems often have a great deal invested in the systems. The prospect of using new technology and of throwing out hardware and software to which they have become accustomed is not always welcome.

The fact that database-driven Web sites are often much cheaper to design, develop, implement, support, and use can be easily obscured when people perceive that their expertise is being questioned. The fact that this is a "people" issue (rather than a technical issue) in no way diminishes its importance. Developing a new system that no one will use is not productive for anyone. When you are replacing or augmenting an old system, remember how much people may be identified with it; they may take statements of fact as personal attacks and may question what to you may be the most obvious statements. The success or failure of a system often depends on managing these issues successfully.

Summary

The remaining chapters in this part of the book provide details of the tools that you need to build your database-driven Web site—in particular, your ISP, database, and application server. The use of Internet standards and protocols means that they should all work seamlessly together and that you can mix and match products and providers.

(That, at least, is the idea. In reality, you always need to check that each component will work with the other components of your database-driven Web site.)

The first step is providing your Internet access: that is described in the following chapter.

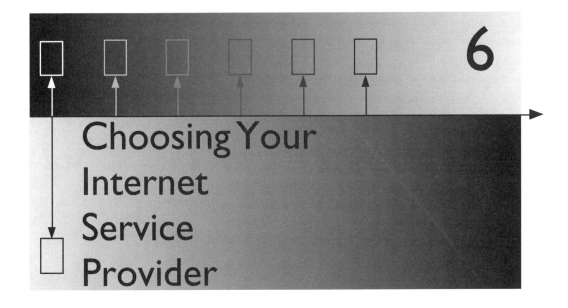

Choosing Your Internet Service Provider

6

This chapter covers the basics of choosing and working with your Internet service provider and database service provider. These may be commercial services, in-house services within your organization, or services that you must provide for yourself and for others.

The combination of services that you need may be provided by one organization or by several; one computer or several may be used. This chapter deals with the basics of how to connect a computer with server software to the Internet (or your intranet); it proceeds through various other services that may be provided and that you may or may not need.

How Many Do You Need?

The diagram previously used to illustrate how you can connect to multiple Internet sites ("Connecting to the Internet" on page 52) is shown again in Figure 6-1: this time it is used to illustrate how you can use several computers to construct your own database-driven Web site.

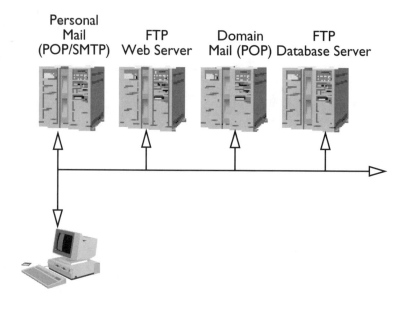

FIGURE 6-1. Internet Services and You

The fact that the same basic diagram can be used to illustrate a number of different activities only underscores the fact that this is the basic Internet architecture that is made possible by standard protocols. The same architecture is used on intranets for the same reason—to take the bother out of network configuration and to allow you to focus on the task at hand.

In this case, the individual layers of connections (physical, TCP/IP, application) are combined into a single set of arrows; what matters here is the fact that all of these computers can talk to one another using Internet protocols. Because of this, it really does not matter where physical walls occur in this diagram. All of these computers could be located in a single computer room; equally, each of them could be located in its own site—perhaps thousands of miles away from the other computers. Furthermore, one or more of these computers could be located within another one: a single computer can run a Web server, a database server, a mail client (POP), and a mail server (SMTP). And any combination is also possible.

"Database server" can refer to the database software itself (Microsoft Access, DB2, Oracle, etc.) or to the computer on which the database runs.

What this means is that you can configure your database-driven Web site from any combination of computers and service providers that is best for you.

How to Get Started

You start by figuring out what you have now. If you have access to the Internet for e-mail, you have the server shown at the left in Figure 6-1 (personal mail). If you have your own Web site, you have the second server shown in Figure 6-1 (the Web server). If you have the ability to upload Web pages to your site, you have FTP access. (If you do not, you either have FTP access provided under a proprietary name or the functional equivalent—unless you are unable to change your own Web pages.)

If you have your own domain name, such as mydomain.com, you have the third server—domain mail. Mail addressed to you@mydomain.com is properly delivered. Normally, it is automatically routed to your personal mail account—which may or may not be on the same computer.

It is common for these three services—personal mail, a Web site, and domain mail—to be provided by a single Internet service provider as part of a package.

If you do not yet have a database server, you need to obtain one in order to produce your database-driven Web site. Your options are simple:

- Your ISP may offer database servers (using one of the connection techniques outlined in this chapter).

- You can find another ISP (or database service provider) to provide that service.

- As part of the previous step, it may be cost effective to reshuffle your Internet services, possibly moving your Web site and domain mail to the DSP.

Whatever you do, remember that you need to construct an environment such as that shown in Figure 6-1; whether you purchase it as part of an all-in-one package from a vendor or construct it yourself, that is what you are looking toward.

Why Domain Names Matter

This brings up the importance of having your own domain name. If you do not have your own domain name, your Web site is addressed as part of your ISP's site—something like www.avendor.com/users/yoursite. If you move your site to another vendor, your address changes to something like www.anothervendor.net/customers/~yoursite. Needless to say, this is not a great way to make it possible for people to find your site.

When you have your own domain name, the change from one ISP to another is done by the Internet addressing agency (www.internic.net in the United States). Your site—www.mydomain.com, for example—is listed in internal Internet tables one day as being located at IP address 123.456.789.0; the next day it is listed as being at 987.654.321.0. Only you, Internic, and the two ISPs involved know this—people who type in www.mydomain.com simply arrive at the new address. (The information is propagated through the Internet's address tables and eventually all Internet sites may have the information—but only you, the Internet addressing agency, and the two ISPs ever need to deal with the issue explicitly.)

When you establish a domain name, there are typically at least two contact people provided for that domain: a technical contact and a billing contact. Often, an ISP will set up your domain name for you. Unless otherwise instructed, they will identify themselves as both contacts. If you are not setting up your domain name yourself, make certain that you (or someone at your organization) is set up as one of the contacts—usually the billing contact.

This is important because either of the two contacts can authorize a change in the domain's address. If your ISP is the only party who can change that address, you may find that they do not act particularly speedily to change your domain's address when you are transferring it to another ISP. Note that neither the new ISP nor you will be able to expedite matters: at that point it is too late. Just specify right up front that it is your policy to be one of the domain contacts. If your ISP has trouble with this, put your checkbook away and go elsewhere. As Figure 6-1 shows, your domain need not be located close to you: find a responsible ISP.

If your domain has already been established and you are not one of the contacts, ask your ISP to make the change now. You can check by looking at www.internic.net to see who the contacts are.

| Mail Accounts | Figure 6-1 shows two mail accounts—a personal mail account and a domain mail account. This is a common situation and represents the difference between sending and receiving mail. |

Receiving Mail

Internet mail is received at the domain to which it is addressed. If mydomain.com is located at IP address 192.168.1.1, all mail sent to any address at mydomain.com goes there.

These addresses are often virtual mailboxes: they are never accessed directly. The mail software may be instructed to forward messages automatically to personal (individual) mail accounts. These accounts may or may not be on the same computer. Thus, mail addressed to webmaster@mydomain.com may go to the computer at 192.168.1.1 only to be forwarded automatically to a mail account such as ttc12345@taconic.net, which is located at a completely different IP address.

For many organizations, the centralized address (mydomain.com) is mapped to any number of individual mail accounts at many different ISPs. Your domain mail must be located at the same IP address as your Web server that uses that domain; however, your personal mail account(s) can be anywhere on the Internet.

Your mail server may use the POP or IMAP protocol to let you retrieve your mail. These protocols affect how you receive your mail from your mail server, but not how it is received by the server from other Internet addresses.

Sending Mail

Internet mail is sent using the Simple Mail Transfer Protocol (SMTP). One of the characteristics of SMTP is that the sending address is not verified as part of the transaction. Thus, nothing prevents the Queen of England from sending mail with a return address of president@whitehouse.gov; by the same token, should the president of France wish to send mail with a return address indicating that it is from the prime minister of England, that is equally possible.[1]

---

1. *Editor's note:* One hopes that the world's leaders have better things to do.

This flexibility makes unsolicited e-mail (spam) possible; it also makes it very easy to manage your e-mail when it involves a domain name. In your e-mail software on your personal computer, you can specify a return address to be used on messages. Even when you are sending e-mail from your personal mail account (which might be ttc12345@taconic.net), you can set your return address to be you@mydomain.com. Thus, you can send mail "from" your domain name while logging on to your personal mail account.

In an effort to reduce spam, many ISPs are allowing mail to be sent only from people connected directly to their mail server. Thus, in Figure 6-1, if you were connected to the computer at the left marked Personal Mail, you could not use standard Internet protocols to send mail from the Domain Mail computer. You would have to dial in—or be otherwise connected—to that computer to do so. However, since you can specify the appropriate return address in your mail, this does not matter from a practical point of view.

Connecting a Server to the Internet

Whether it is a Web server, an e-mail server, or a database server, you need to connect server software to the network. There is only one way to do this: you need to have some kind of telecommunications connection between the computer with the server software and the Internet. Some of the most common connections are described in this section. They include:

- A dial-up (switched) connection such as people use to connect for Web browsing and e-mail through services like America Online and local ISPs.

- A dial-up connection with a static IP address.

- A permanent (nonswitched) connection via frame relay, integrated services digital network (ISDN), or leased lines.

- Colocation in which your computer and its server software are physically located on the premises of an Internet service provider.

- Database hosting in which your database runs on your ISP's (or DSP's) computer on its premises.

As suggested in Figure 6-1, you may use more than one connection for your various server needs.

Dial-Up Connection

The most basic connection for many people is the dial-up connection over a telephone line with a modem that they use to connect for e-mail and Web browsing. You can use this connection to connect your own computer to the Internet, and if you have database server software installed, you can combine your client computer (the one you use for your own purposes) with the basic database server that lets other people access your database.

A dial-up connection is sometimes referred to as a switched connection, reflecting the fact that a circuit is established from source to destination through one or more telephone switches.

Advantages

The advantages of dial-up connections are quite straightfoward.

You May Already Have It Many people already have this kind of connection. Your computer's operating system may incorporate Web server software as well. Even if your operating system does not incorporate Web server software, your database and/or application server may be able to function over any Internet connection—even a dial-up connection.

Note that "function" is a relative term: see "Power and Capacity"under "Disadvantages" on page 77.

Expense For all of these reasons, this may be the least expensive solution. However, be advised that it is likely to be the least useful solution as well when it comes to supporting a database server. For personal e-mail, however, it is often perfectly satisfactory.

Disadvantages The disadvantages of a dial-up connection center around the fact that while you may have such a connection and it is not particularly expensive, it is also not particularly useful for database publishing.

Power and Capacity Using a computer that you use for other purposes (e-mail, Web browsing) may not leave enough processing power or memory to run Web and database server software. Furthermore, a dedicated server (i.e., one that runs only database or Web server software) is likely to be substantially more stable than a mixed-use computer.

Availability Your computer is available on the Internet only when it is connected—that is, when you have dialed in. If people try to connect to your Web site or database at other times, they will not be able to do so.

IP Address A computer's IP address is used when people try to connect to it (even if they use a domain name, it is translated to an IP address). A dial-up connection usually provides you with a different IP address each time you connect; people cannot reliably connect to you unless they know your address.

If you are using a dial-up connection for testing, it is easy to ascertain the current IP address of your computer and to let whoever is testing know what it is.

On Mac OS, use the TCP/IP control panel to see what your current address is; on Windows, use the TCP/IP preferences in the Network control panel to check the address. In either case, make certain that you have dialed into your ISP before checking the address.

Location   Finally, you need to consider the fact that the cost of your connection to the Internet will depend on the distance between you and your ISP (since telecommunications costs are almost always based on distance). This means that the closest ISP is usually one of your first choices. In turn, that probably means that both you and your ISP are on the same power grid, subject to the same weather conditions, and vulnerable to the same disruptions in infrastructure. As you will see later ("Colocation" on page 83 and "Database Hosting" on page 86), there are ways to avoid this constraint and to improve the stability of your database-driven Web site.

Other Considerations   Despite its drawbacks, it is often satisfactory to use a dial-up connection for testing your Web site—particularly for basic testing to see whether things work as you have planned. Also, until you are used to remote administration (running your database server from afar), it can be very useful to connect at will on a computer that you can physically touch.

Cost   Costs in the United States in late 1998 range from $14.95 to $29.95 for unlimited access over a month's time. There is a substantial cost to bringing new customers on line—particularly if they have not used the Internet before or have not used the Internet from the computer they are now connecting. Four or five telephone calls to technical support are not unusual at this stage. Thereafter, things usually go smoothly. As a result, some companies charge a start-up fee (often $20) to absorb these costs. Others do not provide free technical support or limit its availability to certain hours.

It is very hard for ISPs to make money at the low end of this range. For that reason, prices are rising in various ways. The most straightforward is simply to raise the rate toward the high end of the range. Variations include changing unlimited access to a certain number of hours, allowing unlimited access but only during certain hours, and charging for technical support. The market is currently very competitive, and companies are willing to suffer losses to build up customer bases. However, you should be aware that the good deal you have today may not be there tomorrow.

Dial-Up Connection with Static IP Address	This is almost the same as the dial-up connection just described. It differs in that you do not have a different IP address each time you connect. Your ISP guarantees that you will have the same address each time you connect. You pay extra for this.
Advantages	All of the advantages of dial-up connections. In addition, the static IP address means that people can connect to your computer at will (provided that you are connected to the Internet) without having to find out your IP address each time they want to connect.
Disadvantages	All of the disadvantages of dial-up connections. In addition, the added cost of the static IP address may bring this option to a higher cost than some of the connections that follow. If you use an analog router to share a single dial-up connection among several computers using dynamic host configuration protocol (DHCP), the individual computer IP addresses may still be indeterminate unless you specify static addresses in your router—even though you are connecting to a static IP address. If you do not understand this paragraph, it probably does not apply to you.
Other Considerations	Not all ISPs offer dial-up connections with static IP addresses.

Cost	An ISP offering unlimited dial-up access for $29.95 a month (The Internet Access Company—www.tiac.net) offers static IP addresses for the same price, but with a limit of 100 hours. For 300 hours, the price for a static IP address is $49.95.[2]

Nonswitched Connection

You can eliminate the most serious disadvantage of both types of dial-up (switched) connections by using a non-switched connection—a circuit that is open at all times from your computer to the Internet. This may be a connection to an Internet service provider or to an Internet POP (point of presence)—a connection point through an organization that may or may not provide Internet services other than simple connectivity.

A nonswitched connection can be established over a direct connection (a physical line from your computer to the Internet) or through any of a number of technologies that can include ISDN, frame relay, and leased lines.

Advantages

Conceptually, a nonswitched connection is very simple; it also appears to be one simple step beyond the problems of a switched connection.

Availability   A nonswitched connection can be available at all times: you do not have to initiate a telephone call to connect to the Internet.

Reuse of Private Networks   Some organizations have private telecommunications networks that have been implemented using leased lines, ISDN, frame relay, or other technologies. These networks can be repurposed to provide Internet connectivity. This can be done by reprogramming frame relay

---

2. These and other prices given in this chapter are meant to show relative prices in the United States at the end of 1998: they are neither best buys nor endorsements.

connections to connect to an Internet POP or an ISP or by having the telephone company reconnect a leased line so that it terminates at the POP or ISP. In this way, a nonswitched connection between your computer and the Internet can be established.

The connections (leased lines, ISDN, or frame relay) can be made in two configurations. In one, the private network remains, and one computer on it is connected to the Internet. In this way, each of the terminals on the network can access the Internet over the existing private network, and shared private network resources (disks, printers, CD-ROM drives, etc.) can be used with the existing network protocols.

The second configuration involves destroying the private network; in such a scenario, each computer on the network accesses the Internet over a nonswitched line. Each computer on this network can access any other computer by going through the Internet. The only network protocols used are the standard Internet protocols, and access to network resources (disks, printers, CD-ROM drives, etc.) is only via Internet protocols (rather than networking software such as Novell Netware or Windows NT).

A hybrid configuration can be created in which a specific location (an office, a building, etc.) has its own network—a LAN—and that LAN is connected via a router and a nonswitched line to the Internet.

Disadvantages   Although nonswitched connections to the Internet would appear to solve the problems of switched lines (and they do), they are often the most expensive solution.

Running the Database Server   As noted previously, any server—e-mail, Web, or database—works best if it is dedicated to its server functions. If you use the same computer to develop Web sites, keep track of payroll, etc., you are likely to compromise the security of all files and to degrade performance for Internet users.

In addition, a server that is always available on the Internet—as one with a nonswitched line can be—needs support 24 hours a day, 7 days a week (24×7 in common parlance). There is a distinction to be made between support of the network itself, the server computer, and the databases and Web sites on the server. The network and server computer should have 24×7 support unless you are certain that no one will attempt to access them in off hours. This support can be minimal—months may go by without any problems—but it should be available as quickly as possible when it is needed.

Telecommunications Costs   Nonswitched lines are not cheap. They are usually priced by distance—and that distance can vary from a few feet to many miles in rural areas.

Location   As with the switched connections, the fact that telecommunications costs generally increase with distance normally encourages people to use an ISP that is relatively close and subject to the infrastructure problems discussed previously (see "Location" on page 78).

Other Considerations

Nonswitched solutions are very popular with organizations and employees who have been running computers for years. This is the same basic configuration that has been used in remote time sharing for three decades. Jobs (and job descriptions) are in existence, and in many organizations there is a reluctance to change.

Cost

These vary by ISP. The telecommunications costs usually vary by distance; however, one vendor (Bell Atlantic) offers frame relay anywhere within its service area for $208 a month.

Colocation

Recently, Internet service providers have started to provide colocation services. This totally eliminates the cost of telecommunications between the ISP and your server. That is because the server is physically located at the ISP's site.

The maintenance of the network communications and the basic operations of the computer (uninterrupted power, for example) are the responsibility of the ISP. Your maintenance of the server and its software must all be done over the Internet.

Advantages

This is an increasingly popular option, chiefly because of its cost and reliability.

Cost   This is almost always significantly cheaper than a non-switched solution, since there is no telecommunications component to the bill.

Reliability   An ISP that provides colocation services almost always has impressive reliability features—24×7 staff, a several-day backup diesel generator, half-day (or less) response time from maintenance providers, and a staff that specializes in the management of online computers. Such a specialized staff may not be able to provide you with any help on designing a Web page or structuring a database (although such services can be provided by some vendors), but they are likely to know in excruciating detail how to keep network communications and computers functioning through the vicissitudes that plague them.

Location   Because the computer is located at your ISP, you don't have to worry about the distance: you can choose the best colocation ISP that you can find. This might be an ISP in a separate power grid, another time zone—or even another country. If your power or telecommunications are unreliable for any reason, this enables you to avoid those problems. In fact, it may be desirable to deliberately search out an ISP that is distant from your location.

Disadvantages

The disadvantages of colocation center around the fact that it is a different way of working for many people.

Security and Liability   You need to send a computer to your ISP. Although this is a relatively easy task (the monitor can stay home), many individuals and organizations remain reluctant to ship a relatively expensive asset anywhere—much less to a company with whom they may not have done business previously. You can purchase insurance both for the transportation and for the off-site installation (some ISPs will provide this insurance as part of their contract).

In addition, you may be shipping valuable data off to your ISP on the computer's hard disk. It is less easy to insure this data. You can (and must) have backup copies of the data, but you need to assure yourself that the vendor you choose has honest and reliable employees. In fact, this is no different than the precautions that you take with the people who clean your office at night and on weekends: they have access to your computers and data. More than one B movie has featured a cleaning person with a microfilm camera.

Comfort   You may be tempted to laugh, but this is a serious consideration: there is something very reassuring to many people about being able to see their computer. When remote time sharing was first introduced three decades ago, many people were very leery about using a computer that they could not see.

Computer Cost   Finally, colocation means that in shipping a computer off to your ISP, you have one less computer to use in your office as a backup.

*Other
Considerations*

Colocation means that you get out of the hardware business: at your office you have computers that connect over the Internet to your server—wherever it is. All you need are a personal computer, Internet software, and a computer connection. (This connection can be a low-speed switched connection, since it is only for your use: the high-speed connection that supports hordes of users connecting to your database or Web server is located at your ISP.)

This enables you to work anywhere that you can find such a configuration. It also means that you no longer have to support dial-in users, high-speed connections (T1 lines, frame relay, etc.), and the hardware that manages them. If your organization has a long history of managing its own computers and networks, you may be threatening jobs and careers of people who have counted on there always being a need for network support staff. This can become a very serious issue if it is not addressed directly.

Colocation is a relatively new way of working, having been made possible by the increased reliability of hardware and software and the concomitant ability to manage them remotely. Companies are exploring colocation options, and a number of financial variations are emerging. Among them are structures in which the colocated computer is provided by the ISP under a lease arrangement, as well as hybrid services in which the ISP can provide software services. Just to make things harder, each vendor tends to use a different set of terminology and to imply that only it offers this service. In comparing prices and services, stick to your guns and make certain that you get comparable information from all vendors.

Colocation is much less expensive than running your own network operations as you would with nonswitched lines described in the previous section. However, there are sometimes cases in which the nonswitched connection is best for you—often when you have an existing operation and the upheaval of moving everything offsite would be too great. You can mitigate the costs of the nonswitched solution by realizing that you can spread those costs around if you provide colocation services to others. After all, if you have the staff and hardware resources to run a 24x7 operation, you can market that as a side product to your main activity. Remember, however, that if you do so you must compete with organizations that are providing excellent service. If that means improving your operations, it may be a benefit to everyone: you can bring in additional revenues to pay for serious backup generating power, better tele-communications lines, etc.

Cost

These arrangements are often informal (particularly in the education and nonprofit worlds): an organization with Internet access may offer you the space to install your computer in exchange for services that you can offer them. Commercially, rates vary. As an example, Digital Forest (www.digitalforest.net) offers colocation for $300 per month with a $100 start-up fee. Additional services can be arranged such as backups ($20 per month), a range of automated restart options ($10 to $20 per month), and various e-mail options (remember that e-mail for your domain must be delivered to the same physical location as your Web server, although it can be forwarded from there).

Database Hosting

Finally, you can consider database hosting. This is one step beyond colocation: your ISP maintains and owns the computer and takes charge of running the database software and the server software. With colocation, you are in charge of installing and running the basic software; with database hosting, your ISP provides you with tools (generally FTP) to upload your database. From there, the ISP takes charge.

Advantages

There are many advantages to database hosting—chiefly, it is the easiest way to get started.

As a Trial   Since you can access the database host over the Internet, you can choose a database service provider located anywhere in the world. If you have a Microsoft SQL Server database, an Oracle database, or a FileMaker Pro database, use an Internet search engine to find a vendor providing database hosting for that database. You can get a feel for how things will work by opening an account and using your database over the Internet for a few months. (This is also a good way to demonstrate capabilities for your management.) You do not need a domain name—while you are testing it is no problem to use a raw IP address. The cost of such an experiment should be well under $1000—and usually under $500.

Convenience   The computer, database, and database server are all the responsibility of the ISP/DSP. They are responsible for backups, restarts, power, telecommunications, and insurance. Of course, you should make certain that they are capable of providing these services. Do not assume that every vendor has backup power systems in place.

Disadvantages

Nevertheless, there are several disadvantages to database hosting.

Control   Even more than with colocation, you are at the mercy of your service provider. Not only is your computer outside your control, your database is running on someone else's hardware. It is important to satisfy yourself that your service provider takes your data (including its integrity and security) as seriously as you do.

Other Considerations

This is one of the most rapidly growing areas of Internet service. That means that it is highly competitive in terms of price; it also means that many people are just entering the business. Even with the best of intentions, they do not always have the skills and experience to run database systems.

Do not let this deter you. Since your database server need not be located close to you, you can choose from any company in the world.

Cost

This is often the most reasonable choice of all. Netcom (www.netcom.com) offers database hosting with Microsoft

SQL Server starting at $125 per month with a setup charge of $150. Digital Forest (which offers colocation services as described in "Cost" on page 86) offers FileMaker Pro database hosting starting at $50 per month with a setup charge of $60. Each of these services is provided as part of a package that includes a variety of e-mail accounts and/or forwarding, Web sites, etc.

Other Internet/Database Service Provider Services

It may be hard to comprehend, but it has been barely a decade since the Internet was opened to commercial use (before then it was solely for research and educational institutions). It is not even that long that the World Wide Web has been in existence. The phrase "Internet service provider" was unknown 10 years ago, and its meaning—even today—is unclear.

For many people, an ISP is really an Internet access provider: it is the organization that provides connectivity from your personal computer to the Internet. As shown in Figure 6-1 (and others throughout the book), that connectivity need not include any Internet services (such as e-mail, news, and the Web). Those services are provided by some Internet service providers as part of packages (basic or advanced), as well as by companies that bill themselves as database service providers (if they provide database hosting) or enterprise service providers (if they provide the range of services that an enterprise may need).

This range of nomenclature and services reflects an industry (perhaps more than one) that is growing and defining itself daily. The participants arrive on the playing field from many directions: telephone companies add Internet access to their range of services, computer service bureaus add telephony to their products, and start-ups invent totally new ways of approaching the problem.

Two points should remain clear:

1. Whatever the nomenclature, Figure 6-1 represents the architecture (or topology) of your Internet access. It is based on the Internet's protocols (particularly the TCP/IP communications protocol, HTTP for the Web, POP/SMTP for e-mail, and Usenet for Internet news groups).

2. Providing basic dial-in access is very expensive. It requires significant customer support (particularly for new customers), and it is a very competitive market. The lowest rates (under $20 in the United States for unlimited access as of late 1998) are generally not financially tenable for most organizations.

For all of these reasons, a variety of additional services are being offered. Some of them are described in this section. Because basic Internet services are like commodities (they are standardized and interchangeable), you may choose your ISPs based on their support of these additional services if they are important to you.

E-Commerce and Secure Servers	In order to conduct business transactions over the Web, it is usually necessary to implement some form of security for transmissions. Common forms of such security are the Secure Sockets Layer (SSL), secure HTTP (S-HTTP), and Secure Electronic Transfer (SET): they must be implemented within the user's browser as well as within the Web server software at the ISP.

An ISP may offer these and other forms of security and encryption to help you conduct e-commerce over the Web. Often, an ISP that specializes in e-commerce will also offer additional services that may be of interest to you: a common such service is the ability to accept credit cards for transactions. The ISP (or a business partner) allows you to use its merchant credit card accounts to accept payment for your goods and services. For a small organization that does not have merchant accounts established with credit card companies, this can be an efficient one-stop shopping spree to set up e-commerce.

For more information, see "Secure Servers" starting on page 379.

Maintenance and Support

ISPs offer a certain degree of maintenance and support as part of their routine services. They may price off-site backups as an additional fee, and some ISPs provide highly redundant hardware (often in widely separated locations) to help minimize the danger of power outages. ISPs providing services to the largest companies charge rates far higher than those shown previously in this chapter, but they are basically offering an uninterruptible Internet connection.

To help solve the problem of bringing new dial-in customers on line, some ISPs offer a sort of "drive-thru" service. You drop off your computer in the morning and pick it up later in the day. It will have all of the appropriate Internet software installed, modem phone numbers will be set, and you should have nothing to do back at your home or office but to plug it in. Other ISPs will provide house (or office) calls to set up your computers; still others will recommend consultants to do the job. Note that this is usually necessary only if you have not used the Internet before or if you are attempting to install Internet software on a computer that for one reason or another seems reluctant to connect to the Internet. (A common reason is the existence somewhere in the operating system or hard disk of a previously installed Internet connection that rears its ugly head at inopportune moments.)

Site Development Services	Nowhere is it decreed that you must develop your own Web site. You can hire designers to create a Web site for you; you may hire the same people or different ones to maintain it over time. Some ISPs offer Web design as part of their add-on services. ISPs and DSPs may also offer database development services to enable you to take advantage of their Internet database offerings.
Training	Training in using the Internet as well as in developing and maintaining Web and database sites is also provided by some ISPs. This training can be in person or on line. Some ISPs have extensive Web sites that provide very sophisticated training in Internet capabilities.
Hardware	ISPs sometimes sell hardware. In the case of colocation (where your computer is located at the ISP's site), you may find a vendor that leases that computer to you as part of a package. ISPs have also been known to sell modems and other telecommunications items. By the same token, traditional computer vendors may sell Internet services that they provide themselves or through partners.
Cybercasting	Cybercasting (or Webcasting) lets you broadcast video and audio over the Internet. It is typically used to broadcast conferences, sales meetings, and other special events. Using software such as RealPlayer, it can also be used for the routine transmission of video and audio such as radio and television broadcasts.

Cybercasting requires large bandwidth so that people can connect to the event. There are companies that specialize in this technology. If your organization needs such services, you can use one of those companies—or use an ISP that provides such services. This is often a cost-effective alternative to providing high-speed bandwidth to your site for relatively infrequent events.

And More...

Since this area is in such a state of flux, many options are emerging every day. Combinations of the add-on services listed here are provided by existing companies as well as by newcomers with new ideas. Because Internet technology lets you combine services from various vendors in various locations, you can mix and match the vendors and services until you find a mix that suits your needs. Alternatively, you can shop around for a one-stop solution that best fits your objectives.

And if you do not find the particular combination of services that you need, nothing prevents you from putting such a combination together—and marketing it to other people.

Summary

You need to connect yourself to the Internet in order to send and receive e-mail and to maintain your database and Web site. In addition, you need to find a Web server and a database server to host your database driven Web site. These may be found at a single Internet service provider, or you may assemble these services from a variety of vendors.

Now, it is on to your database. Which one should it be?

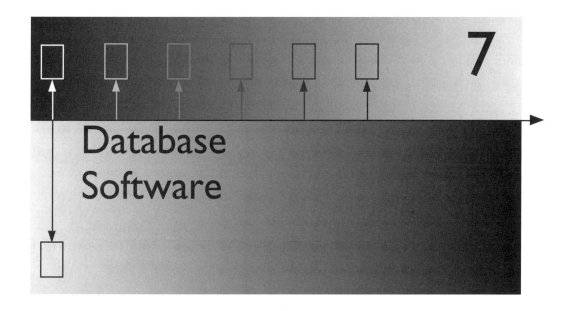

7

Database
Software

The heart of a database-driven Web site is a database. If you are starting from scratch (or from the perspective of a Webmaster who knows little or nothing about databases), you need to be able to evaluate the options and make an appropriate choice.

On the other hand, if your database is a given—either because you already use one, your organization has a particular database installed, or the ISP/DSP that you have chosen supports only certain databases—you need to know how that database can be used to drive a Web site.

This chapter provides an overview of the database software world of the late 1990s. It starts with some of the great secrets of databases, then proceeds to an overview of the types of databases on the market, and concludes with a look at some of the major databases in use to-day. Many of those databases are designed to be supported by pro-gramming staffs (or at least individual programmers); for the two that are designed for end-user support (Microsoft Access and File-Maker Pro), details are provided to show you how to set them up for use on the Web.

The Great Database Secrets

If you are new to the world of databases, there are some aspects of it that may surprise you. Even if you have been around for a while, you may not have noticed three hallmarks of databases when compared with other software products.

- Quality
- Similarity
- Marketing of databases

Quality

Database software is generally among the highest quality software available today. Database software actually does relatively few things: it stores and retrieves data, manages indexing and retrieval of the data, and is responsible for various housekeeping and management tasks. A database management system may well have fewer features and functions than a word processor.

Furthermore, database software has been developed over many decades. The notions of what it should do—and how it should do it—have been discussed, taught, and learned as part of computer science courses. The same is not necessarily true with typical personal computer productivity tools: on the one hand, they are such new products and concepts that standards and expectations have not emerged. On the other hand, the users of many personal computer products are less demanding than the financial institutions, manufacturers, airlines, utilities, and governments that have come to rely on databases for their business operations.

It is disconcerting to veterans of mainframe computers and large database systems to hear personal computer users and consultants say things like, "Just reboot," or "Reinstall the operating system." In environments that manage trillions of dollars of transactions a day (as some of the largest database systems do), as well as systems that may have hundreds or thousands of users connected at all times, rebooting and reinstalling software (much less an operating system) are simply not viable options. As a result, the users of database software have demanded a level of reliability and stability that has not—until now—been demanded of many other software products.

Despite marketing claims to the contrary, you really cannot go wrong choosing any of the major database products on the market today. That is because they are all of high quality—and because they are remarkably similar.

Similarity

Marketing managers might cringe, but the fact is that database management systems are quite similar to one another. As noted previously, the tasks that a DBMS is expected to perform are quite clear by now. The differences among the products have to do with how they go about those tasks and who they are designed for.

The biggest distinction is between DBMS products that have been designed for large computers and those that have been designed for personal computers. Today, the difference in features is rather small; nevertheless, a personal computer–based product is not going to be able to run an international airline's reservations system. By the same token, the overhead and cost of a major mainframe DBMS will be overkill for your personal to-do list.

Marketing of Databases

Personal computer software is often treated much as a commodity: the products are relatively interchangeable, and the product with the most features is often considered the best (particularly if costs are equal, as they usually are for each type of product).

Mainframe software and high-end database software are marketed and purchased quite differently. The feature set for DBMS products is fairly set. Whereas nifty new features in word processing software are added right and left, the purchasers of DBMS products tend to look askance at new features: in every case, the question is, "Yes, but will it slow things up?" In databases, speed is everything (stability and reliability are taken for granted and are not part of most product comparisons).

Within the last few years, the power of personal computers has increased dramatically along with their abilities to network efficiently with one another and with larger computers. As a result, there is a large group of applications that no longer are clearly the province of mainframe databases or of personal computer databases. The personal to-do list is pretty definitely a personal computer project, and the international airline's reservation system is equally clearly a mainframe project. But inventory control systems for a wide array of organizations can live happily in either environment, as can order entry, customer information systems, license and permit information (even for entities as large as states and provinces), and information retrieval systems.

With so many types of projects appropriate for either personal computer or mainframe database systems, the two cultures (which are quite different) are meeting with sometimes dynamic results. Two specific areas are likely to matter to you.

Database Pricing   Shrink-wrapped personal computer products are sold in stores, over the Internet, or through the mail; they also often come preinstalled on new computers. Priced and marketed like commodities, they are assumed to be quite price sensitive. Customers have grown accustomed to buying a word processing product, a spreadsheet, or a database product.

On the other hand, database software that has been designed for use on mainframe computers and in other large installations is often marketed and sold by people. Terms and deals are arranged for each sale, but they often take into account how many people will be using the database software. ("Simultaneous users" and "seats" are terms related to this concept.) When you buy a shrink-wrapped database product to install on your office LAN, you do not think about how many people will use it (except to remember that each user must have a separate copy of the software).

Using a database on the Web poses a difficult pricing problem for this model. Since the Web is essentially stateless (see "Sessions and Transactions" on page 55), each access to the database—from the same person or a different person—appears as a new transaction. The application server software manages these transactions, and from the database's point of view, there is usually only one "user" connected to it—and that is the application server.

For a company that has a price structure based on the number of people using the database, this poses all sorts of problems. Clearly, the one "user" that is the application server does not mean that there is actually one user; equally clearly, the fact that scores of millions of people on the Internet could access the database does not mean that a license should be prepared for those scores of millions.

You may run across this issue particularly if you and your organization are already using a database product and you attempt to modify your license agreement to allow it to be used over the Web. Some companies and some salespeople are adept at working out the appropriate terms; in other cases, you may be presented with estimates (or even bills) for what appear to be ridiculous sums. Over the next few years, as more people use databases on the Web, these issues should be resolved. In the meantime, be aware that they exist—and why they exist. It is not uncommon to wind up with cost estimates from different database vendors that differ by one or two orders of magnitude (for apparently the same functionality).

Platforms and Environments

Most databases run on a variety of hardware and operating system platforms. (In an exception to this generalization, the Microsoft products discussed in this chapter—Access and SQL Server—run only on Microsoft's Windows operating systems.) This is scarcely surprising, since the companies that develop and market databases typically do not develop or market hardware or operating systems (IBM and Microsoft being the main exceptions).

DBMS products today often run on a variety of brands and types of hardware. DB2, for example, runs on everything from IBM's largest computers to personal computers. Oracle also runs on a wide variety of computers and operating systems. One of the attractions of database-centered architectures is that there are so few constraints: you can switch databases, hardware, or operating systems, all the while leaving your basic database design intact. The addition of the Web and its standard protocols extends this mix-and-match approach to almost the entire database project that you design. The freedom and flexibility that come from knowing that virtually any computer running any operating system can access your database is quite valuable. Furthermore, the fact that you can pick up your database and move it to another computer (even another kind of hardware and another operating system) prevents you from being locked into other products that may suddenly become very expensive (or even unavailable).

This flexibility comes at a price: you may have to be more involved with assembling your database environment than you want. There are advantages to one-stop shopping, and it may well be worth it to purchase everything from a hardware vendor or consultant.

Finally, note that this flexibility—which can be quite beneficial to customers—is not always welcomed by vendors of hardware, operating systems, and databases. Today's customer may be tomorrow's customer for a competitor, since change is relatively easy. Vendors often add features to their products that are not duplicated by their competitors; as a result, you can easily design systems that are not portable.

Types of Databases

There are three basic types of databases in use today:

1. End-user tools

2. Programmer tools

3. Custom-written databases

End-User Tools   These products (such as dBase and its associated products, Microsoft Access, and FileMaker Pro) are designed to be able to be used by end users. A reasonably sophisticated personal computer user can design and implement a database project fairly easily. These products ship with templates and examples for standard types of projects, and many people base their solutions on these templates and examples.

Although early versions of these products did not always offer multiuser capabilities or relational database features, today's versions of the products offer most of the standard database functionality that is found in even the largest database management systems.

These products typically include a graphical user interface to use in constructing databases as well as input screens and reports. The latest versions offer Web publishing capabilities.

As noted previously, these products are priced in the same way that other personal computer software is: you buy one copy for each computer that uses the software. (Bulk discounts and site licenses are often available, just as they are for word processors and spreadsheets.) In addition, many of these products come preinstalled on computers either by themselves or as part of a suite of productivity applications.

FileMaker Pro and Access are discussed later in this chapter. They include basic features of application servers (the middleware discussed in the next chapter), and this functionality is discussed at length in "Microsoft Access" on page 101 and "FileMaker Pro" on page 140.

The fact that these products have been designed to make it easy for relatively sophisticated end users to design database projects in no way makes them toys. Their power is quite impressive, and many consultants argue that they are more productive with these tools because so much of the overhead of larger database management systems simply does not exist in the personal computer environment.

Programmer Tools

These databases have often been developed for mainframes or minicomputers. They are designed for use by programmers and database designers (who frequently develop interfaces allowing novices to access their databases).

These products are usually more expensive than the shrink-wrapped end-user tools, and their pricing is often negotiated based on the number of users.

Custom-Written Databases	In addition to commercially available databases, custom-written databases are in use in a number of applications. Sometimes they represent legacy code—old software that has done the job for many years and has no need to be replaced when other tasks have higher priorities. Custom-written databases were often developed to overcome shortcomings in commercial products (such as their inability to store data types such as sound, video, and graphics—limitations that generally have been overcome for most products but that may have posed serious problems when applications were developed).

Microsoft Access

Microsoft Access is an end-user database tool that is distributed as part of the Office Suite. With recent versions, you can use it to publish data on the Web, as shown schematically in Figure 7-1. It runs on the Windows operating system.

(Compare this diagram with the one shown using generic terms in "HTTP and the Web" on page 48.)

There are several important points to note about this architecture:

- The Web server (IIS) can be Microsoft Internet Information Server (on Windows NT), Microsoft Personal Web Server (on Windows 95), or Peer Web Services (on Windows NT Workstation). In this chapter, IIS is used to refer to whichever of these products you are using. (In fact, it is the Internet Database Connector component that is a part of these products that actually does the work.)

- Two mechanisms are available for producing the HTML files that will be delivered to the browser by IIS—one involves a pair of files (IDC and HTX files), and the other involves a single file (an Active Server Page—ASP—file).

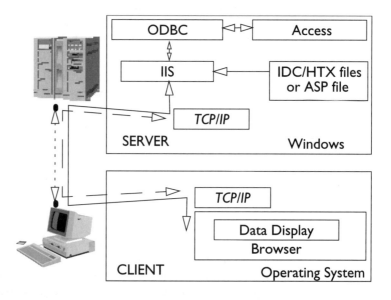

FIGURE 7-1. Microsoft Access: Publishing on the Web

Like FileMaker Pro (see page 140), Microsoft Access is used by end users as well as by consultants and programmers. Because these products are so widely used by nonprogrammers, more detail is given about their workings than for the other products discussed in this chapter.

**Microsoft
Access
Overview**

A Microsoft Access database consists of objects that can be created and modified from the window shown in Figure 7-2. (Unless otherwise noted, all figures in this section use the Event Management template database that ships with Microsoft Access.)

FIGURE 7-2. Objects in a Microsoft Access Database

You select one of the tabs at the top of the dialog box in order to display a list of objects of that type. You can then open, design (or modify), or create new ones. In Figure 7-2, forms are displayed, and the Switchboard form is highlighted.

Tables

Tables are the basic repositories of data in Microsoft Access databases. Like all database tables, they consist of rows and columns; in that way, they are quite similar to spreadsheets, which also are laid out with rows and columns. You can display a table as a datasheet—the simplest way of presenting its data, as shown in Figure 7-3. This is the Payments table from the Events Management template; you can open it from the Tables tab by highlighting Payments and clicking Open.

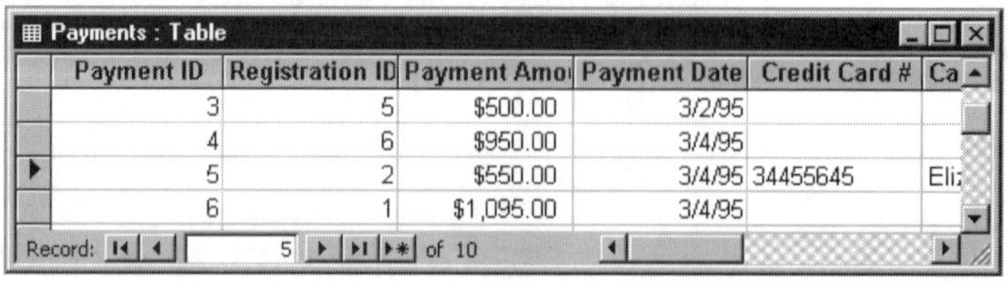

Payment ID	Registration ID	Payment Amo	Payment Date	Credit Card #	Ca
3	5	$500.00	3/2/95		
4	6	$950.00	3/4/95		
5	2	$550.00	3/4/95	34455645	Eli:
6	1	$1,095.00	3/4/95		

Record: 5 of 10

FIGURE 7-3. Payments Table Datasheet

The arrow at the left in Figure 7-3 shows the current record. You can use the arrows at the bottom of the window to navigate through the table.

If you want to enter a new record, you enter it in the first blank row at the bottom of the table. In either a new record or an existing record, you can enter and change data simply by typing the appropriate value in the cell. Figure 7-4 shows the value of Registration ID for Payment ID 5 changed from 2 (as shown in Figure 7-3) to 1. (This means that a specific payment—5, in this case—is to be credited to registrant number 1 rather than to registrant number 2.)

As shown in Figure 7-4, records that have been changed have a small pencil in the left border of the window. When you have completed your changes, you can save them all using the Save Record command from the Records menu.

You can automate this entire process using forms—users need never see datasheets and Microsoft Access commands; nevertheless, they are underneath everything that is happening.

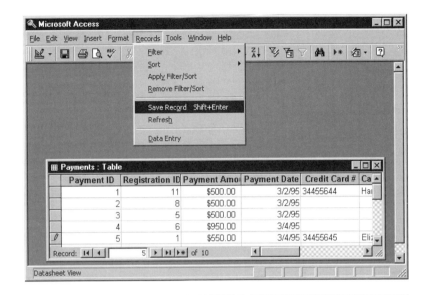

FIGURE 7-4. Changing Data in the Payments Table

You can design your table graphically from a datasheet, as shown in Figure 7-5. You do this by selecting (or creating) a table, highlighting it in the dialog box shown in Figure 7-2, and clicking the Define button.

The interface lets you set a great deal of meta-data about your table; note particularly that in the lower left of Figure 7-5 you can see how you can create automatic edits for your data.

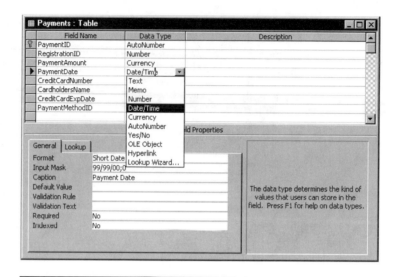

FIGURE 7-5. Designing the Payments Table

Queries

Queries are used to extract information from the tables in a database. In Microsoft Access, you can formulate queries using a graphical user interface. You click the Queries tab in the database window (Figure 7-2) and then click New or Define to create a new or modify an existing query.

The query definition window is shown in Figure 7-6. This is the Sum of Payments Query from the Event Management template.

As defined here, the query retrieves data from two fields—the Registration ID and Payments. The Registration IDs are to be shown in the first column of the query result table; in the second column is the sum of all payments for that registrant.

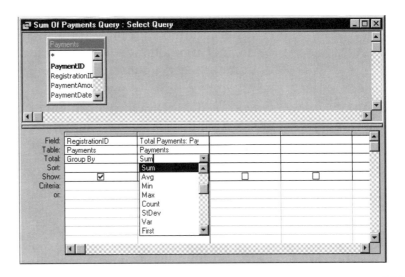

FIGURE 7-6. Microsoft Access Query Definition

If you open the query with the Open button, you see the results shown in Figure 7-7. If you have not used Microsoft Access (or a similar database) before, you can quickly get the hang of how it works by opening a table and a query based on that table.

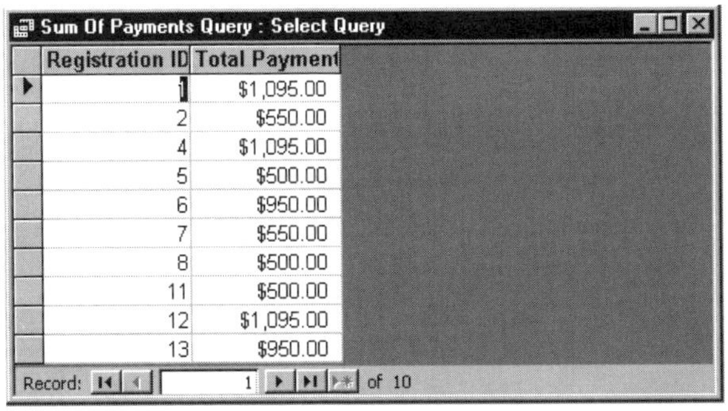

FIGURE 7-7. Microsoft Access Query Results

Then, change data in the table (don't forget to save the changed records), and refresh the query—using the Refresh command from the menu (you can also close and reopen it). You should see the data change automatically in the query.

Criteria for Queries   The query shown here selects all the data and performs a basic aggregation—summing all payments for a given registrant. You can create queries that select only certain data—data that meets one or more criteria. Figure 7-8 shows how you specify such criteria.

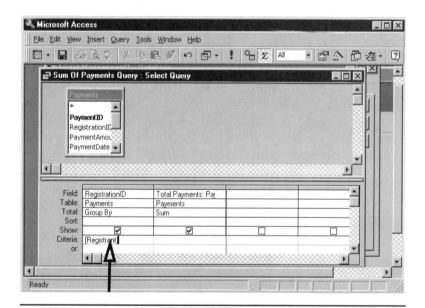

FIGURE 7-8. Query with a Criterion

In this case, a criterion is established. Only those values of RegistrationID that meet the criterion will be shown. Microsoft Access will automatically prompt the user for the value to be used; you enter the name of the criterion (in this case "Registrant") as shown in Figure 7-8 (the arrow points to the name of the criterion that you enter).

Note that you can establish criteria even for data elements that are not shown. The Show checkboxes toward the bottom of each column determine whether data is used only for selection criteria or is also displayed.

After this, when you open the query, Microsoft Access will pose a dialog box. In order to edit the criterion's parameters properly, you need to specify their type. You do this as shown in Figure 7-9. (You open the Query Parameters dialog box from the Parameters… command in the Query menu.)

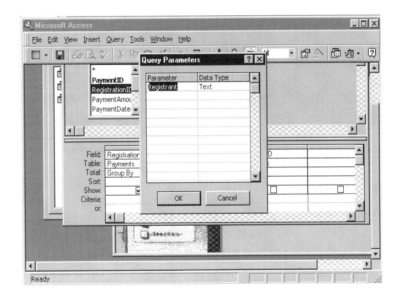

FIGURE 7-9. Setting Query Parameter Data Types

After this, when you open or run the query, you are first presented with the dialog box shown in Figure 7-10. Microsoft Access uses the information that you have provided about the type of the parameter to edit the entry. If it is not valid, the appropriate error message is displayed.

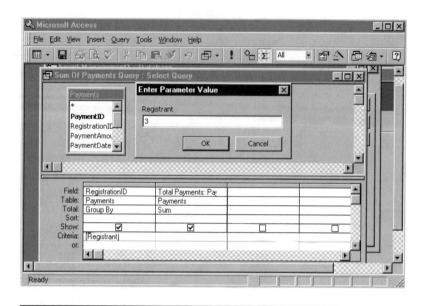

FIGURE 7-10. Entering the Parameter Value for a Criterion

Forms

A typical Microsoft Access Form is shown in Figure 7-11.

Although it presents some of the same information shown in the table and query, it presents it in a much simpler way for users to view it. The graphics make the display not only more attractive but also easier for most people to use than the work-horse graphics of the previous figures.

You can use controls in forms (such as the button in the lower left of Figure 7-11—highlighted with the arrow) to add programming actions to your forms. For this, you most often use Visual Basic (for more information see "Visual Basic" on page 113).

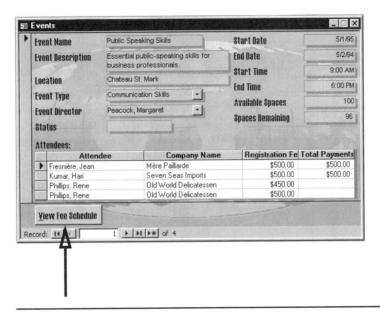

FIGURE 7-11. Events Database Shown in an Access Form

Since a form can contain such active controls—and need not display any data whatsoever—you can construct forms such as the Main Switchboard form for the Event Management template, which is shown in Figure 7-12: all it does it is let the user open other forms.

Reports   Reports are similar to forms in that they combine data with graphics; they differ in that they are designed for output only. You cannot add interactive controls (such as buttons) to reports, nor can you enter data into them.

Reports are not part of Microsoft Access on the Web.

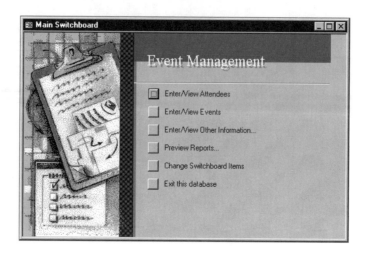

FIGURE 7-12. Switchboard for Event Management Database

Macros

Macros let you automate certain tasks that a user would normally perform with the mouse and keyboard. They can be linked to controls (such as buttons) so that they execute automatically on a mouseclick or other event. They can also be added to the menu bar.

Macros can be useful for performing very simple tasks (such as opening a form), but the Visual Basic programming language is much more powerful and in the long run is easier to maintain.

Modules

Modules contain Visual Basic code that you can write (or import from other sources). This code consists of routines that are executed when specific events occur. These routines may be associated with a particular Microsoft Access form or report (class objects) or they can be associated with the database as a whole (standard objects).

These routines are often used to enhance the user interface, making buttons perform appropriate actions and manipulating data in response to user actions. On the Web, the entire interface is replaced by HTML pages; as a result, many of these routines are unnecessary (or cannot be used because the events that initiate them do not occur in the Web environment).

However, you should have a general understanding of how this code works (if only to be able to sidestep or duplicate it as necessary in the Web environment).

Event Driven　The most important feature of this structure is that it is event driven: these routines execute only when a specified event occurs. Each object in Microsoft Access has a number of predefined events associated with it. For example, a button has an event that is triggered when you click on it; a form has events that are triggered when it is first opened, then when its data is loaded, and finally when it is closed. You can associate a routine with any of these events, as well as with the events of the database itself (which is how you can display a standard form or do other processing automatically whenever the database is opened).

Visual Basic　Visual Basic is the programming language that is used for these modules. It is thoroughly object oriented and can be developed using the sophisticated graphical programming interface provided.

A typical module window is shown in Figure 7-13.

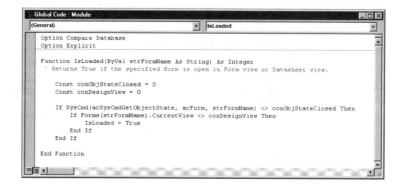

FIGURE 7-13. Visual Basic at Work

Using ODBC

Internet Information Server (or Personal Web Server) needs to connect to your Microsoft Access database as well as to the files that it will use to produce the HTML files that will be downloaded to the user's browser (see the figure "Microsoft Access: Publishing on the Web" on page 102). The design that is used has an intermediary—Open Database Connectivity (ODBC) as shown in that figure.

The reason for the use of an intermediary is that the Internet Information Server can connect to any database (that conforms to ODBC) without knowing its inner details. ODBC has a driver for each type of database that it supports; those drivers let ODBC carry out whatever functions are requested by the Internet Information Server.

This is a common architecture, and it is implemented by many vendors in many ways—sometimes in more than one way by a single vendor. In this case, newer technologies from Microsoft including OLE DB and ActiveX Data Objects (ADO) may be used instead of or in addition to ODBC.

Note that the ODBC driver for Microsoft Access may require separate installation: see your documentation or use the online help for further details.

Before you can use your Microsoft Access database on the Internet, you need to create an ODBC data source. You do this by double-clicking the ODBC icon from the Control Panels folder. This opens the dialog box shown in Figure 7-14.

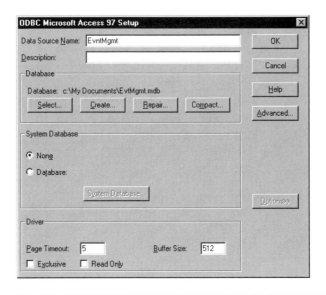

FIGURE 7-14. Setting up ODBC

You assign a name to your database and locate it on your hard disk. To locate it, click the Select button to open the window shown in Figure 7-15. If you cannot select Microsoft Access files in the file type selector in the lower left of that dialog box, you do not have the Microsoft Access ODBC driver installed. Review your documentation or online help to find where the driver is located in your software product.

FIGURE 7-15. Selecting a Database for ODBC

The whole idea of ODBC is to enable you to access a database through a data source name (DSN) rather than through a specific file name. To use this feature appropriately, create a DSN that is meaningful rather than descriptive of a file's location.

Thus, you might create a DSN such as Calendar. In your ODBC setup dialog, you can select a database called CalendarTest for that DSN. Later, you could change the database to CalendarProd (the production version of that database). This enables you to keep all of your other database-related files the same even as you switch databases (or move them from one disk to another).

Publishing on the Web

There are three ways to publish Microsoft Access databases on the Web:

1. You can use static HTML to display data from your database on Web pages. This method only displays data—it cannot be updated.

2. You can use IDC/HTX files to display data and to allow updates to it. This technique works with most Internet software.

3. You can use Active Server Pages (ASP) to display and allow updates to your data. This mechanism is not supported in all Internet browsers for forms that require the HTML Layout ActiveX control; in practice, this is the case for pages based on Microsoft Access forms that are saved as Active Server Pages.

You can create the necessary files to publish your database on the Web either manually or by using the Publish to the Web wizard. You can combine these methods by using the wizard to create basic files that you modify manually as you see fit. (It can also be very useful to run the wizard to create files that you use for reference or as a tutorial as you manually create your own files.)

In this section, the Publish to the Web wizard is presented, followed by discussions of the three publishing methods—static HTML, IDC/HTX, and ASP.

Remember that IDC/HTX and ASP files are used by the Web server to generate the HTML that is downloaded to users' browsers. Although HTML is part of these files, it is not downloaded directly to browsers; it is input to the Web server.

Publish to the Web Wizard

The wizard is a good way to take a database (or components thereof) and generate files that can be used to publish it on the Web or for basic reference.

Note that the wizard may not be installed automatically during your Microsoft Access installation; it may need to be installed manually from a value pack. See your documentation for further details.

Once the wizard has been installed, you can launch it by choosing Save As HTML from the File menu.

Using the Publish to the Web Wizard   The first step is shown in Figure 7-16. This screen provides an introduction to the wizard and gives you the option of using stored publishing parameters that you have set in a previous session. (You store these parameters at the end of your work with the wizard—see "Publish to the Web Wizard—7" on page 124.)

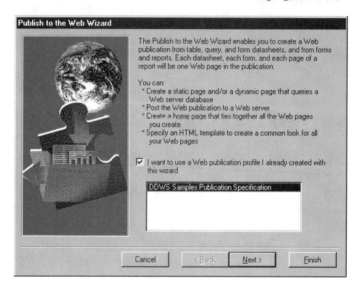

FIGURE 7-16. Publish to the Web Wizard—1

The next screen lets you select the database objects that you want to publish. You can choose a single table, form, or query, or any combination that you want. Figure 7-17 shows this screen.

Having selected the objects that you want to publish, you move on to the screen shown in Figure 7-18. Here, you are able to specify a default HTML document as a template for your pages (you can also select an option to use different templates for different pages). This allows you to create a template for your site (or for sections of it) that provides uniform graphics and design features.

It is much, much easier to use a template in this way than to add your logo, standard navigation buttons, etc. to each and every page of your site.

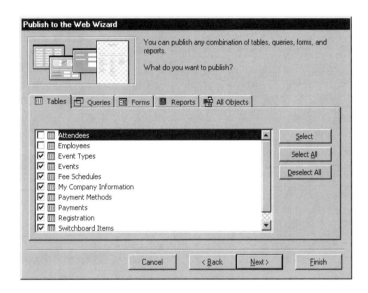

FIGURE 7-17. Publish to the Web Wizard—2

Next, you choose the type of pages that the wizard will generate, as shown in Figure 7-19. As noted there, static HTML pages can be used to display any object in your database, but they do not allow any updates; dynamic pages query your database as they are produced for a user, allow updates, and can be used only for tables, queries, and forms. (These types of pages are discussed later in this section.)

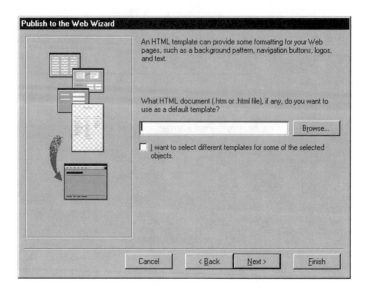

FIGURE 7-18. Publish to the Web Wizard—3

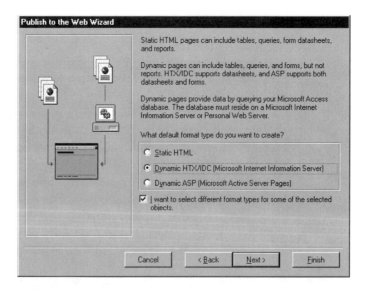

FIGURE 7-19. Publish to the Web Wizard—4

As with the templates in the previous screen, you can choose an option to use different types of pages for different database objects.

If you chose the option to use different types of pages for different database objects, you next see the screen shown in Figure 7-20. In this window, all of the objects that you selected for publication are listed. You can highlight each one and select a format type from the three options at the right.

By selecting a default option in the screen shown in Figure 7-19, you can quickly use this screen to select a few objects that use a different type of publication. (Often, the combination will be static HTML for certain pages and either HTX/IDC or ASP for the others. Mixing HTX/IDX with ASP is not particularly common.)

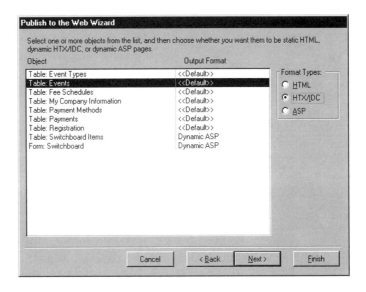

FIGURE 7-20. Publish to the Web Wizard—Choosing Types of Files

Also at this point, you may be presented with the screen shown in Figure 7-21. If you have set any pages to use dynamic HTML (IDC/HTX or ASP pages), the wizard needs to know what ODBC data source will be used to generate those pages when users ask for them. You enter that information in this screen.

Note that you can enter that information even if the data source does not yet exist: it must exist only when people actually use your pages.

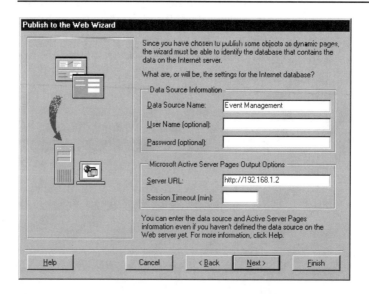

FIGURE 7-21. Publish to the Web Wizard—Specifying a Data Source

On the screen shown in Figure 7-22 you can choose where on your hard disk to save the files that the wizard creates. You can also choose to run automatically the Web publishing wizard, which will move the files to your Web server. Figure 7-23 shows the next step in the process: you can ask the wizard to create a home page for the pages that it is generating here. You can name that page as you see fit. (As you can see, the wizard actually can create an entire site for you.)

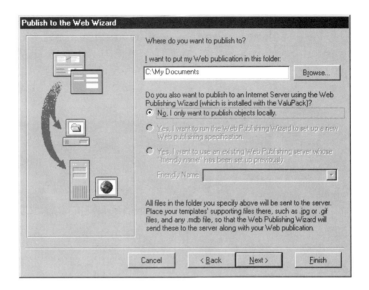

FIGURE 7-22. Publish to the Web Wizard—5

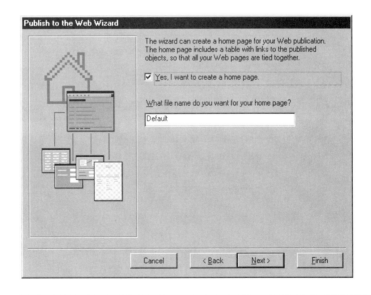

FIGURE 7-23. Publish to the Web Wizard—6

You can save the publication settings that you have used in this session in a profile, as shown in Figure 7-24. If you do so, you can then use that profile by entering its name in the first wizard screen.

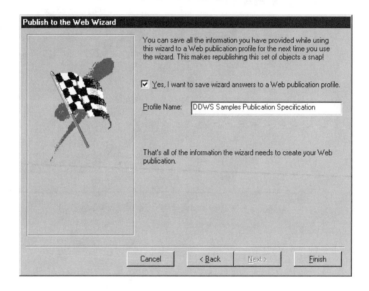

FIGURE 7-24. Publish to the Web Wizard—7

Static HTML

This is the simplest way to publish data on the Web. You use Microsoft Access to display the data that you want to publish (by running a query, opening a form, or displaying an entire table); then, you simply save that window as an HTML file, using the Save As HTML... command from the File menu as shown in Figure 7-25.

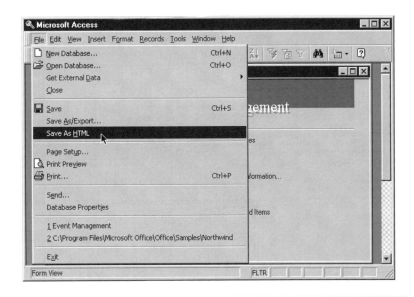

FIGURE 7-25. Save As HTML

As with all Save As commands, you will be prompted for the location and name of the file to be created. (If the Publish to the Web wizard has been installed, you will be prompted through the screens shown in the previous section.)

If you were to save the Events table from the Event Management template using the Save As HTML command, an HTML file would be created that would look like Figure 7-26 when displayed in a browser.

Note that you can display HTML files in a browser without being connected to the Internet. All major Internet browsers provide the ability to do this, but they use different commands to access files on your computer. See their documentation or online help for further details.

This is the data from your database as it exists at the time that you save the HTML file. Subsequent changes to that data in the database do not affect the HTML file.

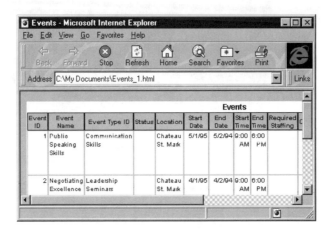

FIGURE 7-26. Events Table in Web Browser

As noted previously, you can use the Publish to the Web wizard to save multiple tables, forms, and queries to a number of Web pages that it will automatically generate. As a result, you can automatically create the HTML page shown in Figure 7-27 from the Event Management template database.

This page is the automatically generated default home page (like the Main Switchboard form shown in Figure 7-12) that lets you select from among the automatically created HTML files for the objects in the Event Management template database that you chose to publish with the Publish to the Web wizard.

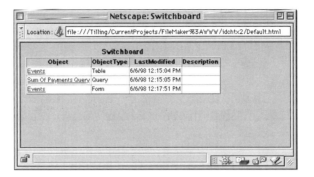

FIGURE 7-27. Default Home Page for Switchboard

Using IDC/HTX Files

The combination of Internet Database Connector (IDC) and HTML Extension (HTX) files lets you publish a table, query, or form datasheet. You specify a name for the files, and two files—one with a suffix of .idc and the other with a suffix of .htx—are automatically created.

The IDC/HTX combination works with all browsers, and it is similar to the way in which other databases on other systems generate dynamic database-based pages.

The rest of this section describes IDC/HTX files. You may never see them and certainly may never create them manually. They are created by Microsoft Access. Nothing prevents you from creating them manually—or from modifying the generated files. Do not let this section scare you: if it does, just skip it and rely on the Publish to the Web wizard and default layouts.

Connecting to IDC/HTX Data The user is able to connect to your data by typing in a URL for the .idc file followed by a question mark. In practice, rather than typing in the URL, users typically click on a link in another file in order to get to your page.

If you ask the Publish to the Web wizard to create a default home page, it will automatically generate such code for the IDC/HTX file(s) that it is creating. Of course, you can create such code yourself: it is very simple.

Here is the code for the default home page generated by the Publish to the Web wizard and shown previously in Figure 7-27.

HTML code is discussed later in this book (see "HTML for Database Designers" on page 233), but even without knowing much about it, you can easily pinpoint the crucial lines of code in this file—and you can change them if you need to do so. The most important lines of code are underlined, and comments have been added for each one.

```
<HTML>
<HEAD>
<META HTTP-EQUIV="Content-Type" CONTENT="text/html;char-
set=windows-1252">
<TITLE>Switchboard</TITLE>'
```

This is the title of the page; it is displayed in the browser's window title.

```
</HEAD>
<BODY>
<TABLE BORDER=1 BGCOLOR=#ffffff CELLSPACING=0><FONT FACE="Ari-
al" COLOR=#000000><CAPTION><B>Switchboard</B></CAPTION>
```

This is the caption for the table; it is displayed in boldfaced text.

```
<THEAD>
<TR>
<TH BGCOLOR=#c0c0c0 BORDERCOLOR=#000000 ><FONT SIZE=2
FACE="Arial" COLOR=#000000>Object</FONT></TH>
<TH BGCOLOR=#c0c0c0 BORDERCOLOR=#000000 ><FONT SIZE=2
FACE="Arial" COLOR=#000000>ObjectType</FONT></TH>
<TH BGCOLOR=#c0c0c0 BORDERCOLOR=#000000 ><FONT SIZE=2
FACE="Arial" COLOR=#000000>LastModified</FONT></TH>
<TH BGCOLOR=#c0c0c0 BORDERCOLOR=#000000 ><FONT SIZE=2
FACE="Arial" COLOR=#000000>Description</FONT></TH>
```

These are the column headings in the table. If you want to change them, just type over the underlined text. Likewise, you can change the font and color for the text—but that requires a minimal (very minimal) knowledge of HTML.

```
</TR>
</THEAD>
<TBODY>
<TR VALIGN=TOP>
<TD BORDERCOLOR=#c0c0c0 ><U><FONT SIZE=2 FACE="Arial" COL-
OR=#0000ff><A HREF="Events_1.idc?">Events</A></FONT></U></TD>
```

This is the underlined link you click on to open the Events idc page. It is a very important line of code, and it is one that you will see (and write) frequently. The name of the file that has been created is Events_1.idc (the companion file is Events_1.htx)—that is the name that was typed into the Save As file dialog box. You create a link to the file with this line of code; the text that will be displayed is "Events." A link to the same page with the text "Click Here to See Events" would look like `<A HREF="Events_1.idc?">Click Here to See Events</A>`. If you feel that you could create such links on your own just by blindly following this formula, you are absolutely right.

```
<TD BORDERCOLOR=#c0c0c0 ><FONT SIZE=2 FACE="Arial" COL-
OR=#000000>Table</FONT></TD>
<TD BORDERCOLOR=#c0c0c0 ><FONT SIZE=2 FACE="Arial" COL-
OR=#000000>6/6/98 12:15:04 PM</FONT></TD>
<TD BORDERCOLOR=#c0c0c0 ><FONT SIZE=2 FACE="Arial" COL-
OR=#000000><BR></FONT></TD>
```

Referring back to Figure 7-27, you will note that there are three columns in the table next to the name of each page: the object type, date of last modification, and a description. That text is generated automatically with these three lines of code.

Note that the Publish to the Web wizard generates an unnecessary line of HTML for the description—which in this case is blank. All automated generators do this. You can clean it up manually or not as you see fit.

```
</TR>

<TR VALIGN=TOP>
<TD BORDERCOLOR=#c0c0c0 ><U><FONT SIZE=2 FACE="Arial" COL-
OR=#0000ff><A HREF="Sum Of Payments Query 1.idc?">Sum Of Pay-
ments Query</A></FONT></U></TD>
<TD BORDERCOLOR=#c0c0c0 ><FONT SIZE=2 FACE="Arial" COL-
OR=#000000>Query</FONT></TD>
<TD BORDERCOLOR=#c0c0c0 ><FONT SIZE=2 FACE="Arial" COL-
OR=#000000>6/6/98 12:15:05 PM</FONT></TD>
<TD BORDERCOLOR=#c0c0c0 ><FONT SIZE=2 FACE="Arial" COL-
OR=#000000><BR></FONT></TD>

</TR>

<TR VALIGN=TOP>
<TD BORDERCOLOR=#c0c0c0 ><U><FONT SIZE=2 FACE="Arial" COL-
OR=#0000ff><A HREF="Events 2.idc?">Events</A></FONT></U></TD>
<TD BORDERCOLOR=#c0c0c0 ><FONT SIZE=2 FACE="Arial" COL-
OR=#000000>Form</FONT></TD>
<TD BORDERCOLOR=#c0c0c0 ><FONT SIZE=2 FACE="Arial" COL-
OR=#000000>6/6/98 12:17:51 PM</FONT></TD>
<TD BORDERCOLOR=#c0c0c0 ><FONT SIZE=2 FACE="Arial" COL-
OR=#000000><BR></FONT></TD>
```

The second and third lines of the table are created in exactly the same way: their links are underlined in the code shown here.

```
</TR>
</TBODY>
<TFOOT></TFOOT>
</TABLE>
</BODY>
</HTML>
```

This is an example of how you can use the Publish to the Web wizard files to learn more about using IDC/HTX (and ASP). Generate code automatically, and then look at it. It will always help If you open the code in a Web browser so that you can compare the code with what is actually produced.

Creating the IDC/HTX Files   You use the Save As/Export: To An External File Or Database (.*.htz/*.idc) command from the File menu to create these files (unless you use the Publish to the Web wizard). Microsoft Access can create the files for you, but it will need some information that is not part of the database. In particular, you will be asked to specify:

- The DSN (data source name) that you used—or will use—in ODBC.

- The user name and password for the database (if security is in place).

- The HTML template to be used in generating the HTX file. This template lets you standardize the look of all of your HTX pages so that they have common backgrounds, logos, etc. This template is optional.

Inside the IDC File   The IDC file—which is the one that you connect to with a link—contains the basic information to let the Web server generate the appropriate HTML page. Here is the IDC file that is generated for the Events table, provided that you have decided to name the Event Management template database EventManagement (in ODBC setup, as described in "Using ODBC" on page 114).

```
Datasource:EventManagement
Template:Events_1.htx
SQLStatement:SELECT * FROM [Events]
Password:
Username:
```

You can try this yourself: create a database from the Event Management template, and then export the Events table—you should generate this file exactly.

Note that an SQL statement that you may never have seen before has been generated here automatically. Note also that it uses some Microsoft Access–specific variations of SQL.

If you are wondering what a query looks like in an IDC file, here is the IDC file for the Sum of Payments query:

```
Datasource:EventManagement
Template:Sum Of Payments Query_1.htx
```

```
SQLStatement:SELECT DISTINCTROW [Payments].[RegistrationID],
Sum([Payments].[PaymentAmount]) AS [Total Payments]
+FROM Payments
+GROUP BY [Payments].[RegistrationID];

Password:
Username:
```

The only thing that may be at all perplexing is the SQL statement itself. It is generated automatically from the graphical query that was described (see "Queries" on page 106).

Inside the HTX File   The HTX file is somewhat longer, since it contains the HTML that is used by the Web server to generate the page that is returned to the user's browser. Here is an annotated example—it is the HTX file that is generated for the Event Management template database. (The results are shown in Figure 7-26.)

```
<HTML>
<HEAD>
<META HTTP-EQUIV="Content-Type" CONTENT="text/html;char-
set=windows-1252">
<TITLE>Events</TITLE>
</HEAD>
<BODY>
<TABLE BORDER=1 BGCOLOR=#ffffff CELLSPACING=0><FONT FACE="Ari-
al" COLOR=#000000><CAPTION><B>Events</B></CAPTION>

<THEAD>
<TR>
<TH BGCOLOR=#c0c0c0 BORDERCOLOR=#000000 ><FONT SIZE=2
FACE="Arial" COLOR=#000000>Event ID</FONT></TH>
<TH BGCOLOR=#c0c0c0 BORDERCOLOR=#000000 ><FONT SIZE=2
FACE="Arial" COLOR=#000000>Event Name</FONT></TH>
<TH BGCOLOR=#c0c0c0 BORDERCOLOR=#000000 ><FONT SIZE=2
FACE="Arial" COLOR=#000000>Event Type ID</FONT></TH>
<TH BGCOLOR=#c0c0c0 BORDERCOLOR=#000000 ><FONT SIZE=2
FACE="Arial" COLOR=#000000>Status</FONT></TH>
<TH BGCOLOR=#c0c0c0 BORDERCOLOR=#000000 ><FONT SIZE=2
FACE="Arial" COLOR=#000000>Location</FONT></TH>
<TH BGCOLOR=#c0c0c0 BORDERCOLOR=#000000 ><FONT SIZE=2
FACE="Arial" COLOR=#000000>Start Date</FONT></TH>
<TH BGCOLOR=#c0c0c0 BORDERCOLOR=#000000 ><FONT SIZE=2
FACE="Arial" COLOR=#000000>End Date</FONT></TH>
<TH BGCOLOR=#c0c0c0 BORDERCOLOR=#000000 ><FONT SIZE=2
FACE="Arial" COLOR=#000000>Start Time</FONT></TH>
```

```
<TH BGCOLOR=#c0c0c0 BORDERCOLOR=#000000 ><FONT SIZE=2
FACE="Arial" COLOR=#000000>End Time</FONT></TH>
<TH BGCOLOR=#c0c0c0 BORDERCOLOR=#000000 ><FONT SIZE=2
FACE="Arial" COLOR=#000000>Required Staffing</FONT></TH>
<TH BGCOLOR=#c0c0c0 BORDERCOLOR=#000000 ><FONT SIZE=2
FACE="Arial" COLOR=#000000>Confirmed</FONT></TH>
<TH BGCOLOR=#c0c0c0 BORDERCOLOR=#000000 ><FONT SIZE=2
FACE="Arial" COLOR=#000000>Available Spaces</FONT></TH>
<TH BGCOLOR=#c0c0c0 BORDERCOLOR=#000000 ><FONT SIZE=2
FACE="Arial" COLOR=#000000>Event Description</FONT></TH>
<TH BGCOLOR=#c0c0c0 BORDERCOLOR=#000000 ><FONT SIZE=2
FACE="Arial" COLOR=#000000>Employee ID</FONT></TH>

</TR>
</THEAD>
```

The format of all automatically generated HTX files is exactly the same, so it can be worthwhile to look at this one. In addition to the standard HTML overhead, this file contains a table. The section of code immediately preceding this paragraph defines the head of the table: the underlined text is the column headings.

In a normal table, each row of data would then be entered into the HTML file. In an HTX file, only a single row is entered. It contains some special tags that the Web server uses to merge the database data with this template. The special tags are delimited by <% and %> rather than the simple < and >.

The <%BeginDetail%> tag introduces this special row, which instead of containing data contains placeholders for all of the data that will be returned. The <$EndDetail%> tag terminates that row. Within the row, data elements are referenced as shown in the underlined code here:

```
<TBODY>
<%BeginDetail%>
<TR VALIGN=TOP>
<TD BORDERCOLOR=#c0c0c0  ALIGN=RIGHT><FONT SIZE=2 FACE="Arial"
COLOR=#000000><%EventID%><BR></FONT></TD>
<TD BORDERCOLOR=#c0c0c0 ><FONT SIZE=2 FACE="Arial" COL-
OR=#000000><%EventName%><BR></FONT></TD>
<TD BORDERCOLOR=#c0c0c0 ><FONT SIZE=2 FACE="Arial" COL-
OR=#000000><%EventTypeID%><BR></FONT></TD>
<TD BORDERCOLOR=#c0c0c0 ><FONT SIZE=2 FACE="Arial" COL-
```

```
OR=#000000><%Status%><BR></FONT></TD>
<TD BORDERCOLOR=#c0c0c0 ><FONT SIZE=2 FACE="Arial" COL-
OR=#000000><%Location%><BR></FONT></TD>
<TD BORDERCOLOR=#c0c0c0 ALIGN=RIGHT><FONT SIZE=2 FACE="Arial"
COLOR=#000000><%StartDate%><BR></FONT></TD>
<TD BORDERCOLOR=#c0c0c0 ALIGN=RIGHT><FONT SIZE=2 FACE="Arial"
COLOR=#000000><%EndDate%><BR></FONT></TD>
<TD BORDERCOLOR=#c0c0c0 ALIGN=RIGHT><FONT SIZE=2 FACE="Arial"
COLOR=#000000><%StartTime%><BR></FONT></TD>
<TD BORDERCOLOR=#c0c0c0 ALIGN=RIGHT><FONT SIZE=2 FACE="Arial"
COLOR=#000000><%EndTime%><BR></FONT></TD>
<TD BORDERCOLOR=#c0c0c0 ALIGN=RIGHT><FONT SIZE=2 FACE="Arial"
COLOR=#000000><%RequiredStaffing%><BR></FONT></TD>
<TD BORDERCOLOR=#c0c0c0 ALIGN=RIGHT><FONT SIZE=2 FACE="Arial"
COLOR=#000000><%Confirmed%><BR></FONT></TD>
<TD BORDERCOLOR=#c0c0c0 ALIGN=RIGHT><FONT SIZE=2 FACE="Arial"
COLOR=#000000><%AvailableSpaces%><BR></FONT></TD>
<TD BORDERCOLOR=#c0c0c0 ><FONT SIZE=2 FACE="Arial" COL-
OR=#000000><%EventDescription%><BR></FONT></TD>
<TD BORDERCOLOR=#c0c0c0 ><FONT SIZE=2 FACE="Arial" COL-
OR=#000000><%EmployeeID%><BR></FONT></TD>

</TR>
<%EndDetail%>
</TBODY>
<TFOOT></TFOOT>
</TABLE>
</BODY>
</HTML>
```

What happens is that for each row of data returned, the Web server replaces each placeholder (such as <%AvailableSpaces%>) with the value of that data item for the row of data.

What You Need   You can create IDC and HTX files on any computer running Microsoft Access. To publish them on the Web, you need to place them on a Microsoft Windows NT Server running MS Internet Information Server version 1.0, 2.0, or 3 or Windows 95/Windows NT Workstation running Personal Web Server.

Parameterized Queries   If you have a query that contains a parameter for a criterion (see "Criteria for Queries" on page 108), you can specify that parameter in the URL for your page. Instead of creating a link such as Events_1.idc? create a link such as `Events_1.idc?EventID=2`. (This is discussed further in "Requesting a Resource on the Web" on page 256.)

Active Server Pages

You can save table, query, and form datasheets as Active Server Pages (ASP). There are advantages to using ASP over the IDC/HTX combination, not least of which is that there is only one file to keep track of. The Publish to the Web wizard can output either type of file, and—as with IDC/HTX files—you most likely will find yourself using those files either untouched or with minor modifications. Most people do not find themselves writing ASP files from scratch.

Creating the ASP File You need to provide the same information that you do for IDC/HTX files. In addition, you will need to provide the URL for the server where this file will be located.

Connecting to an ASP File You use the same type of addressing for ASP files as for IDC/HTX files. Thus, this link opens an ASP file:

```
<A HREF="Events_1.asp">Events</A>
```

The question mark, however, is not needed.

Inside the ASP File ASP files consist of code in addition to HTML. The file that is generated from the Events table in the Event Management template database is shown here. A discussion of the ASP code is beyond the scope of this book, but you can spot some of the highlights and may well be able to modify such code on your own.

```
<HTML>
<HEAD>
<META HTTP-EQUIV="Content-Type" CONTENT="text/html;char-
set=windows-1252">
<TITLE>Events</TITLE>
</HEAD>
<BODY>
<%
Param = Request.QueryString("Param")
```

```
Data = Request.QueryString("Data")
%>
<%
If IsObject(Session("EventManagement_conn")) Then
    Set conn = Session("EventManagement_conn")
Else
    Set conn = Server.CreateObject("ADODB.Connection")
    conn.open "EventManagement","",""
    Set Session("EventManagement_conn") = conn
End If
%>
<%
    sql = "SELECT * FROM [Events]"
    If cstr(Param) <> "" And cstr(Data) <> "" Then
        sql = sql & " WHERE [" & cstr(Param) & "] = " & cstr(Data)
    End If
    Set rs = Server.CreateObject("ADODB.Recordset")
    rs.Open sql, conn, 3, 3
%>
```

This is the SQL query that was written to the IDC file in the previous section. The balance of this code adds optional parameters to the query and then runs it.

```
<TABLE BORDER=1 BGCOLOR=#ffffff CELLSPACING=0><FONT FACE="Ari-
al" COLOR=#000000><CAPTION><B>Events</B></CAPTION>

<THEAD>
<TR>
<TH BGCOLOR=#c0c0c0 BORDERCOLOR=#000000 ><FONT SIZE=2
FACE="Arial" COLOR=#000000>Event ID</FONT></TH>
<TH BGCOLOR=#c0c0c0 BORDERCOLOR=#000000 ><FONT SIZE=2
FACE="Arial" COLOR=#000000>Event Name</FONT></TH>
```

These are the column headings; they are identical to those shown previously, and most of them have been omitted.

```
</TH>

</TR>
</THEAD>
<TBODY>
<%
On Error Resume Next
rs.MoveFirst
do while Not rs.eof
```

Inside the <%BeginDetail%> and <%EndDetail%> combination used in the HTX file, a programming loop is created; it iterates through the data until the end of file is encountered. The loop code is terminated in this file with a loop that is double-underlined in the code that follows.

```
 %>
<TR VALIGN=TOP>
<TD BORDERCOLOR=#c0c0c0  ALIGN=RIGHT><FONT SIZE=2 FACE="Arial"
COLOR=#000000><%=Server.HTMLEncode(rs.Fields("EventID").Val-
ue)%><BR></FONT></TD>
<TD BORDERCOLOR=#c0c0c0 ><FONT SIZE=2 FACE="Arial" COL-
OR=#000000><%=Server.HTMLEncode(rs.Fields("EventName").Val-
ue)%><BR></FONT></TD>
<TD BORDERCOLOR=#c0c0c0 ><FONT SIZE=2 FACE="Arial" COL
```

This code is repeated for each of the fields to be displayed in the table. The remaining lines have been omitted.

```
</TR>
<%
rs.MoveNext
```

This advances to the next record.

```
loop%>
</TBODY>
<TFOOT></TFOOT>
</TABLE>
</BODY>
</HTML>
```

What You Need   To use an Active Server Page, a copy of the database and Active Server Page must be on a Microsoft Windows NT Server running Microsoft Internet Information Server version 3.0 and ActiveX server. Forms need the ActiveX HTML Layout Control; this is currently not supported except on Internet Explorer.

Publishing Your Files

You can publish your files on your own computer if you have the Personal Web Server installed. This is useful for testing and debugging what you have done; it is not appropriate for many users to access, but at this stage of the game that is not likely to be your main worry.

If you have the Microsoft Internet Information Server or Windows NT Peer Web Server installed, you can publish your files using the techniques you normally use. This section is designed for people without those resources and without the expertise (their own or someone else's) that IIS and Personal Web Server entail.

If you are not connected to a network—and you do not have to be to use Personal Web Server—you can connect to your Web pages using the following steps.

1. Move your Web pages into the C:\Webshare\Wwwroot folder. It is easiest to keep each site or subsite in its own folder within this folder. (For IIS and Peer Web Services, use the C:\INetpub\Wwwroot folder.)

2. Set the privileges for your static HTML pages to Read Only (Read for IIS and Peer Web Services); for dynamic HTML pages set the privileges to Execute Scripts (Execute for IIS and Peer Web Services). The wizard normally takes care of this step for you, so you can skip it unless you have problems later.

3. Set your computer's IP address to the artificial IP address used by Personal Web Server. To do this, in the \Windows directory, rename Hosts.sam to Hosts (i.e., drop the .sam suffix). Open Hosts, and add 127.0.0.1 to your computer's name. Close and save Hosts.

4. In the Network control panel, change the following properties of the TCP/IP Dial Up Adapter: IP address property sheet should be set to Specify an IP address; IP Address box should be 1.2.3.4; Subnet mask should be 255.0.0.0.

5. With your browser, connect to http://1.2.3.4. You should see the files in your Wwwroot directory. At that point you should be able to use all of your pages

and navigate from one to the other as you wish. Because you are not connected to a network, you will not be able to connect to other Web pages.

6. When you are finished, reset the Navigator control panel's IP Address property sheet to Obtain an IP Address automatically (from Specify an IP address set in step 3).

If you are using your Web server software for the first time, it is always best to install one of the samples that comes with it in order to test that your configuration is correct. If a sample does not work, it is highly unlikely that your own pages will work properly. Configuring a Web server is not always an easy task, but once it has been set up properly, publishing files is as easy as dragging them into a folder—usually a folder called Wwwroot.

Upsizing Microsoft Access Databases

The architecture that is used to publish Microsoft Access databases on the Web (including the Internet Information Server and ODBC) has been generalized by Microsoft to allow the same architecture to function with other types of databases. As a result, it can be relatively easy to migrate from Microsoft Access to Microsoft SQL Server (see "Microsoft SQL Server" on page 166 later in this chapter).

If you are planning to upsize your Microsoft Access database, it is best to do it as a test at the beginning of your project and then periodically throughout your project as you make changes. Upsizing is a fairly straightforward process, but there are a few gotchas (such as different formatting of dates in queries) that can be an annoyance. It is generally easier to know these in advance—even if you do nothing about them—rather than to suddenly discover that what you thought would be a simple process is a major undertaking.

FileMaker Pro

FileMaker Pro, like Microsoft Access, is used by many consultants and end users in addition to professional programmers. It is known for its ease of use and simple yet powerful interface. It runs on both the Windows and Mac OS operating systems.

As with Microsoft Access, you can publish FileMaker Pro databases on the Web.[1] Although there are many differences in how the two products act, the overall structure of Web publishing is the same for both. Figure 7-28 shows the architecture of Figure 7-1 renamed with FileMaker Pro names.

Microsoft Access relies on the generalizations of Microsoft Internet Information Server (or Personal Web Server) as well as ODBC. FileMaker Pro's approach is different: it provides a way to publish their databases easily to the Web, and integration with other types of databases can be done very simply within the Web site and HTML pages. Thus, where you saw the generalized Microsoft Internet Information Server and ODBC in Figure 7-1, you see FileMaker Web Companion in Figure 7-28. When properly configured, FileMaker Pro can run as a Web server by itself.

FileMaker Pro 4.1 provides ODBC access for its databases. Thus, you can import any ODBC data (including Microsoft Access data) into FileMaker Pro 4.1 databases; from there, the data can be published using FileMaker Pro's Web publishing capabilities. This is a further example of the interoperability of products within the world of database-driven Web sites.

Within FileMaker Pro, a separate component called FileMaker Web Companion handles the actual interaction with the data-

---

1. For further details, see *FileMaker Pro 4 and the World Wide Web*, Jesse Feiler, FileMaker Press, 1998.

base and with CDML format files—the FileMaker Pro functional equivalent of IDC/HTX and ASP files for Microsoft Access.

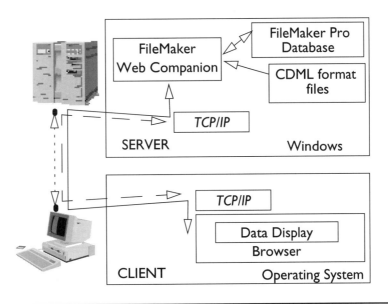

FIGURE 7-28. FileMaker Pro Web Publishing Architecture

FileMaker Pro Overview

In the FileMaker Pro world, the significant objects are:

- Databases
- Relations
- Layouts
- Searches
- Scripts

Leaving aside subjective issues such as the relative quality of the user interfaces, FileMaker Pro differs significantly from Microsoft Access in the basic units it deals with. Microsoft Access uses the SQL standard of tables within a database; for FileMaker Pro, each table is its own database. This has advantages and disadvantages—and, in practice, you can accomplish the same goals with both designs. In this section, the FileMaker Pro terminology is used: a database is what Microsoft Access and SQL-based databases would call a table.

Databases

A FileMaker Pro database contains not only its data but also the meta-data and structural information that describes the data and helps you manipulate it. In Microsoft Access, tables live within a database, and that database object can store information about all of the database's tables; in FileMaker Pro, all such information is stored in each database.

You can define fields in a FileMaker Pro database much as you do in a Microsoft Access database—compare Figure 7-29 (FileMaker Pro) with Figure 7-5 (Microsoft Access).

Again, you can create a variety of entry options for each field in your database, as shown in Figure 7-30, and you can specify a variety of automatic validity editing options as shown in Figure 7-31. Calculations are also available to be used in editing data and in automatically generating data for fields.

Since each FileMaker Pro database has its own environment (as opposed to being part of a shared environment in Microsoft Access), you can create fields that have constant values for all records in a database (globals) as well as special summary fields that have meaning only within the context of sorted and summarized layouts.

FIGURE 7-29. Define Fields Dialog Box for Asset Management Database

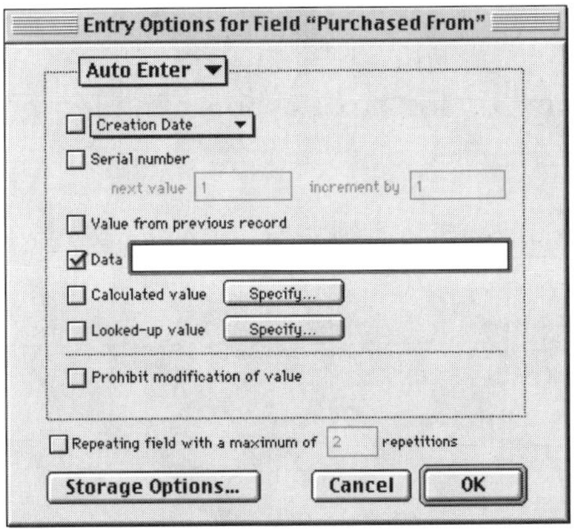

FIGURE 7-30. Define Fields—Entry Options for Auto Entry

Experienced database designers almost always prefer to use entry options to produce the highest quality data. It is much easier to prevent errors than to have to write scripts or macros to catch them after the fact.

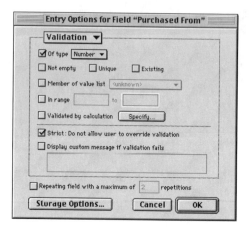

FIGURE 7-31. Define Fields—Entry Options for Validation

Relations

Relations between databases are very easy to create in File-Maker Pro. From the Relationships… command (found in the Define submenu of the File menu), you open the Define Relationships dialog box as shown in Figure 7-32.

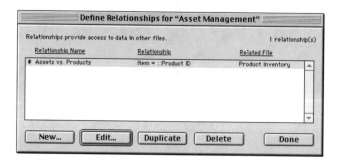

FIGURE 7-32. Define Relationships Dialog Box

When you start, there are no relationships; you click the New... button to create the first one, and you open the dialog box shown in Figure 7-33.

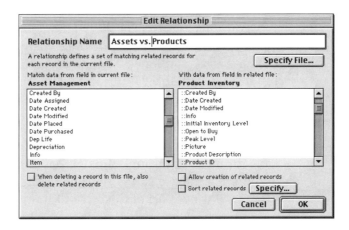

FIGURE 2-33. Edit Relationship Dialog Box

You enter a name for the relationship at the top of the dialog box. Then comes the heart of the relationship: using the Specify File... button, you select the database that you want to relate to. You will see the fields in the master database (the one you are working in) at the left; the fields of the related database are shown at the right. (Related fields are always shown with a :: prefix.)

In relational databases, the relations between and among tables are specified in queries—that is, as data is entered or retrieved. In FileMaker Pro, the relations are specified independently of queries; they may be used as needed within queries and layouts.

Layouts

FileMaker Pro lets you create layouts for the entry, display, and manipulation of data. There are two parts to a layout:

1. A layout determines which fields from the database

and its related databases the user can use in that layout.

2. The layout contains whatever graphical designs you choose.

For example, Figure 7-34 shows the Event Schedule example Form layout that is used for data entry. FileMaker Pro layouts are very similar to Microsoft Access forms—as well as reports and databases. In fact, all representations of a FileMaker Pro database are visualized with layouts

The status area at the left of the window (outlined with a dotted line) can be shown or hidden by the user. It contains controls for moving through the database as well as information about the database status with regard to sorting and finding records. It is not part of the layout for an individual database.

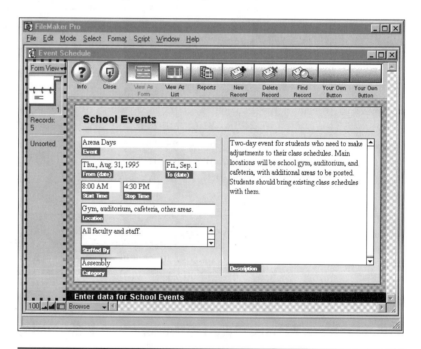

FIGURE 7-34. FileMaker Pro Asset Management Example Layout

Searches

FileMaker Pro—like any database—is designed to manage data efficiently, and that includes searching. The FileMaker Pro Find command lets you find sets of data within your database. In FileMaker Pro, Find is a menu command; you enter your Find criteria (your query, in other words) into a layout that looks just like a data entry layout. The only difference is that the data is used for searching rather than for entering data.

Scripts

FileMaker Pro provides an extensive scripting language. You can attach scripts to graphical elements and to logical events. The scripts can do a variety of chores such as opening other databases, setting display and layout options, and even sorting the database.

Modes

The final aspect of FileMaker Pro that you need to know about is its modes. These allow you to browse records, entering and modifying data; find and search for data (these are synonymous terms); preview reports that are designed to be printed on paper; and create and manage your layouts.

Publishing on the Web

FileMaker Pro's Web publishing capabilities are among the most powerful of any database, if only because so many choices are provided. To publish a FileMaker Pro database on the Web, you can use any of these techniques:

- Instant Web Publishing. You do this by enabling your database for Instant Web Publishing and specifying the layouts to be used for various standard functions (data entry, retrieval, sorting, etc.). When users connect to your FileMaker Pro computer over the Web, they get HTML pages with data and update capabilities without your writing any code or managing any files.

- Home Page FileMaker Pro Assistant. FileMaker Pro's companion product, Home Page, provides an assistant that walks you through the creation of Web pages (or a complete site) for your database. As with Microsoft Access, you can use those pages as they are or modify them before placing them on the Web.

- Home Page Graphical Editor for FileMaker Pro. Home Page contains tools that let you graphically design database Web pages.

- Custom Web Publishing. You can create files that will be used as input to FileMaker Web Companion for it to combine with your database. You can create these using any text or HTML editor.

Samples of each of these techniques are shown in this section.

Instant Web Publishing

Instant Web Publishing is the fastest way to put a database on the Web. You set up FileMaker Pro Web Companion once on the computer you are using as a server (which might also be the computer you are developing your databases on), and it does the rest.

Everything that Instant Web Publishing does is dynamic—created on demand. For example, the home page shown in Figure 7-35 lets users go to any of the databases on that computer that have Instant Web Publishing enabled. Rather than being constructed as static HTML, this page is generated whenever you connect to the computer, and it reflects the Instant Web Publishing databases then available.

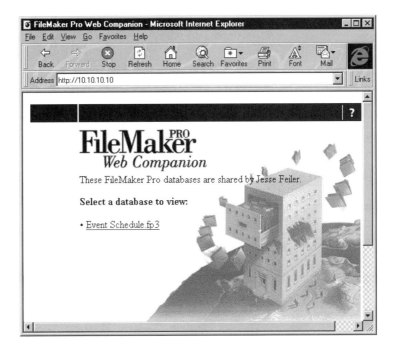

FIGURE 7-35. FileMaker Web Companion Home Page

For each database that you publish using Instant Web Publishing, you can specify how each of four primary functions will be displayed:

1. Tabular display of records

2. Single record views

3. Data entry

4. Searching and sorting

Figure 7-36 shows a tabular display of records generated automatically by Instant Web Publishing.

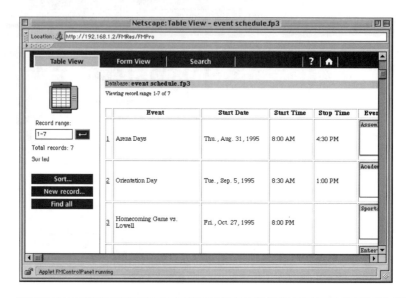

FIGURE 7-36. Instant Web Publishing Table Display of Records

You can also specify that data be able to be modified, and Instant Web Publishing will generate an HTML page such as that shown in Figure 7-37. Note that you can determine which fields are shown in each of these types of views as well as the privileges (updating, view only, etc.) that will be available for each field and view.

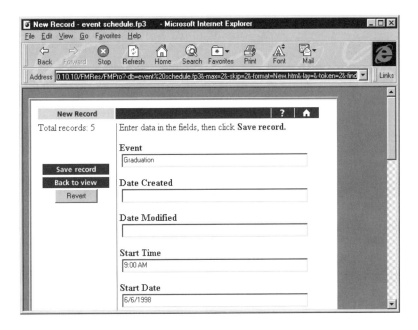

FIGURE 7-37. Instant Web Publishing Data Entry Page

For many people, this is all that they want to do when they publish a database on the Web: let people browse it and possibly update it. The graphics are default FileMaker Web Companion graphics, but that is satisfactory for many purposes. Furthermore, remember that you can integrate Instant Web Publishing with other Web sites—either located on the same server or elsewhere.

However, for many people, a more sophisticated database site is needed.

FileMaker Pro Connection Assistant

The FileMaker Pro Connection assistant walks you through the creation of a database Web site much as the Microsoft Access Publish to the Web wizard does. The Home Page File-Maker Pro assistant focuses somewhat more intensely on the functionality of your site. For example, as shown in Figure 7-38, you can specify the types of pages to be generated.

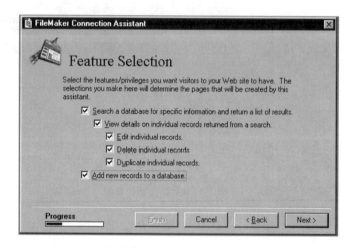

FIGURE 7-38. Feature Selection in FileMaker Pro Connection Assistant

As you can see from Figure 7-39, you can not only specify the fields that are shown on each type of page but also rename them for display and specify the types of entry formats that will be generated.

You can also specify page styles and other formatting choices as you use the assistant.

The resulting database Web site will contain all of the necessary navigation tools to handle the features that you have requested. Even so, this may not be sufficient for your purposes. You may need to modify the files that have been created or even to start from scratch for a particularly difficult problem.

In such cases, you can use the graphical editor in Home Page (FileMaker Pro's companion product).

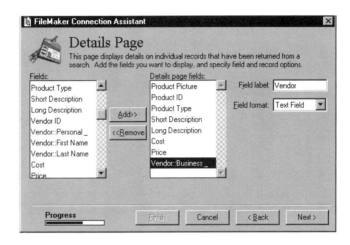

FIGURE 7-39. Specifying Fields in FileMaker Pro Connection Assistant

Home Page Graphical Editor for FileMaker Pro

Home Page lets you create and modify HTML pages using either a graphical user interface or a text-based editor. Both have been enhanced to be able to handle the FileMaker Pro syntax. Just as Microsoft Access has IDC/HTX files, FileMaker Pro uses its own syntax to enhance HTML—CDML. The functionality is much the same, as it has to be since the basic architecture of databases on the Web is similar regardless of product.

Just as HTX files are used as input to IIS, CDML files are used as input to FileMaker Web Companion. Both provide basic HTML and custom database formatting to be merged with the database data and sent to the user's browser as a finished HTML page.

Figure 7-40 shows how you can edit the CDML tags in Home Page.

FIGURE 7-40. Editing CDML with Home Page

The page itself is shown in the background; the small gray boxes represent CDML elements; you can double-click on each one and edit its contents. The elements shown here identify the database (-db), layout (-lay), and CDML format file (-format) that are used in processing this page. An additional error page (-error) is specified: it is shown by FileMaker Web Companion if an error is encountered during processing.

Custom Web Publishing

If you want, you can work totally within the text-based world of HTML and CDML. The structure of CDML files is very similar to that of the files that you have seen previously.

Start by looking at a page that is generated dynamically by FileMaker Web Companion and is shown in Figure 7-41. It is laid out by using HTML tables (for more information see "Tables" on page 246). In the center of the table (in the area surrounded by the line indicated by A) is data from the database.

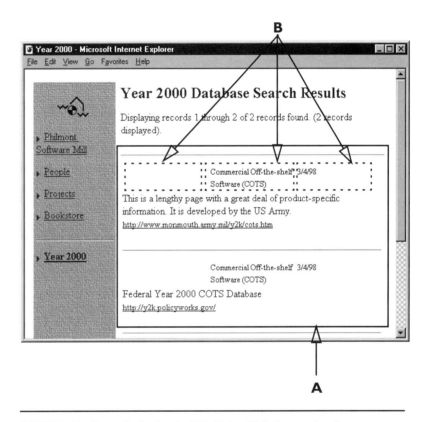

FIGURE 7-41. Dynamically Created FileMaker Web Companion Page

It is coded in the CDML format file in the excerpt that follows:

```
<TABLE BORDER=0 WIDTH="100%">
[FMP-RECORD]
```

Within this table, each record retrieved from the database is shown in its own section of the table. Note the double-underlined companion to this tag at the end of this section of code.

Everything between those two tags is repeated for each record of data.

Each data record consists of four rows in the HTML table. The first row has three cells (indicated by the arrows B):

1. The cell on the left contains the name of the product that this record pertains to. It may be blank.

2. The cell in the middle contains the subject of this record. It also may be blank.

3. The cell on the right contains the date the data was entered; it is never blank (data entry options guarantee that).

Here is the code for the first row. The underlined code uses FileMaker Pro's CDML syntax: it displays data from database fields entitled Product, Subject, and Date Entered. In addition, it tests to see if either Product or Subject is blank. The rest of the code is standard HTML code.

(Note how similar this is to the Microsoft Access HTX code shown previously in this chapter—see "Inside the HTX File" on page 132.)

```
<TR>
  <TD VALIGN=top WIDTH="31%"
  <P>
  [FMP-IF: Product .neq. ]
    <FONT SIZE="-1">[FMP-FIELD: Product]</FONT>
  [/FMP-IF]
  </P>
  </TD>

  <TD VALIGN=top WIDTH="31%">
  <P>
  [FMP-IF: Subject .neq. ]
    <FONT SIZE="-1">[FMP-FIELD: Subject]</FONT>
  [/FMP-IF]</P>
  </TD>

  <TD VALIGN=top WIDTH="31%">
  <P>
```

```
<FONT SIZE="-1"> [FMP-FIELD: Date Entered]</FONT>
</P>

</TD>
</TR>
```

The second row of each data record's section of the table contains the single field Message. Here is its code, with the section that inserts the Message field underlined.

```
<TR>
  <TD COLSPAN=3 WIDTH="93%">
  <P>[FMP-FIELD: Message, Break]</P>
  </TD>
</TR>
```

In the third row, a link to a URL is displayed—both as text and as a link (an HTML anchor element). Here is the code that does that (note that if the field—called Reference—is blank, nothing is displayed). This is basically the same syntax as that shown previously for HTX files (see "Connecting to IDC/HTX Data" on page 127 and "Connecting to an ASP File" on page 135).

```
<TR>
  <TD COLSPAN=3 WIDTH="93%">
  <P>[FMP-IF: Reference .neq. ]
    <P><A HREF="[FMP-FIELD: Reference]"><FONT SIZE="-1">[FMP-
FIELD: Reference]</FONT></A>
  [/FMP-IF]
  </P>
  </TD>
</TR>
```

Finally, the fourth row of each data record's display consists solely of a line—a horizontal rule in HTML terms. Here is the code (it is pure HTML and has nothing to do with databases at all):

```
<TR>
  <TD COLSPAN=3 WIDTH="93%">
  <P><BR><HR></P>
  </TD>
</TR>
```

```
[/FMP-RECORD]
</TABLE>
</P>
```

Although there are many similarities between Microsoft Access and FileMaker Pro when it comes to publishing databases on the Web, the fact that there are so many similarities is a reminder that this is truly a vendor-neutral technology. A point-by-point comparison of the two products is beyond the scope of this book (and more appropriate to a barroom brawl, in any event). If a single comparison had to be made, it would be that Microsoft Access is a bit more oriented to code and text (traditional programmer-type features) and that FileMaker Pro is a bit more oriented toward graphics and end-user features. This is a *very* broad generalization.

Publishing Your Files

Publishing your files with the FileMaker Web Companion is very simple because you do not have to worry about configuring a separate Web or database server. These are the steps you take:

1.   Set up the FileMaker Web Companion on the computer you will be using as a database server. (You do this once for all databases that you will publish.)

2.   Set up each database for sharing with the FileMaker Web Companion.

3.   Let people access your site.

At this point—subject to security constraints, of course—users will be able to connect to your database with their browsers.

Setting Up the FileMaker Web Companion   From the Preferences command of the File menu, you select the Plug-Ins tab in the Preferences dialog box to see the Web Companion settings as shown in Figure 7-42.

As you can see from the figure, you have a variety of fairly sophisticated options regarding security, logging, and administration; you can use them or not as you see fit. In order to enable Instant Web Publishing, you merely check the appropriate box. If you do so, anyone who connects to your computer will see the dynamically created home page shown earlier.

FIGURE 7-42. Configuring the FileMaker Web Companion

The FileMaker Web Companion is designed to be able to run on a computer that is running other Web or database servers. As a result, it lets you set the TCP/IP port number (in the lower left). Within a URL (such as http://www.filemaker.com or http://192.168.1) a number of ports may exist. Each port is a separate communications path; messages coming into the URL are routed to a single server for each port.

Normally, you do not worry about ports: each Internet protocol has its own default port (for the Web, that default port is 80). Thus, connecting to http://www.filemaker.com is the same as connecting to http://www.filemaker.com:80. In the case where a single computer is going to be hosting two or more servers for a single protocol, each server other than the default one must have its own port number. If you are running a Web server on your computer (such as Microsoft Internet Information Server), port 80 will usually be taken by that server. In such cases, you simply set FileMaker Web Companion to use another port (591 has been registered by FileMaker and should not be used by any other servers). When telling people your URL, provide them with the port number as part of it: http://www.mybusiness.com:591.

If you are not running other servers on your computer, you do not need to worry about the port number.

That is all that you need to do to enable FileMaker Web publishing on your computer. (Of course, you need a connection to the Internet or an intranet; that connection will provide you with the IP address or domain name that you can use to identify your computer. See "Choosing Your Internet Service Provider" on page 69 for more details.)

Setting Up the Database   Setting up your database is done by marking it as being shared by the FileMaker Web Companion. From the Sharing... command in the File menu, you open the dialog box shown in Figure 7-43.

Note that a database that is shared over the Web is not opened as a multiuser database: multiuser databases are shared over LANs by FileMaker Pro's standard network sharing software. A database that is shared over the Internet with the FileMaker Web Companion is opened for a single use: the FileMaker Web Companion. (Refer to the diagrams in this chapter for a reminder.) It is the FileMaker Web Companion—or other Web server software—that manages multiple users. The database itself has only the single user.

You enable the FileMaker Web Companion by checking the box. (If the FileMaker Web Companion is not listed or is grayed out, your software has not been installed properly: repeat the process.)

In the lower right of the dialog box, you can click the Set Up Views… button to open the dialog box shown in Figure 7-44.

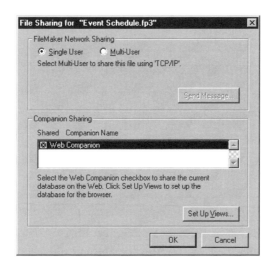

FIGURE 7-43. FileMaker Web Companion Sharing Setup

For each of the four standard views in Instant Web Publishing (see "Instant Web Publishing" on page 148), you specify a layout to use. This layout determines which fields will be available in that particular view. The graphical elements of the FileMaker Pro layout (your form or report design) are not used in Instant Web Publishing—only the fields that you have selected for the layout are used.

By default, FileMaker Pro includes all database fields on the layouts that you have selected; specifying individual layouts lets you include fields from related files as well as letting you control the formatting of fields (the layout field formats are used for the pages that are generated by the FileMaker Web Companion).

Figure 7-45 shows the Instant Web Publishing sort options.

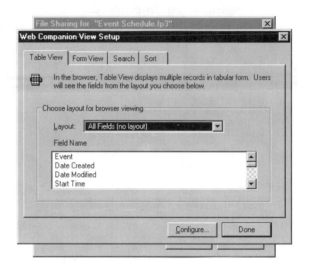

FIGURE 7-44. Instant Web Publishing—Selecting Layouts for Display

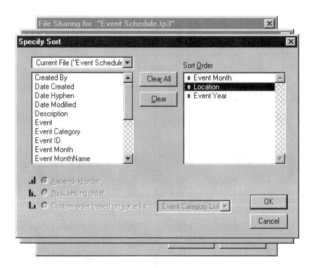

FIGURE 7-45. Instant Web Publishing—Creating a Sort

Let People Access Your Site   If you are using a default home page, all you need to do is to give people the address of your computer (either as an IP address or as a domain name). If you use a port other than the standard port (for example, if you use the FileMaker Pro alternative of 591), include that in your address.

If you do not use the default home page or if you want to let people execute queries as part of their URL, you need to provide them with additional parameters. Just as with Microsoft Access, you can specify a searchpart that follows a question mark at the end of a URL. The text there is interpreted by the Web server and sent on to the database. That is how you can wind up with a URL such as `http://www.yourdomain.com/FM-Pro?-db=y2kdb&-format=newrec.htm&-view`.

Whereas with Microsoft Access you specify the ASP or IDC file as part of the URL, with the FileMaker Web Companion, you direct all messages to FMPro—the FileMaker Web Companion. After the question mark, you specify the format files and other options that you want to be executed. (In effect, the contents of the IDC file are provided in the URL to the FileMaker Web Companion.)

Databases for Programmers

It is tempting to suggest that these products lie at an opposite pole from Microsoft Access and FileMaker Pro. Those products were designed originally for personal computers; they now provide sophisticated and high-performance features over local networks, intranets, and the Internet. These products, on the other hand, were developed originally for mainframes and minicomputers (with the exception of Microsoft SQL Server). They are the workhorses for large organizations throughout the world.

In fact, the differences between products such as Microsoft Access and FileMaker Pro lie primarily in the fact that whereas Microsoft Access and FileMaker Pro have been developed so that end users and nonprogrammers can use them to create databases, these products have been designed for programmers and database administrators to use in developing major database projects. In terms of functionality and capabilities, there is far less difference today between those products than one might expect. This is good news if you are looking for a database to drive your Web site. If you already have a database, you can probably use it to drive your Web site. For most of the operations that support Web sites, any of the databases described in this chapter (as well as a host of others) will do the job.

Even quite sophisticated database features are available in one form or another in all of these databases. Triggers—routines that automatically run when certain data conditions occur, referential integrity—certain data consistency rules that you declare for a database, and security down to the field level can all be implemented in these databases. This is worth stressing because the early versions of a number of these databases—including the largest ones—did not implement some of these features fully. If you looked at a database a few years ago and decided that it did not provide the features that you needed, you might want to look at the current version: you may be very pleasantly surprised.

Where distinctions need to be made, it is primarily with regard to issues such as security, processing power, speed, and system administration that choices matter. The performance of Microsoft Access is not going to be acceptable for a database that must respond to hundreds of thousands of requests a day; by the same token, DB2 is likely to be substantial overkill for a database that must respond to fewer than a hundred requests a week (which is the case for many infrequently used databases on the Web). Of course, if you happen to have DB2, adding your small project to its environment is far from overkill—it is usually a very simple procedure and one that can be accomplished with a minimum of effort.

And there is one other area of difference: cost. Not only are databases for programmers more expensive than end-user databases (often by one or more orders of magnitude), their features are also provided as separate products, rather than in a shrink-wrapped carton.

DB2

IBM's DB2 Universal Database is their primary database product for transaction processing as well as for analysis and decision support. Originally developed for mainframes, it is now available throughout their product line (on OS/390, MVS/ESA, VSE and VM, and OS/400) as well as on computers from a variety of manufacturers running OS/2, Windows, and AIX (IBM's version of UNIX).

It is a fully relational database (as are all of these); it was one of the first databases to bring SQL to the attention of many programmers. Today, its features reflect its heritage: its support for sophisticated roll-back and roll-forward recovery, parallel processing, automatic optimization of queries, and clustering of processors makes it one of the most important databases in the world.

It is at the heart of many third-party products, and it is supported by a good number of the application servers discussed in the next chapter (including those from IBM as well as other vendors).

Oracle

Oracle's history is similar to that of DB2: it runs on a wide variety of platforms and was one of the first major SQL products. It, too, is at the heart of many third-party products, and it can interact with most of the application servers discussed in the next chapter through its support of industry-standard interfaces and protocols (including Java).

| Microsoft SQL Server | Microsoft SQL Server was originally developed through relationships between Microsoft and Ashton-Tate (developers of dBase) and Sybase. It was initially designed to run on personal computers using the OS/2 operating system; today it is designed primarily for Windows NT, although the most recent version will run on Windows 95 and Windows 98. |

You can upsize Microsoft Access database to Microsoft SQL Server (subject to the constraints mentioned previously—see "Upsizing Microsoft Access Databases" on page 139). It is often the product of choice for installations that are growing up from personal computer–based products; it also has an established role in distributed computing environments within large organizations. It is a commonly available database product offered by many ISPs that are providing database hosting services.

Other Products

As noted previously, the database market is fairly mature. All of the products at each segment of the market are roughly comparable in terms of price and features. This may make it difficult for vendors to make a profit (the market is also relatively saturated—most companies that are going to have a database already have one).

All of this is good news for you: it is hard to go wrong with any database that you select—at least in terms of its capabilities. (You can make the most awful mess of your own database design with any product on the market, but that is your problem.)

What this means is that if you have a database—either in your own organization or offered by an Internet database provider—you can use it to drive a Web site. If you do not have a database available to you, you can choose whichever one you want without having much of a problem.

The only exception to this is if you are choosing a database that will be used by end users or nonprogrammers to develop databases. In those cases, the choice is usually between FileMaker Pro and Microsoft Access. Since both are priced competitively, and since both can import and export data from the other, base your selection primarily on the ease of use for the people who will be using the database. This is not an absolute—it is more like choosing a comfortable desk chair. Get the one that feels right.

The Warning

There is only one point you should worry about in choosing a database. Most databases let you import data or convert existing data to their own format. Make certain that your database lets you export data to a standard format. It is your data; do not sell it to a vendor.

Summary

Today's databases are powerful and efficient tools that let you manage large amounts of data easily. The market is mature and competitive, which leads to the situation in which basic functionality is sophisticated and common to most of the major products.

However, databases cannot do everything—particularly on the Web. They need software to integrate their functionality with that of Web servers. Many databases—both large and small—have such features built into them; however, separate products called application servers are often used to integrate databases with the Web. That is the topic of the next chapter.

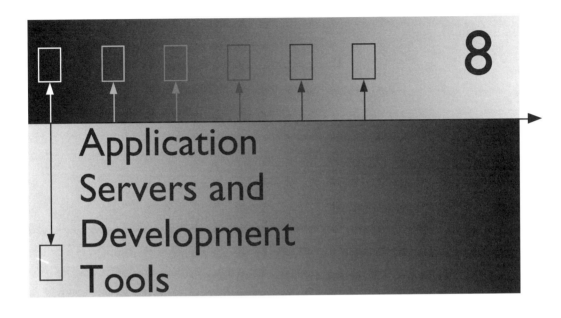

Application Servers and Development Tools

8

This chapter deals with the final piece of the puzzle: the application server that you actually use to produce the HTML that is downloaded to users. Application servers are one of the areas of the Internet that are being developed and marketed most aggressively today. They are a critical piece of the developing dynamic Web in which pages are no longer handcrafted but rather are created on the fly.

As with all of the other components of database-driven Web sites, application servers may be the starting point for your Web site—in which case you find an ISP that runs your application server of choice and a database that works with it, or you may start by selecting an ISP and a database—in which case you need to find an application server that completes the puzzle. (Single-vendor solutions—

whether from IBM, Microsoft, or another company—sometimes provide a turnkey approach that makes your life easier; they also sometimes lock you in to technology and pricing that are less advantageous than customized solutions. You need to evaluate each case on its own merits, giving appropriate weight to the comments and suggestions of the people who will actually work with the products involved.)

This chapter provides an overview of application servers and the types of tools available to develop for them. Finally, there is an example of the use of one of the new breed of application servers and its development tool.[1]

Where Is the Application Server?

The application server is the component of Figure 8-1 shown in black. As discussed previously, it interacts with HTML file templates, the database, and the Web server in order to produce HTML that is downloaded to the browser on a user's (client) computer—HTML that has no vestige of databases or special processing.

The application server may be part of the Web server, as it is with Microsoft Internet Information Server. A variation on this scenario is provided by FileMaker Web Companion, which is a dedicated Web server itself, often running alongside another Web server with its own TCP/IP port (591) rather than with the standard HTTP port (80).

The application server may become part of the Web server by being provided as a plug-in to the server. With the application server as a plug-in, code (often created by a third party) is executed by the Web server software when appropriate. In a

---

1. For more on this topic, see *Application Servers: Powering the Web-Based Enterprise* by Jesse Feiler, Morgan Kaufmann, 1999.

variation on this, the application server may run as a separate application; it communicates with the Web server using a standard protocol for such processes—the common gateway interface (CGI).

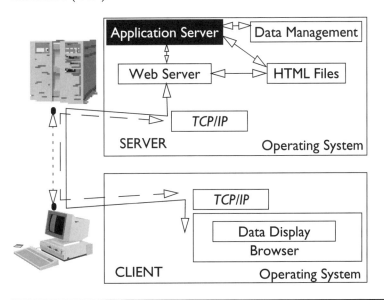

FIGURE 8-1. Application Server

As a result, you may not be able to see your application server—it might be inside your Web server. Nevertheless, it is there.

Tools for Working with Application Servers

Application servers need to combine three types of functionality:

1. They need to interact with the database.

2. They need to create HTML for downloading—often from template files.

3. They need to provide some basic programming features—such as looping through all records that satisfy a search criterion. (HTML itself is static and does not provide if statements, loops, and other programming features.)

Tools for working with application servers (whether stand-alone or part of a Web server) all need to handle these three functions. They typically favor one function over the others, being focused on the database, HTML, or programming, while still providing all three functions—which they must, since the end result is always HTML that is downloaded to a user's browser and the raw data almost always comes from databases.

| Database-Centric Tools | Most databases today come with some kind of "black box" Web site generator. The most commonly used databases on personal computers (Microsoft Access and FileMaker Pro) both provide wizards and assistants that will create Web pages for you. You go through a series of screens selecting the database data that you want to work with, specify parameters and queries, and the appropriate files are created for you. All you have to do is to upload them to the correct folder on your Web server. (See "Publish to the Web Wizard" on page 117 and "FileMaker Pro Connection Assistant" on page 151 for more details.) |

Third-party products provide similar functionality for these and other databases. The emphasis here is on providing automated (or nearly automated) tools so that people who are comfortable with a database can effortlessly create what—to them—may be those mysterious things called Web pages.

Database-centric tools typically work behind the scenes to create HTML and HTML-based files such as those described in the following section. The fact that you do not see them does not mean they are not there.

HTML-Centric Tools

Other people find no great mystery or terror in Web pages, although databases may spook them quite a bit. For them, a wide array of tools is available to let them stay within the comfortable world of HTML and still deal with databases. There is an inherent conflict between the statelessness of the HTTP protocol and the Web in general and the need to carry out what may become intricate processes and procedures—the very essence of stateful programming. Accordingly, extensions to HTML provide the sorts of programming tools essential for these tasks.

Some of them were discussed in "Using IDC/HTX Files" on page 127, "Active Server Pages" on page 135, and "Custom Web Publishing" on page 154. The HTML extensions that provide implicit looping through a set of retrieved records as well as IF statements all strive to turn HTML into a programming language. Cold Fusion from Allaire Corporation is a popular third-party tool in this category.

Programmer-Centric Tools

All that matters in Figure 8-1 is that somehow or other a string of HTML is returned to the user. One way to generate that string is to write a program that does that. Such a program needs the following characteristics:

- It must be addressable in the URL; that is, the user must be able to request it. Using the techniques discussed in "Sending Data to Web Sites with HTTP and Forms" on page 255, you can construct URLs that the Web server will interpret as requiring it to launch a program on the Web server. For this to happen, you must often place the program in a specific directory—often called cgi-bin.

- The program must be able to run on the Web server. If your Web server runs Windows NT, it cannot run a program written to run on Unix; likewise, a Unix Web server cannot run a program written to run on Mac OS. If the program requires run-time support (such as programs and scripts written in Perl or Java applets), that support must be provided on the Web server. None of this needs to be available on the user's computer.

Not all ISPs allow you to run all types of programs on their servers. However, if you are working on an intranet that you control (or that your organization controls), you may have no problem arranging for a program to run on the server. In fact, if you have existing software that performs database accesses, you may be able to run that software with few if any modifications.

Using programs to generate the HTML (and do any necessary database accesses) provides you with the greatest range of opportunities—and often the greatest cost. You need to find programmers adept at Java, C++, Perl, Visual Basic, or some other programming language. For many organizations, this is a daunting (and unnecessary) expenditure. For others, however, there may be someone—perhaps you—who is far more comfortable writing traditional computer code than mucking about with HTML (which can seem pretty lame next to an object-oriented programming language). If this is your situation, forget about fussing with database- or HTML-centric tools, and just write your code.

Because so many Web servers need to interact with programs that run on the server, the common gateway interface (CGI) has been specified to create a standard for passing information between the Web server and these application programs.

Which Tool Is Right for You?	You can find a variety of tools to work with application servers. Most of the tools are designed to work with specific servers; many of the tools and servers come in a package from a vendor.

In such cases, you will typically find that the pricing for the application server part of the product is much higher than that for the development tools. Before selecting a tool, check its pricing—not just for the development portion but also for the deployable application server. Because the pricing of server-based software is still in a state of flux, you may find products that are prohibitively expensive to deploy, and you should know this before you start a project.

You may also find an ISP (or your own organization) that already has deployed a certain application server; in such cases, you usually have no choice but to use that tool. If you prefer to use another tool, you can check with the vendor of your preferred tool: you may find a list of ISPs that have already licensed the application server and that will provide you with Web hosting services and access to that application server for a very modest fee.

It all comes down to what development tool and application server are most convenient to be used by you and your organization and which products will correctly interact with your existing Web server and database (if any).

Finally, remember to consider scalability—whether you can increase (or decrease) your performance needs by large amounts. Almost all databases and application servers feature scalability; you can find examples of very small Web-based applications and very large Web-based applications developed with the same tools and running on the same servers. However, you should be very careful: try to find someone who has actually scaled a project from small to large (or large to small) using the tools you are considering. It is easy to create large or small projects, but the gotchas are mostly in the scaling process itself. And, for some reason, vendors tend to be rather overoptimistic in this particular regard.

Tango Enterprise

Tango Enterprise (from EveryWare Development, Inc.) combines an integrated development environment (IDE) with an application server. Tango Studio is the development tool, and Tango Server is the application server. The process of developing a database-driven Web site using Tango is described in this section.

Why Tango?

Unlike the operating system arena or the Web browser field, the application server and tool market is populated by a very large number of vendors and products. You will find offerings from IBM, Microsoft, Netscape, Sun, and Apple next to products from companies you may never have heard of. The reliance on Internet standards to power database-driven Web sites makes it possible for small companies with specific focuses to make their mark.

In time, some of these companies will fall by the wayside; some of the products will fail, and others will be incorporated into other vendors' products—perhaps even replacing some of them. The situation is extraordinarily dynamic, even for the Web. (This is partly because application servers are at the heart of e-commerce, the next frontier of fortunes, according to the always-prescient financial analysts.)

Tango comes from a relatively small company that has been developing software (including database software) for a number of years. It is now in its third major release and has a worldwide installed base of over 5,000 users. It sports a development environment that is the type that most developers today prefer (and even those who do not prefer it recognize that graphically oriented development interfaces are here to stay).

Unlike a number of the other products in this category, Tango runs on a wide variety of operating systems (Sun Solaris, AIX, Silicon Graphics Irix, Windows NT, Windows 98, and Mac OS). It comes with full ODBC support, as well as native interfaces to DB2 and Oracle. Its server handles multithreading well and takes advantage of multiprocessor machines.

Its pricing is just about in the middle of the range of these products: Tango Development Studio is $695, and the Tango Server is $2500 (Mac OS) and $5000 (Windows NT/95).

The Tango Workspace

One of the problems with HTML-centric tools is that they tend to help you create disorganized code very quickly. HTML is very good for creating Web pages, but even the simplest page soon turns into a monstrous amount of code. When you add applets and scripts that may be in external files, you can quickly confuse yourself and others.

Tango lets you create projects that you manage in the Tango Workspace as shown in Figure 8-2.

FIGURE 8-2. Tango Workspace: Projects

A Tango project has a number of files in it—each file represents a single action and has a suffix of .taf (Tango action file).

Such a file may display a single Web page—or it may create and display a variety of Web pages as a user carries out a fairly complicated action. (For more information, see "Defining Actions" on page 180.)

In addition to Tango action files, each project may have a variety of data sources; a typical list of data sources is shown in Figure 8-3.

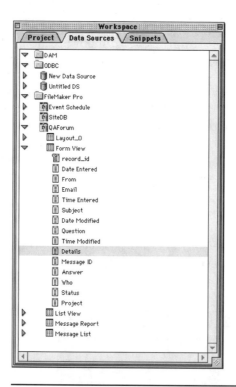

FIGURE 8-3. Tango Workspace: Data Sources

You can see that data sources for native protocols (such as FileMaker Pro in this case) and for ODBC are all shown in this list. Within a single table (such as QAForum), you will find a variety of views (such as Form View). Underneath each view, you will find the field names. Tango retrieves all of this information from the database: when you create a new data source, you specify its location, and Tango does the rest.

The data source display is very useful in developing your projects: whenever you want to access a database field, you just drag that appropriate field from the data source display into your Tango action file.

Finally, you can put snippets of HTML code into your project as shown in Figure 8-4. Many such snippets come with Tango; you can add snippets such as standard page headers and footers, common instructions, and so forth to the project so that you can then use them in your Tango action files. Changing the snippets causes the action files to use the new snippets—you do not have to modify the project or the action files.

FIGURE 8-4. Tango Workspace: Snippets

All of this is the sort of development environment that most programmers use today; even for nonprogrammers, the concepts are not particularly daunting. Furthermore, in the case where a number of people are working on a project, programmers or database administrators can create projects with data sources and snippets ready for use by nonprogrammers.

Defining Actions

The core of Tango's development environment is the Actions palette, which is used to create action files. The Actions palette is shown in Figure 8-5.

FIGURE 8-5. Tango Actions Palette

You drag actions into a Tango action file window as shown in Figure 8-6.

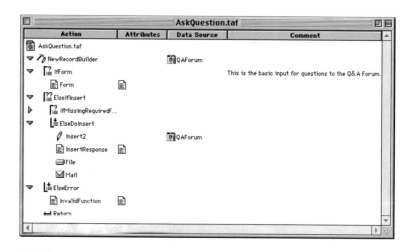

FIGURE 8-6. Tango Action File

This particular action file is used to handle online updates to a question and answer forum. A form is created to collect the necessary information from users; then a test is done to see if any required fields are missing. If they are not, the data is inserted into the database. All of this is done just by dragging actions from the Actions palette into the Tango action file. (Two commonly used actions are at the right of the palette— they are used to insert records and to search the database.)

You can find this application on the Web. You can ask questions and—subject to time constraints—get answers from the author of this book. The database is updated for every question, and only when the Status flag is changed to "Answered" (from "Unanswered") are the questions (and answers) displayed for anyone to see. The HTML page that handles the status change and the entry of answers is located on a server different from the one on which the database is stored; this is one way of preserving security. Note also that this database may run using Tango or using FileMaker Web Companion; it may even be a Microsoft Access or Oracle database. The same application and same database structure are used in all cases; what happens to be available at any given time depends on the research being done on the site. The address of the site is http://www.philmontmill.com/ddws/.

What is important is that no code—no HTML, Javascript, Visual Basic, or C++—is used to handle this process. Once the data sources and snippets (if needed) are set up, you can create this type of database-driven Web page in no more than 5 minutes. In addition, the visual structure of the Tango action file—with automatically indented actions, arrows that let you show or hide sections of the code, and graphical programming symbols—helps you see what is going on. This is something that is almost impossible when you are working with text-based HTML. Even working with a graphical interface to HTML, you are usually looking at the page image, and all of your extensions for database access are hidden from view.

To make your life even easier, you can specify properties, including comments, for any action, as shown in Figure 8-7. It cannot be stressed too much that you must make your Web pages easy to maintain and modify. Most of the Year 2000 computer problem arises from the fact that no one thought the code they were writing two and three decades ago would still be in use today. It is—and most of it is poorly documented. Do not do this to your junior colleagues!

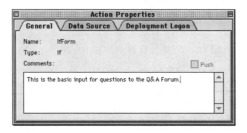

FIGURE 8-7. Action Properties

Manipulating Data

All data manipulation is handled with this graphical interface. If you drag the NewRecord action into the Tango action file, the basic shell of a new record process is created. When you double-click the resulting action, you see the dialog box shown in Figure 8-8. From the data sources (Figure 8-3) you drag the fields you want for the data entry form into this window. (By using the data sources, you can create this form without worrying about where the data sources are or the structure of their databases. Tango like many tools of this nature—interposes its interface between you and the nitty–gritty of the database.)

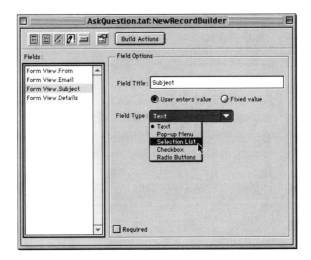

FIGURE 8-8. Specifying User Entry into a Form

Figure 8-9 shows how you can specify that a field is to have a fixed value; the pop-up menu in that figure shows the default values that you can automatically insert. You can also, of course, specify a literal value by simply typing it into the field.

While Tango interposes its interface between you and the database and other details you may not care about, it does generate HTML code automatically that you can then edit (by double-clicking the HTML icon in the attributes column next to an action).

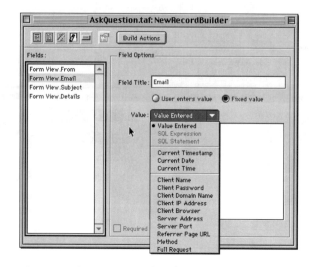

FIGURE 8-9. Specifying a Value to Be Placed in a Form

The HTML code generated automatically in this case is shown here:

```
<!DOCTYPE HTML PUBLIC "-//W3C//DTD HTML 3.2//EN">
<HTML>
<HEAD>
    <TITLE>New Record</TITLE>
</HEAD>
<BODY>
<FORM METHOD="POST" ACTION="<@CGI><@APPFILE>?
    function=insert&<@USERREFERENCEARGUMENT>">
<TABLE>
<TR VALIGN=TOP ALIGN=LEFT>
    <TD>
        <B>From: </B>
    </TD>

    <TD>
        <INPUT NAME="From" TYPE=TEXT SIZE=40 MAXLENGTH=255>
    </TD>
</TR>
<TR VALIGN=TOP ALIGN=LEFT>
    <TD>
        <B>Email: </B>
    </TD>
```

```
    <TD>
       <INPUT NAME="Email" TYPE=TEXT SIZE=40 MAXLENGTH=255>
    </TD>
</TR>
   … similar code omitted…
</TABLE>
<INPUT TYPE=SUBMIT VALUE="Save"> <INPUT TYPE=RESET VALUE="Reset
Values">
</FORM>
</BODY>
</HTML>
```

This is an important point to watch out for. Many graphical and automated development tools generate code that can then be modified only by returning to the underlying source code (Cobol, HTML, or whatever). This has been true for several decades; make certain that you can not only create but also modify the code that you generate graphically.

Also automatically generated are the conditional statements necessary to test for required fields. You can create these automatically by simply checking the Required box in the lower left of the screens shown in Figures 8-8 and 8-9. That is all that is needed. If, however, you want to check to see what Tango has done (or if you feel that you want to modify it), you can double-click the IfMissingRequiredField action (which was generated automatically) to reveal the window shown in Figure 8-10.

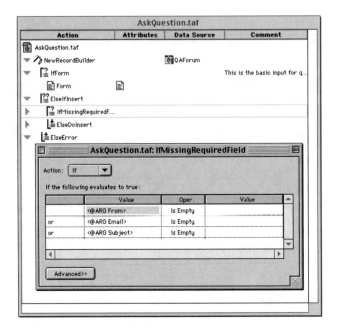

FIGURE 8-10. Test for Missing Data

And, if this graphical depiction is not sufficient for you, you can click the Advanced>> button in the lower left of the screen in order to view the HTML code that has been generated. But the point is that nothing needs to be done beyond checking the Required box in the initial field description window.

Sending Mail and Writing to Files

Development tools like Tango usually include features to handle operations that are frequently performed by application servers. For example, if you drag the Mail action from the Actions palette into the Tango action file, you can cause Tango to send an e-mail message. You can fill in the form (shown in Figure 8-11) to specify that it should use certain values from the input form and certain constants in the e-mail message it generates.

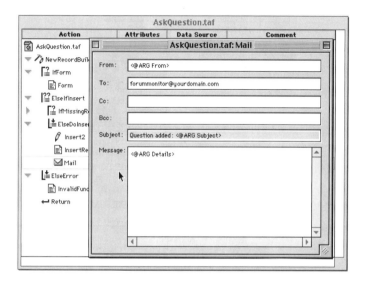

FIGURE 8-11. Mail Response

You may want to compare this with the Perl script shown in "Automatically Sending E-Mail" on page 468 that does the same thing.

And just to show you that the world does not begin and end with databases, Tango includes a read from/write to file action as shown in Figure 8-11. This is convenient for creating a log file. If, as shown here, you send an e-mail confirmation and write a log file entry for every database update you do, it is unlikely you will ever lose data.

FIGURE 8-12. Write to File

Summary

Application servers and their development tools are usually closely intertwined; they often come as a single package. The application server itself must also be able to coexist with your database and Web server (not to mention your ISP and its standards).

All of this may be daunting, but remember that you are rarely going to be starting from scratch: this is the environment that you will be working in, and it may all be ready for you. (That is one reason for using an ISP that is experienced in database hosting—even if you have your own network facilities. The schematic used on the opening pages of the chapters in this book, representing a variety of servers, is not there for decoration: it is the model for what many of these sites look like.)

With your ISP (or DSP), database, and application server, you are now ready to get to work. The next part of the book provides a fairly detailed overview of databases as they exist today and as they relate to the Web.

How to Do It: Setting Up and Using a Database

SQL and Relational Databases

9

Today's databases are primarily relational—all of the databases discussed in this book are. They are accessed in most cases either with proprietary graphical interfaces or with the industry standard SQL. This chapter provides an overview of relational databases and of SQL—with particular emphasis on the aspects of both that are most relevant to database-driven Web sites.

If you are one of the people whose eyes glaze over at the mention of databases, you can skip this chapter—but it represents a brief summary of what databases today really are. There is a lot of confusion about databases (and many people like to promote even more—possibly by way of making themselves more important as database gurus). The issues are really quite simple, and it is quite easy to learn enough about databases to use them successfully with your Web sites. Furthermore, if you have been feeling put upon by someone who knows what a sensitive cursor is (and refuses to tell you), this chapter reveals the mystery (see "Sensitive Cursors" on page 211).

What Database-Driven Web Sites Need from Their Databases

As pointed out earlier (see "Databases on the Web" on page 3), there are four primary ways of using databases to drive Web sites. Each of these has different database needs:

Publishing Data on the Web

In this case, you often have a relatively large amount of data. The database may have been created for purposes other than Web publication, and it may have complex relationships among its data elements. Your job is often to facilitate access to such an existing database (or to parts thereof).

These projects have some typical database characteristics:

- These are often large databases.

- Often the database predates the Web project. The mission of the Web site is to allow access to an already existing database.

- Queries are likely to be at least partly generated by users. Instead of providing buttons on your Web site that automatically retrieve all records related to zebras, you are likely to provide a form into which users can type zebra, snake, ice cream, or whatever they want to search on.

- Since queries are not predictable, you may need to manage special cases including massive successful results ("14,235,634 records found"), repeated failures due to user error ("no entries for zebra"), and counter-intuitive results ("zebra—see under circulation"[1]). In such cases, the messenger—the Web site—is often blamed.

- Furthermore, you need to be able to pass information about unsuccessful queries on to the user if you cannot handle them automatically. If the user has constructed a bizarre query, there is more likelihood of the user's being able to handle the resulting mess than there is of your HTML page being able to do so.

Sharing Data	Here, you are typically concerned with a relatively small amount of data that is relatively simple—interoffice messages, bulletin boards, etc.

Among the database characteristics involved with using databases to share data are the following:

- As part of such a project, you often design and implement the database.

- The database is likely to be quite simple: each entry is likely to be one item (a message, a bulletin board posting, etc.), and the other fields in the database are supporting information (date entered, recipient, subject, etc.).

- Queries are likely to be predictable (by date, subject, and a free-form scan of text within messages) and can be implemented on your Web site with buttons rather than data entry fields.

---

1. This result can occur when the British usage of zebra as in "zebra stripes"—a pedestrian walkway—is mixed with the use of circulation as in traffic.

E-Commerce

This may entail aspects of both of the previous cases: you may interact with a large customer or inventory database as well as with a separate database containing sales information—which components can be put together with one another, advertising copy and images, etc.

In addition to those issues, database used for e-commerce Web sites often need to address these characteristics:

- They need to implement security with regard to all aspects of their operations.

- They need to manage transactions—multiple database accesses that must be treated as a single unit (such as a sale).

- Their operations need to be recoverable in the case of hardware or software failures after a customer believes that a transaction has been completed.

Keeping Web Pages up to Date

In these situations, the fact that you are using a database is usually irrelevant (and often invisible) to the user. As a result, you have several special points to consider:

- Performance must be as fast as possible. (Since there is no clear benefit to the user from using a database, it is inappropriate to ask the user to suffer from more sluggish performance than would be the case if a database were not used.)

- You generally design and create your own database; you can implement it in whatever way is easiest for you (and most convenient for driving the Web site).

- The database should be hidden; this means that no strange error messages ("unfermented primary database key found") should appear before the user's eyes.

General Database Needs	In most cases, your database-driven Web site needs a reliable, fast database manager; your demands will probably not be particularly great. Except in the case in which you publish a database and let users do their own searches, you will not wind up using complex outer joins, recursive table expressions, or sensitive cursors. (Even in these cases, you will likely not be involved—you will let users type in their complex outer joins, recursive table expressions, or sensitive cursors and let them have it out directly with the database.)

What you need to worry about are the basics of databases. If you think of databases as little more than automated file storage mechanisms, that is usually sufficient. (For some reason, the word "database" scares many otherwise reasonable people. They have decided at some point in their lives that databases are too complicated for them to understand, and they tune out whenever the subject comes up. This is an irrational reaction.)

You will also need to worry about the issues involved in physically placing your databases on your Web site (see "Setting It Up" on page 311) and issues involved in database security (see "Security" on page 355).

The Relational Model

There is a specific (if changing) conceptual model underlying today's databases—the relational model. As noted previously ("The Great Database Secrets" on page 94), databases differ from some other contemporary software in that they are based on such a model—and it is a model that is studied extensively in universities and other institutions that are not necessarily engaged in the development of commercial products. (There is absolutely nothing wrong with the development of commercial products; however, there is a distinction between a conceptual foundation based on mathematics and computer science and one based on marketing strategies.)

Almost all current databases are built on the relational model. You may use one that uses proprietary terms invented by marketing folk instead of the terminology described here, but you should be able to map the two sets of terms to one another.

The Relational Model in Two Simple Points

You can sum up the relational model in two simple points:

1. All data in a relational database is stored in tables—two-dimensional structures with rows and columns (like spreadsheets).

2. Everything that you do to a table results in another table (which—if it has a single column and row—may contain one data value).

From these two simple points, a number of important consequences ensue (including many books, a wide variety of products and careers, and a large number of dissertations).

There are three parts to the relational model, two of which matter to you:

1. Objects—the database structures in which data is stored.

2. Integrity—rules governing the content of the database. (This is the part that you can safely ignore.)

3. Operators—the commands that manipulate the data in the database.

These parts of the relational model are discussed briefly in the next sections.

The reason for this discussion is that you may need to translate between conflicting sets of terminology: that of the database world, that of the programmer, that of the mathematician or set theorist, and that of the Web world. The concepts are quite simple, but none of these worlds has felt inclined to adopt another's terminology.

Objects

Data in a relational database is stored in tables (see the first point in the previous section). Tables are the most important objects in the relational model—except they are called **relations**.

By convention, each row of the table represents one observation or data record (such as one individual's data). It is called a **tuple**.

Each column of the table contains the data for a field—a specific type of data (such as age or telephone number) for each of the rows. Each column or field is called an **attribute**.

In most tables, one (or more) of the columns contains identifying information—a value that is unique for each row. This might be a person's social security number, a name (although names are often not unique), a serial number, or any other information that uniquely identifies that row. This is called a **primary key**.

Should you wish to complete your overview of the objects in the relational model, you can add these definitions:

- A **domain** is the universe of legal values for an attribute (or field or column). All valid part numbers, all valid social security numbers, and so forth are valid domains. Domains are a concept that is implemented only indirectly in most relational databases—but it is a very important concept when it comes to ensuring data integrity. ("Green" is not normally considered to be in the domain of birth dates.)

- The number of rows in a table (relation) is its **cardinality**.

- The number of columns in a table (relation) is its **degree**.

Integrity

This part of the relational model deals with rules of integrity that relate to the use of keys to identify (and therefore to retrieve) rows of data within a table. You may hear talk of unique keys, candidate keys, foreign keys, and referential integrity: all refer to database integrity and to the identification of records within tables.

For the purposes of almost every database that you deal with on a Web site, it is sufficient to identify a unique key for each row—some value that can identify that row when you need to locate it.

Operators

Operators come in two flavors in the relational model: algebraic and calculus. For your purposes, it is sufficient to remember that all operations on tables (relations) in the relational model produce other tables. The resultant tables may be larger than the original table (as is the case when you combine several tables into one), or they may be smaller (as is the case when the resultant table has a single row and column—one value).

The operators that you need to know about are described later in this chapter in "SQL" on page 207.

Normalization

In the cases where you create databases to drive your Web site, it is useful to know something about normalization—the process of structuring a database's tables in such a way that they are most efficient. Normalization has a significant basis in database theory; database software is usually optimized to handle the processes needed to store and retrieve normalized data.

There are five forms of normalization. You probably normalize data now without knowing it; you need not normalize your data (and if you do, you need not say that you have done so). Nevertheless, it is useful to know the correct terminology. It is very easy to set up all of the database fields shown in this section.

First Normal Form (Eliminate Repeating Groups)

Imagine a database record layout that lets you store your appointments for a given day as shown in Table 9-1.

Appointment Database
Name
Date
Appointment 1 time
Appointment 1 title
Appointment 1 location
Appointment 2 time
Appointment 2 title
Appointment 2 location

TABLE 9-1. Appointment Database with Repeating Groups

This may look simple (and in fact it is the type of database layout that almost everyone creates when they are starting).

Note, however, that there is a repeating group of fields—the time, title, and location of each appointment. This is almost always a problem for the following reasons:

- Since each record contains all of the fields, if you ever need as many as 10 appointments for one day, every record must have space for 10 appointments. This can be an enormous waste of space.

- It is very difficult to use search mechanisms efficiently on this structure. If you are looking for a specific appointment, you wind up searching for a condition in which Appointment 1 name = X or Appointment 2 name = X, etc.

- Getting around this problem brings out the most imaginative ideas in users and database designers. In the example given here, typical work-arounds include having two records for the same day (so as to double the limit of appointments), using two names for one person (for the same reason), piggybacking two appointments in one entry, and others too disturbing to mention.

The correct implementation of this structure is to use two related tables. The structure is shown in Table 9-2.

Name/Date Database	Appointment Database
Sequence Number	Sequence Number
Name	Appointment time
Date	Appointment title
	Appointment location

TABLE 9-2. Normalized Appointment Database

The relationship between the two databases is provided by a sequence number that is unique for each record in the Name/Date database. Every appointment for that person and that date is stored in the Appointment database; each record in the Appointment database has a sequence number in it that matches a Name/Date database sequence number. (These sequence numbers are unique within the Name/Date database, identifying a single person and date; within the Appointment database, they are not unique, since many appointments can exist for a single person on a given date.)

Note that this structure doesn't waste space—there are only as many appointments for a given person on a given date as actually exist (if any). Furthermore, there is no limit to the number of appointments that can exist.

Violating the first normal form is the most common mistake that people make in designing databases. However (as always in database design, there is a "however"), you should remember two important points:

1. Not all databases support relations such as that used to link the sequence number in the two databases shown in Table 9-2. If you are working with old databases—or databases derived from old databases—do not automatically assume that people didn't know what they were doing.

2. The definition of a repeating group is far from clear. Table 9-3 shows two sets of data fields. Do you think that the fields in the first column represent a repeating group? The same information can be presented in a way that appears to be a repeating group (the first column) and that appears to be unique data fields (the second column). This is a common situation.

In general, the trade-off is simply stated: repeated groups take up more disk space and are harder to work with, while nonrepeating groups use slightly more processing time (to perform the relationship) and use less disk space. Although you may need to do some experiments for yourself in very time-critical applications, in most cases the cost of normalizing data is well worth it.

Phone 1 Name (fax, home, office, etc.)	Fax phone number
Phone 1 Number	Home phone number
Phone 2 Name (fax, home, office, etc.)	Office phone number
Phone 2 Number	
Phone 3 Name (fax, home, office, etc.)	

TABLE 9-3. Identifying Repeating Groups

Second Normal Form (Eliminate Redundant Data)

As soon as you start creating a database project with several related databases, you will encounter the temptation to store data in two places: don't do this. In the example shown in Table 9-2, you can blithely violate the second normal form by adding a Name field to the Appointment database. The Sequence Number lets you match up a Name/Date database record with the appropriate Appointment database records; using that relationship, you find the appropriate name from the Name/Date database for a given Sequence Number. Stashing the name in the Appointment database as well may seem like a good idea, but it is not.

The most common reason given for violating this rule is efficiency: "Why should I have to look up the name from another database, when I can just as easily keep a copy in the Appointment database?" The answer is that as soon as you have redundant data in your design, you need to worry about keeping it synchronized. Violation of the second normal form is what lets you have two different names at your bank, two different account numbers for a single credit card, or a multitude of different mailing addresses for a single mass marketer.

There is a reason for violating this rule—and it is a very important consideration. The advantages of storing each data value once (and only once) include not only reduced storage space but also the fact that a change to the data value—such as a change of address or change of name—need be entered only once; it is propagated through the entire database project as various related databases pick up the revised data.

If you are using related data in an invoice database, it is important that the values not change after the invoice has been accepted. A change to your mailing address a week after you have ordered an item should not affect the records of a shipment that has already been dispatched. More important, a change in the price of an item that you have ordered and paid for should not be reflected on the invoice when it is subsequently printed and stuffed in the carton in which the goods are shipped.

There are two standard solutions to this problem:

1. When you want to freeze the value of related fields (such as a price at the moment when a sale is consummated), you can copy all of the data in the invoice record to a new database that contains all of the invoice's data with no relations. This violates a whole host of database design considerations but is a realistic and practical solution to the need to keep a copy of the data as it was at a given time.

2. You can add validity dates to the related data items, indicating that the price, item name, address, etc. are valid from a certain date and time until another one. Then, when you get the related data, you get the data that falls within the appropriate range based on the invoice date and time. This is a more complicated method than the first one, and if it fails it can lead to the display of incorrect data. The first method—dupli-

cation of data when it is accepted for processing—cannot display incorrect data.

Third Normal Form (Eliminate Fields Not Dependent on the Key Field)

There may be relationships within the data that you store in a database record (the most common is the relationship between a ZIP or postal code and a town name). In this case, data is dependent on (varies in accordance with) another field in the record. Storing both elements is redundant and wasteful; in addition, it can lead to incomplete data in the database.

In a database that stores both postal code and town names, you can search for one and find the other—given the postal code you can find the town and vice versa. This is often useful, but it works only for the towns and postal codes that are used in addresses in the database. If you order merchandise over the telephone, you will learn that most telemarketers have a separate database of all postal codes for all towns—regardless of which codes and towns are used in their customer database; you provide your postal code and they confirm the town that you are in.

Violating the third normal form can create databases in which people rely on incomplete data. On the other hand, violating the third normal form when the data items are very small (as in postal codes) can sometimes simplify the design of a database project sufficiently that it is worth the risk.

Fourth Normal Form (Separate Multiple Relations)

This rule is very simple to demonstrate using the Appointment database from Table 9-2. If you enter an appointment that consists of a meeting with Jill for 2 PM on Tuesday in your office and another appointment that consists of a meeting with Joan for 2 PM on Tuesday also in your office, is that a joint meeting with both Jill and Joan or a conflict of two separate meetings?

Fourth normal form requires that there not be two types of relationships within the same database; thus this must be two separate and conflicting meetings.

This explanation of fourth normal form is overly simplified; for more details consult a book on database design. For practical purposes, you can avoid running amuck in fourth normal by keeping your databases simple.

Fifth Normal Form (Use Common Sense)

The traditional definition of fifth normal form has to do with the need to isolate semantically related relationships; it is usually covered in textbooks with a brief parenthetical note and then ignored. Another way of looking at fifth normal form is in a broader sense that covers all of the other rules as well: do what makes sense. The way in which you design a database has to do with the data and the use to which it will be put. Issues of efficiency sometimes suggest that you unnormalize data to save processing time and use more disk space. Similarly, issues of security may dictate that you separate logically related fields so that you can enforce necessary procedures.

For all of the normalization rules, do what makes sense. Remember, though, that database software works most efficiently with database projects that are normalized. Also be careful to do real-life testing before assuming that one database structure is more or less efficient than another. Most actual experiments have shown that the performance gains achieved by using nonnormalized data are minimal.

SQL

Originally, SQL was an acronym for "Structured Query Language"; it was designed to be a language to manipulate relational database data. Over time, SQL has become a non-acronym, and its goal has become that of manipulating something called SQL-data—that subset of relational data that it handles properly (it cannot properly handle all aspects of the relational model).

SQL is the language that is used most frequently to manipulate databases today. It is a text-based language and is often inserted into code written in traditional programming languages (such as Cobol, Fortran, C, C++, and Ada). However, much database manipulation is done using visual programming languages and tools; in such cases, SQL may be used as a text-based insert (you type it into a box on a syntax diagram), or it may be used in a graphical form. In all cases, however, the basics are the same.

SQL is very powerful; even so, it does not fully implement all of the features needed for the relational model. But you need not worry: you need only a small subset of SQL (in fact, no more than six commands).

The Basic Rule of SQL

Remember the basics of the relational model:

- Everything is a table.

- The results of all operations are tables.

These basics give rise to a very important point: operations within a relational database occur on groups of records (i.e., tables) and result in further groups of records (i.e., tables) that may incorporate changes. In other words, you do not use SQL (or the relational model) to handle individual records.

How This Works in Traditional Programs

In traditional programming (such as that which preceded the adoption of relational databases in the 1980s), programmers wrote code like this:

- Get the first record which is…

- Do something to it.

- Get the next record which is…

- Do that to it.

- Repeat until there are no more records which are …

These loops formed the basis of well-structured programs in the 1980s and 1990s. However, their code mixes two operations: the retrieval of data and its processing.

With relational databases, the code becomes much simpler:

- Get all the records which are…

- For each of them, do something to it.

There are no intermediate tests (except to see if all the records have been used), and in fact the relational database supports very efficient retrieval of each of these records after the major database retrieval ("all the records which are…") has been done.

Why This Matters for Database-Driven Web Sites

You will see this model over and over in products that support the use of databases on Web sites. A query (the data retrieval) is specified in one way or another. Then, for each of the records that is returned, HTML is generated to display that record. In FileMaker Pro, such code is delimited by [FMP-RECORD] and [/FMP-RECORD]; in Microsoft Access, it is <%BeginDetail%> and <%EndDetail%>; and in Tango, it is <@ROW> and </@ROW)>.

This works very well when what you are doing is retrieving a set of data. However, there are times when you need to retrieve an individual data item (such as the name that will be shown at the top of your HTML page). In such cases, you need to do exactly the same thing: retrieve all the records that conform to a certain criterion and process each of them in turn. It is your responsibility to create a table which has a unique identifier so that when you specify that identifier you get only one row. The code that you will write to display the results of the database query will be capable of displaying multiple records—and that is probably not what you want to do if you are simply trying to retrieve the title to place on your Web page.

You are always asking for "all the records which are..."; it is your database design that guarantees in some cases that one—and only one—record fulfills that requirement. See "Tango Enterprise" on page 176 for an example that includes both unique and nonunique keys of retrieval.

Cursors

Cursors are SQL constructs that are used to implement the logic described in the previous section. A cursor is associated with a table—which is often created as the result of some database operation (such as finding all records which are...). The cursor can be positioned on, after, or before any row in the table. When it is so positioned, the data for that row can be manipulated by the program, and the cursor is typically advanced to the next row.

The most significant database access occurs when the cursor is opened—that is, when its associated table is constructed via a query. Subsequent accesses (retrieving each row) typically involve much less database horsepower.

Why This Matters

Since the major processing occurs once, it is most efficient to get the most out of that processing. You can certainly write perfectly good code which uses cursors to evaluate the data that is retrieved (if the data to which the cursor points has certain characteristics, do X); however, in almost all cases databases work more efficiently if you move those evaluations into the original query. In other words, if you want to find all customer records with balances that are over two months old and subsequently mark the customers that have a history of late payments, it is best to form a basic query that retrieves all customers with balances over two months old *who also* had such late balances in the past year. The alternative (retrieving the customers with late payments and checking each one for previous late payments) is less efficient.

Because databases are often designed to work in this way, you may find that you are working with a process whose timing is very uneven. The time it takes to perform the initial—and complex—query may be noticeable to the user; the time to retrieve each additional row from the cursor is often unnoticeable. In such cases, it makes sense to plan ahead in designing your Web site: know when the major database accesses occur and present messages to users so that they know time will pass before they get a response. (See "Timing and Performance" on page 224.)

Sensitive Cursors

The issue of sensitive cursors can now be explained. If the data to which a cursor points changes (due to another user's activities), those changes may or may not be reflected in the data that you are retrieving. (Remember that the major data retrieval occurs when the cursor is opened.) If you declare a cursor to be sensitive, it reflects such changes; insensitive cursors do not.

Select

Whether you type your query in text (as in the previous examples) or design it using a graphical user interface, you are usually creating SQL queries. (Even in those cases when you are not, the designers of the database often think in SQL terms and they map their query language to SQL either consciously or unconsciously.)

The most basic SQL statement is the Select statement; it operates on one or more tables and creates a result—a new table. Although the Select statement can be very complicated, its basis is quite simple:

```
Select
column(s)
```

```
FROM table(s)
<WHERE condition>
<GROUP BY condition
    <HAVING grouped characteristic>>
```

The basis of relational databases in general and SQL Select statements in particular is mathematical set theory. Concepts of sets, unions, and intersections are at the heart of these operations.

SubQueries Since the result of a Select statement is a table, you can use a Select statement in the From clause of a Select statement, as in

```
Select Name, Age From
    (Select Name, Age, Address From Customers Where Age > 18)
```

(Although in this case the statement could be expressed in a single Select statement, many complex statements benefit from this multilayered construction of Select statements.)

Select * Instead of specifying the columns to be retrieved, you can ask for all columns of a table to be selected by using an asterisk—

```
Select * from Customers
```

(This is the shortest Select statement that can be constructed— it returns all rows and columns from the table mentioned in the Select statement.)

Where Conditions Where clauses can specify comparison values (such as Age > 18) as well as set operations such as IN. You can create a temporary table (using a Select statement, of course) and use that temporary table to test whether rows from your primary select statement will be used.

Group By/Having The Group By clause lets you group the returned rows by some value (often a calculated value, such as a sum or average). When the Having clause is used as well, you can include only the rows from groups having certain characteristics (a sum greater than X, an average less than Y, etc.).

Examples of Select Statements

Here are some typical Select statements:

```
Select Names from Customers
```

This could select all customer names from a Customers table.

```
Select Names from Customers where Balance > 100.00
```

This could select all customers with balances greater than 100 from a Customers table.

```
Select Names from Customers where Balance > 100.00 ORDER BY Bal-
ance
```

This query is the same as the last except that the results will be sorted from smallest to largest balance.

Queries can operate against several tables at the same time; in such cases, column names need to be qualified with table names as in this query and the relationship between records in the two tables needs to be expressed. In this query, records are drawn from both the Customers and the Accounting tables; the tables are matched on a field called ID that exists in both tables:

```
SelectNames, Balances from Customers, Accounting Where Custom-
ers.ID=Accounting.ID.
```

It is the section Customers.ID=Accounting.ID that links the records from the two tables (assuming that a unique customer ID exists in both Customers and Accounting—and that it is the same ID for both files).

Some database software allow you to specify such relations explicitly in the database design (FileMaker Pro is one of these); others let you specify the relations only in queries—as they are needed.

Why This Matters   All of this is background for you: most database-driven Web sites use only the simplest SQL queries. However, you do need to pin down a few facts.

You Need the Queries   You need the queries that will generate your Web pages. These may already be known to database designers in your organization; if you are creating your own databases, you will need to create the queries. As you design your Web pages, look at every item that will come from a database and make certain that you have the query (or can create it). If you cannot construct the query that gets your data, you cannot construct the Web site.

Two types of queries are typically used on database-driven Web sites:

1. Standard queries that return a variable number of rows are used to answer user queries or to present dynamic database information (as in, "Here are all of today's messages").

2. Specialized queries that return a specific number of items are used to build Web pages. Such cases are demonstrated in "Tango Enterprise" on page 176 and "Totally Database-Driven Web Sites" on page 435.

In either case, you will need the query sooner or later.

Table and Field Names   If you are going to be writing the query yourself, you will need table and field names to use. They may not be self-evident from their names; also, it is common to find fields that appear to be similar (or even identical) but are not. If you are new to the world of databases, you may be expecting a degree of uniformity that does not exist; if you are an old hand at databases, you probably know that users and managers have a perverse desire to "refine" database designs. Both situation can occasionally result in counterintuitive database structures.

Common Keys   Linking two tables together using a common key (such as the ID field in the Customers and Accounting tables of the previous section) is called a join. (It joins two tables based on a shared key value which lets you rely on the fact that the balance for ID# 14356 belongs to the name associated in another table with that same ID.)

In cases in which you are building a Web site on existing database tables, you may find yourself attempting to gather and display data that has not been gathered and displayed in the applications that run against the database elsewhere in your organization. It is not uncommon for you to discover that you do not have shared keys—the ID numbers in the customer table differ from those in the accounting table. This is a very frequent problem in large (and not so large) organizations. If you are using preexisting databases, have no qualms about asking what the shared keys are—and be prepared to discover that the accounting systems do not really talk to the customer support systems and that they in turn do not communicate easily with analytical systems.

Stand Your Ground   Creating database-driven Web sites is often a collaborative effort, and the parties to the collaboration often come from different worlds (databases on the one side, Web design on the other). The database queries are the interface between the two worlds. Whichever side of the fence you are on, you must understand the query—what the Web page needs and what the database can provide. It is in no way a poor reflection on anyone if they do not understand the language from the other side of the fence. If you are the Web page designer, you must get the query that will get the data you want; if you are the database designer, you must generate the query that will give the Web page designer what is required. This may take some time, but it is key to the success of the project. Get the query, run it interactively if you can, and examine the results. Make certain that everyone is happy.

Insert	The SQL Insert command inserts a row of data into a table. The data must often adhere to certain edits (such as having a unique key, having numeric values for certain fields). You will often use an Insert command to add data to your database-driven Web sites, although the application server you use will often generate it for you automatically.
	Commonly, the data that is inserted into the database is collected from a user using an HTML form—see "Sending Data to Web Sites with HTTP and Forms" on page 255.
Delete	The SQL Delete command deletes a row of data that is specified using the appropriate unique key. Again, edits may come into play to prevent you from deleting part of related records in several tables (referential integrity).
	As with Insert, you often do not see this code—it is generated for you by your application server software.
Update	The SQL Update command modifies data in an existing row of a table. You can use variations of the Update command to perform mass updates (such as multiplying all values by a constant). The difference between Insert and Update is that Insert creates a new row and Update modifies an existing row.
Create	A variety of SQL Create statements let you create the objects of relational databases. These include tables as well as subsidiary structures such as views and indexes.
Views	Views can be considered temporary tables. The result of a select is always a table; such a table can be saved as a view. It

does not actually exist as a table, but you can refer to the view as if it were a table. Each time you refer to the view, the Select statement that created it is effectively reexecuted, along with its conditions and criteria.

Indexes

Database software uses whatever information it has at hand to fulfill your queries. It can create indexes to the data in the database—and you can create indexes yourself. This can be useful when you know how the data will be retrieved.

Create statements (as well as views and indexes) are frequently used in database-driven Web sites, but you rarely worry about them. Your database administrator usually takes care of creating them as needed; you may get involved if performance is sluggish—views and indexes can speed up processing.

Summary

The widespread use of SQL and relational databases means that the ways of storing and manipulating data are fairly standard. In addition, the basic techniques for programming database-driven applications are not proprietary to an individual vendor's architecture. This makes it possible to discuss general principles of database programming, which is exactly what the next chapter does.

Programming with Databases

10

Alan Turing and John von Neumann are considered two of the most important developers of modern computers. Both realized that a computer could store data in electronic form and that it could store instructions in electronic form—and that the instructions could act upon stored instructions in precisely the same way in which they could act upon data. In the 1940s, the ability to treat data and computer instructions as (sometimes) interchangeable made modern computers possible.

Within two decades, however, this flexibility started to cause problems, and designers (particularly designers of operating systems) starting erecting barriers to the manipulation of computer instructions as if they were data (the famous cry of "no non-reentrant code" *was first heard at this time). Within not too much more time, the modification of program instructions within applications (rather than just within operating systems) started to cause problems. The development of database software—in which the data was physically removed from the application software—helped to rebuild the wall that Turing and von Neumann had demolished.*

Database programming consists of this very rigid distinction between data and the instructions that act upon it. The pendulum of computer science development continues to swing back and forth between this pole and the other pole—that at which data and instructions are indistinguishable. (In some ways, objects—particularly distributed objects—represent this opposite pole: the union of data and instructions.)

Meanwhile, back in the world of Web page design, the distinction between data and computer instructions started out not mattering very much. Recent developments (such as applets and XML) are raising these barriers again as ontology does appear to recapitulate phylogeny in the world of software design.

This chapter covers four major topics in database programming:

* *Result Sets*

* *Timing and Performance*

* *Transaction Processing*

* *The Data and Nothing But the Data*

Result Sets

As noted previously, relational databases manipulate tables: data is stored in tables, and the results of database operations are other tables (which, when they contain a single row and column, are single values). All of this is based on the mathematics of set theory—unions, intersections, and logical operations on elements of sets that have certain properties and attributes. The resultant tables can be called **result sets**.

Procedural Programming	This type of computer processing environment differs from the procedurally based world that preceded it. The computer code that is generated looks quite different. Typical procedure-based code is structured like this:

```
Get a data record.
Check to see if condition X is met; if so do A, if not do B.
If the results of A are of type T, do C, else do D;
    if the results of B are of type T, do C, else do E.
Get the next record.
```

Database Programming	Database programming tends to move all of the condition checking into the database query itself. Thus, you wind up with several sections of code of this nature:

```
Get all data records in which condition X is met and
    where the results of A would be T.
Do A and C for all those records.

Get all data records in which condition X is not met and
    where the results of B would be T.
Do B and C for all these records.

Get all data records in which condition X is met and
    where the results of A would not be T.
Do A and D for all those records.

Get all data records in which condition X is not met and
    where the results of B would not be T.
Do B and E for all these records.
```

Differences between Procedural and Database Programming	The database code has these obvious differences from the procedural code: • It is longer.

- The choice logic (testing conditions) is separated from the executable logic, and

- Once execution begins for any condition (the underlined lines of code in the previous example), it continues without interruption or further testing.

- Some commands may be executed twice. The italicized lines in the previous example show the evaluation of a process (A or B), which is then actually performed in the underlined code that follows the test.

For these reasons, many people consider database programming to be less efficient than procedural programming. However, just as programmers chose procedural programming over its predecessors (which in turn appeared to be more efficient), database programming offers advantages in that it is easier to understand, easier to debug (since there are fewer branches in the code), and much easier to maintain over time.

Why This Matters

This matters to database-driven Web sites because you must be able to structure your Web pages in this way. In fact, because of the nature of HTML, you really have no choice in the matter—you cannot write traditional procedural code on them. The typical Web page as constructed by an application server is generated as shown in Figure 10-1.

You send an HTTP request to the Web server (usually by typing in a URL or clicking on a link). The Web server, together with the application server (which may be a plug-in or part of the Web server) then constructs the page—all of this is shown inside the dotted box of Figure 10-1.

You may provide HTML excerpts or stubs to be used as headers and footers and as templates to surround data returned from the database. However, the database queries are specified as part of the original HTTP request to the Web server: there is no further interaction with the user until the page is returned. Many pages encapsulate only one query; those that do incorporate more than one (as the figure shows) need to have both specified in the original HTTP request.

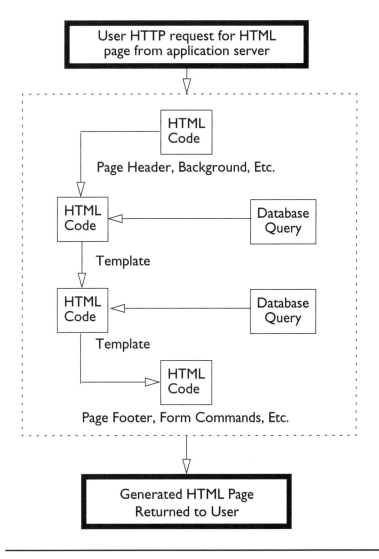

FIGURE 10-1. HTTP Request for Generated HTML Page from Web and Application Server

Once you have started to generate an HTML page for a user, you cannot stop in the middle for database accesses and queries. (You can make a subsequent query dependent on the results of a first query on the page, but that is not the same as interacting with the user.)

Thus, you need all the information for your query (or queries) when you start to generate the page. This includes passwords, options (number of records to retrieve), and all other parameters for the query. (See "Sending Data to Web Sites with HTTP and Forms" on page 255 and "Cookies" on page 374 for how to implement this.)

Not only do you need the information, but you need to be able to find it in the database. Having people type in their passport ID numbers will not help you to retrieve any information about them if the passport ID numbers are not in the database. As you start to design your Web pages, keep this in mind and make certain that you know what you will need to retrieve the data you need—and that is in the database. (In large enterprises, it can be a very time-consuming process to change database designs.)

Some application server products do allow you to interrupt this processing to perform intermediate actions and tests on data as it is retrieved and as HTML is generated. In such cases, the complexity of the project quickly mushrooms.

Timing and Performance

Looking back at Figure 10-1, another point should become clear: the process of generating the database-driven Web page is almost always substantially longer than the process of returning a prefabricated Web page (all that is required in that case is to transmit the text of the HTML on the page). Some old-fashioned HTML coders will immediately thumb their noses and say, "See? This database stuff is just an inefficient waste of time."

What matters in general is that the total time is usually less, but it is spent in different ways. The feel of a database-driven Web site will be very different from that of a Web site without a database, and that in turn will feel different from a database-driven application that doesn't use the Web (or even a graphical user interface). Beware of jumping to conclusions based on timing and performance of small pieces of the application.

Automating Web Page Production	The fact that database-driven Web pages take longer to generate than simple HTML pages means no more or less than that: the total cost (and complexity) of a database-driven Web site is almost always less than that of a traditional site. However, those costs increase and decrease in different places:

- The cost of coding HTML pages by hand is substantially reduced with database-driven Web sites.

- The computer resources needed to deliver database-driven Web pages are greater than those for traditional HTML pages. You either need more powerful computers or you need to accept slower responses. (Note: the final HTML page that is generated is typically not much bigger for database-driven Web pages than for manually written Web pages. As a result, it is only the computer resources—not the telecommunications link—that need upgrading.)

You are simply automating the production of Web pages, and it should not be surprising that you need greater computer resources and fewer human resources to do so (that is the history of all automation efforts).

Interface Adaptations	In addition to realizing that you may need more computer power for your database-driven Web sites, you should consider the user's experience in browsing through the site. Even with very fast computers, a lot of work is needed to generate each page; furthermore, the Web server (and application server) needs access to the database in order to fulfill users' requests: all of this takes time.

Remember what database accesses are required for individual pages on your site. When a page presents a search interface that lets users browse the database, the production of that page is usually quite simple: database access is needed only for the results. Users who have formulated their query and asked for a database search are not likely to complain about a pause at that point.

For other purposes, however, the possible delay in generating the Web page needs to be addressed with an adaptation. Here are some that you can use:

- Frames. When you use HTML frames, the page that is generated is actually produced from several separate pages. You can use frames that do not rely on database access to return a banner or navigation frame quickly while the database access is still being carried out. Thus, the user sees part of the page (and a usable part—not just a background) very quickly.

- Redirection. You can use the redirect command to send the user to a new page automatically. This is commonly used when a Web site has moved—the user types in www.olddomain.com, and a page with a redirect statement there automatically sends the user on to www.newdomain.com after a brief pause. Use the first page for welcome and identification; while the user reads it, the redirect command is executed (and with it the database access). Then the full database-driven page is automatically displayed.

- Set Home Pages. On intranets, set default home pages to your site's home page. When people start their browsers, they will automatically be connected to your site and the database accesses will occur as part of the start-up process (often before people have found a safe spot for the coffee cup).

Whatever you do, do not let a user type in your URL (or click on a link) and sit there with nothing happening while your application server and database go about building some gargantuan structure.

Transaction Processing

Transaction processing is the collection of a number of operations into what appears to be a single process: that single process either succeeds or fails. When you are working with transactions, you do not worry about leaving an inventory record in one condition while an account balance record is in another: if they are part of a transaction, the charge to a customer account occurs in the same process as the shipment from inventory.

Transaction processing can be implemented at a variety of levels:

- Many databases support transactions themselves, allowing you to specify which operations will be part of the transaction.

- Some application servers and application development tools (such as Tango) let you create transactions at that level.

- You can create your own transactions. While this is not particularly difficult to do, it involves creating temporary flags to mark transactions as pending or complete.

It is likely that you will have a choice of how to implement transaction processing. What you should remember, though, is that transaction processing is relatively expensive. It is one of those cases in which operations are performed twice—or even three times—during the process of carrying out the transaction and leaving proper traces behind so that the transaction can be undone if necessary.

The two critical parts of a transaction are its **commitment** (on successful preparation of the transaction) and its **rollback** (in the case of failure). Failure can be anything from corruption of a disk or database to a user cancellation of the process. Because transaction processing is relatively expensive, make certain that you use it correctly. If you have a set of related operations that should be carried out but that do not need to be rolled back as a single operation in the case of failure, you do not need transaction processing. The critical thing to remember with transaction processing is that the rollback must be necessary (in the case of problems). Grouping operations together logically into a transaction is a waste of expensive computer time.

Note also that transaction processing can degrade database performance for other processing that occurs while the transaction is being handled. At the critical moment of the transaction, a single-thread operation must occur: the database must write to its log and verify that that write statement has been executed correctly.

Transactions always involve database updates; there is no data retrieval process that cannot be repeated, and so retrieval can never require a rollback. (You may want to lock the database or parts of it during a retrieval to prevent updates while you are retrieving data, but that is not the same as a transaction.)

The Data and Nothing But the Data

Database-driven Web sites often merge data from databases with data that is contained in standard HTML pages. (Your name and address, for instance, may be part of your HTML page rather than being retrieved from the database.) Since it is almost always easier to type information into an HTML page than to enter it into a database (and to plan for its retrieval), you may find that with time more and more of your site's data finds its way from the database environment into the HTML environment. Knowing that this is a danger, you should be able to guard against it.

Whereas it is almost always easier to enter data into an HTML page than into a database, it is almost always easier to maintain it when it is in a database. This is a typical short- versus long-term trade-off, but the long-term benefits of database-driven Web sites are so great that you should be ever vigilant.

Summary

Database programming is somewhat different from procedural programming—the step-by-step processing of data as you encounter it. The principles of database programming—particularly result sets and transaction processing—make it quite amenable for use with Web sites.

This part of the book has focused on databases. In the next part, you will find chapters on HTML and Web technologies.

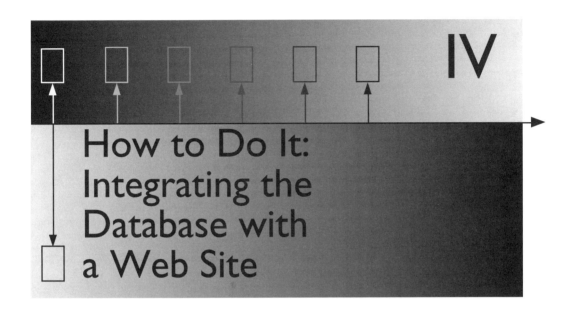

How to Do It: Integrating the Database with a Web Site

HTML for Database Designers

HTML—hypertext markup language—is the language used for Web pages. This chapter provides a summary of HTML's structure and a step-by-step walk-through of one of the HTML pages that ships as part of the Shopping Cart example with FileMaker Pro.

The page in question has no database access involved—you could use it with any database (or in fact in any environment whatsoever). It is typical in that it displays several images and contains a scripted button that changes color as the mouse is moved over it.

Although many books have been written on HTML, this brief summary of HTML may well be enough for you to do much of your work: rarely do HTML programmers and designers start from a blank piece of paper (or blank screen). You usually start from an existing HTML document—from an example, from Home Page, or from another project. The development of most HTML (as of most computer programs) consists largely of modifying and extending existing code. In short, you probably don't need to know how to develop a Web site from scratch; instead, you need to be able to understand how an existing site is designed and implemented so that you can build on the existing work.

HTML Overview

HTML is one of several Structured Generalized Markup Languages (SGMLs). Originally, these languages were designed to integrate content and formatting information into a single text-based document. The formatting information (used to "mark up" the document, as copy editors would say) was enclosed in distinctive characters—typically < and >.

There are other ways of formatting text-based documents:

- The formatting information can be kept separate from the document's content. In such a structure, the formatting information (fonts, paragraph spacing, etc.) is kept—often in binary form—in one part of a file; each piece of formatting information is associated with one or more parts of the document itself—often using character position numbers.

- Formatting information can be integrated into the text but kept in binary or other nontext formats.

Word processing programs often use the first of these methods. The use of nontext formatting information means that the documents are not easily read by humans; this is an advantage for proprietary word processing formats.

Markup Information	As markup languages have evolved, the information that is provided has been of several kinds:

- Formatting information—including fonts, indentations, headings, etc.—has been present from the start.

- Structural information—often having no visible representation—has been added.

- Meta-information—information about the document (author, etc.)—is needed to categorize and organize documents.

The ratio of markup information to content in documents is becoming greater and greater. The original notion of adding a few formatting codes to the text of a document has mushroomed; as a result, one of the primary benefits of SGMLs—the ability to read the content and the markup information easily—has been lost.

Managing Markup Information	For this and other reasons, the trend in SGMLs is to break a single document into many parts. This is done in various ways:

- Formatting information is gradually being moved to style sheets. The details of formatting information—font sizes, colors, etc.—are placed in files that can be referenced from basic HTML documents. This allows the detailed formatting information in the style sheets to be reused; it also allows alternate formatting to be applied based on user choices of style sheets. It also makes the basic HTML document much shorter and clearer.

- A relatively new SGML called XML (Extensible Markup Language) has been developed that focuses on data, content, and structure rather than the presentation aspects of documents. Elements can be defined by users and can reflect the data that is involved. Thus, whereas standard HTML has elements such as paragraphs and tables, a user of XML can define an element such as name or city.

• Images, applets, and scripts are placed in separate files. They can be included using standard HTML syntax.

When developing a site, the use and reuse of images, applets, and scripts is an easy way to keep your files easily readable and understandable. In addition, it makes it easier to keep your site consistent and up to date because changes to a single graphical element that may appear on several pages can be made in a single file that is included several times.

The actual presentation of information in a user's browser is a combination of separate strands of content, structural information, styles, and data (such as database information, as distinct from the surrounding content which might be logos, informational text, etc.). This combination is made in two locations: at the Web server that assembles the Web page and at the browser that displays the page. Style information (including preferred fonts) may be part of the user's environment, whereas content and data are almost always assembled by the Web server.

It is important to keep this model of the dynamic combination of strands in mind: not only is it what is happening, but also it can make it easier to track down problems (that peculiar font may have been someone's browser choice, not the aberration of the Web page author), and it can make multiperson projects easier to manage.

Elements

HTML documents consist of elements. An element consists of content that is surrounded by starting and ending tags. Together, the three components (start tag, content, and ending tag) are referred to as a single element.

Thus, a paragraph in HTML consists of text such as the following:

```
<P>
This is a paragraph.
</P>
```

Some elements are not allowed to have content—for example, a line break element specifies a line break but contains no content. (What would the content be?) These elements contain no ending tag—again, the line break element is an example of an element with no ending tag. The line break is simply inserted in one place in the HTML document.

Other elements have optional content (the body element is one such). Elements with optional content do have ending tags—how else would a browser know where the end of the optional content is?

Elements can be contained within one another—a paragraph may be placed within a column or table, for example. However, not all elements can be placed within all other elements.

Except within content, capitalization, spacing, and text styles have no meaning in HTML. If you are using a text-based browser (or the HTML edit mode of Home Page), the HTML code is often formatted using color and indentations to make it easier to read. If you are modifying existing HTML code, one of the first things you may want to do is to make the elements clear by lining up starting tags (such as <P>) with ending tags (such as </P>). Having done so, you will see the structure of an HTML page become clear; modifying an existing page (which is what a great deal of HTML authoring is all about) then becomes a matter of focusing on one or two specific elements that need changes, additions, etc.

Tags

Tags delineate the start and (optionally) end of HTML elements. They are embedded in brackets < and >. Capitalization does not matter, but spaces between multicharacter tags should be eliminated (e.g., the break tag —
—should not be written <B R>).

Attributes

HTML elements may have attributes in addition to content. (Some elements that are not allowed to have content may have attributes, and vice versa.) Attributes are such items as margins, fonts, file names, and colors that should be associated with the given element. Attributes are of the form

```
attributename=attribute value
```

Attributes are separated by spaces. Thus, the HTML code

```
<IMG SRC="images/header.gif" ALT="4.0"
    WIDTH=99 HEIGHT=67 BORDER=0 ALIGN=top>
```

consists of:

- An IMG (image) element. The IMG element is defined as having no content and no ending tag.

- An SRC (source) attribute, which specifies the file in which this image is located. (This is not the element's content—content is placed physically within the tag; a reference to a file is an attribute.)

- An ALT (alternate) attribute, which is a text string that browsers can use to display instead of the image if the user has opted not to use graphics.

- WIDTH and HEIGHT attributes, each of which specifies a dimension of the image.

- A BORDER attribute, specifying the width of the border to be placed around the image.

- An ALIGN attribute, indicating how the image is to be aligned with surrounding text.

| HTML Documents and Their Editors | HTML documents are text documents—they contain no binary information. Special characters are coded using numerical character references and character entity references. |

Characters—whether typed directly or specified with references—may occur as part of quoted strings. All characters that are not part of quoted strings are HTML syntax (such as <P>, <BODY>, and the actual text of a Web page). Thus numeric character references and character entity references ultimately are enclosed in quotation marks—but they may adjoin standard characters, as in the character string

```
Copyright © 1999 Philmont Software Mill
```

which is typed as an HTML string thusly:

```
"Copyright &copy; 1999 Philmont Software Mill"
```

Numeric Character References

Characters have numeric equivalents. Although it is easiest to describe the letter A by typing A, many characters—particularly in nonroman alphabets—cannot be described by typing a single key. In such cases, it is necessary to use the numeric equivalent. These numeric equivalents are typically expressed in hexadecimal or decimal notation. In hexadecimal, each roman character consists of two digits, each of which can have the value 0–F (in the sequence 0, 1, 2, 3, 4, 5, 6, 7, 8, 9, A, B, C, D, E,F). In decimal, each roman character consists of one digit with the value 0–255. Unicode and double-byte characters use four hexadecimal digits and corresponding decimal values.

A numeric character reference for the character å is å in hexadecimal and å in decimal. The difference is the presence (or absence) of the X immediately following the &#. Capitalization has no effect on numeric character references. å is the same as å.

Character Entity References

Certain commonly used characters can be described by symbolic references. For example, the copyright symbol ©, which cannot by typed with a single keystroke, can be described using the character entity reference © which is much easier to remember than its numeric character reference (© or ©).

Hexadecimal Values

It is sometimes necessary to type numeric values that cannot be expressed in binary digits; this is often the case in describing a color, which may be specified as three hexadecimal values. To do so, the value is typed in quotation marks, starting with a # and with two hexadecimal digits per value, as in the following example:

```
BGCOLOR="#ABCDEF"
```

The three hexadecimal values specified here are AB, CD, and EF.

Creating and Editing HTML Documents with Graphic Editors

It would seem that since HTML documents consist entirely of text characters, a simple text editor would be the best tool to use to create and edit them. In fact, there are three primary reasons why a graphic editor such as Home Page is preferable:

1. With special characters, documents quickly become very hard to read; a graphical editor can convert the special characters described in the previous section into their values (and their colors).

2. The HTML elements—particularly when embedded within one another—can be hard to locate. The visual elements are easily seen.

3. Most important, the end result of the process is not an HTML document (the input to the user's browser) but the graphical depiction of the HTML document (the output from the user's browser). A "perfect" HTML document may not look the way you want it to.

Creating and Editing HTML Documents with Text-Based Editors

Nevertheless, there are many reasons for using text-based HTML editors. These include familiarity with them, a preference for manipulating the HTML code directly, and the need for people with different software environments to collaborate on a single Web page. Home Page provides both graphical and text editing features.

An HTML Example

The easiest way to get a general understanding of HTML is to look at the code that underlies a simple page. For example, the home page of the FileMaker Pro Shopping Cart example, is shown in Figure 11-1.

There are four major elements in the page:

1. The background image.

2. The Knitting Factory image.

3. The Enter button.

4. The FileMaker Pro logo at the bottom.

Clicking either the Knitting Factory image or the Enter button creates a new record in the Orders.fp3 database. (It is not uncommon for the behavior of buttons such as OK, Enter, and Start to be duplicated by logos and background images: basically, the theory is that a click anywhere on the page should have some default action.)

FIGURE 11-1. Default.Html Page

There are two sources of movement on this page. The File-Maker Pro logo at the bottom is an animated gif—an image that automatically refreshes itself in various ways, simulating movement. In this case, the FileMaker Pro logo rises from the globe. The second source of movement is the Enter button: as the mouse is moved over the button, it changes color. This is done with a JavaScript (which is described in "Enhancing the Interface with Scripts" starting on page 294).

The source code for this page is shown and annotated in this section. The JavaScript section is omitted (but is shown in the chapter on "Scripting for Database Applications" starting on page 281).

Note that this is a walk-through of real HTML code. It is neither the simplest nor the most complicated such code around. The purpose of the walk-through is to give you a sense of what HTML looks like and what it does.

The HTML Source Code

All HTML files consist of the element <HTML> as shown at $\overline{1}$. Note that the file does not *start* with an HTML element, it *is* an HTML element. The starting tag is at $\overline{1}$, and the ending tag is at $\overline{\overline{18}}$. All other elements are contained within the HTML element.

Comments start with <!-- and end with -->. Often, they are generated automatically by your editor (as at $\overline{\overline{2}}$). As with all computer code, more comments are better than fewer. When you look back at the code weeks (or months) from now, you may not remember what you had in mind.

```
1<HTML>
2<!--This file created 2/16/1998 12:37 PM by Home
    Page version 3.0-->
```

Head Element

The Head element starts at $\overline{\overline{3}}$ and ends at $\overline{\overline{6}}$. An HTML head contains information about the document itself. The Title element ($\overline{\overline{4}}$) is used by browsers to title their windows (see Figure 11-1) as well as to identify bookmarks and histories. The next elements in this section are generated by Home Page; you need not worry about them and you do not need to enter them if you are constructing an HTML file by hand.

The final section of the Head element is the definition of the JavaScript used to animate the Enter button. This element is shown at $\overline{\overline{5}}$ and is described in "Enhancing the Interface with Scripts" starting on page 294.

The Head element is technically optional, but it should be contained in all HTML elements, if only to specify the Title element. Only one Head element is allowed inside an HTML element.

3`<HEAD>`
    4`<TITLE>Welcome to the Knitting Factory</TITLE>`
    `<META NAME=GENERATOR CONTENT="Home Page 3.0">`
    `<X-CLARIS-WINDOW TOP=42 BOTTOM=613 LEFT=4 RIGHT=534>`
    `<X-CLARIS-TAGVIEW MODE=minimal>`
    `<!--This is the main entry point for the Knitting`
        `Factory shopping cart solution. This page simply`
        `contains 4 images. When two of the images are`
        `clicked, they'll create a new record and take you to`
        `the search page.`
    `-->`

    5`<SCRIPT LANGUAGE="JavaScript">`
    `<!--Hide from older browsers`
        `…`
        `(See "Enhancing the Interface with Scripts" starting on`
`page 294 for the code that has`
        `been removed here)`
    `//End hiding-->`
    `</SCRIPT>`
6`</HEAD>`

Body Element

After the Head element, HTML elements contain a single Body element, which starts at **7** and ends at **17**. The starting Body tag (**7**) contains two attributes—the background color for the body and the background image for the body. These attributes are commonly used for Body tags to provide a default look to a Web site or page.

The color—as are all colors—is specified as three hexadecimal values, each represented by two hexadecimal digits. Using a graphical editor makes all of this transparent to you: you select a color from a color wheel or other color picker, and the software figures out what the actual numbers are.

The background image is a gif (graphical interchange format), one of the standard file formats for Web images. (The other commonly used format is JPEG.) For the sake of convenience, most Web site designers place all of their images into a single folder—usually called images. Thus, this file is headerbg.gif, located in the folder images, which is assumed to be in the same location as the page itself. Figure 11-2 shows the file and folder layout.

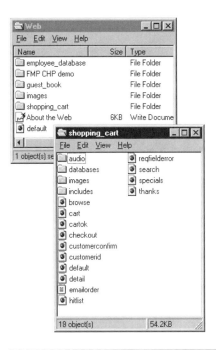

FIGURE 11-2. File/Folder Structure

7<BODY BGCOLOR="#6666CC" BACKGROUND="images/headerbg.gif">

The Center element, which starts at **8** and ends at **16**, contains the balance of the elements—in fact, all of the visible content of the page. It simply specifies that all elements should be centered on the page.

Tables

Starting at **9**, a series of elements are used to define an HTML table; these elements and their tags are italicized throughout the file. The Table element contains two rows (the TR elements), each of which contains a single cell (the TD—table data cell—elements). The first row contains the Knitting Factory logo and the Enter button; the second contains the FileMaker Pro logo at the bottom of the page.

Tables are used in two general ways in HTML:

1. Tables can be used to display tabular data: this is the purpose for which they were designed. New versions of HTML make it possible for browsers to display table data dynamically, rendering the rest of the page while database accesses continue.

2. Because tables provide a way to structure pages into grids of rows and columns, they can be used—as they are here—simply to position elements on a page. Automated HTML generators (like Home Page) rely heavily on tables to let you create good-looking pages.

If you are using a graphical editor like Home Page, the table elements will be created automatically as you draw your page. If you are creating an HTML page manually, you are likely to use tables far less. For now, you can safely skip over the italicized portions of this code and focus on the content.

8 `<CENTER>`

9 `<TABLE BORDER=0 CELLSPACING=0 CELLPADDING=10 WIDTH="100%">`
`<TR>`
`<TD ALIGN=center VALIGN=top BGCOLOR="#FFFFFF">`

10 `<P>`
11 `<A`
  12 `HREF="FMPro?-db=Orders.fp3&-format=search.htm&-new"`
    `onmouseover="return setimg('enter',true)"`
    `onmouseout="return setimg('enter',false)">`
  13 `<IMG SRC="images/kf.gif" ALT="The Knitting Factory"`
    `WIDTH=341 HEIGHT=250 BORDER=0 ALIGN=bottom>`

14 `</A>`

15 `<BR>`

```
<A
    HREF="FMPro?-db=Orders.fp3&-format=search.htm&-new"
        onmouseover="return setimg('enter',true)"
        onmouseout="return setimg('enter',false)">
    <IMG SRC="images/enter1.gif" ALT="Enter"
        WIDTH=75 HEIGHT=41 BORDER=0 ALIGN=bottom
        name=enter>
</A>
</P>

</TD>
</TR>

<TR>
<TD ALIGN=center VALIGN=top>
<P><NOBR>
    <IMG SRC="images/BannerAnim.gif"
        ALT="Powered by FileMaker Pro"
        WIDTH=230 HEIGHT=90 BORDER=0 ALIGN=top>
    <IMG SRC="images/header.gif" ALT="4.0"
        WIDTH=99 HEIGHT=67 BORDER=0 ALIGN=top>
</NOBR>
</P>

</TD>
</TR>
</TABLE>
```

16 `</CENTER>`

17 `</BODY>`

18 `</HTML>`

Paragraphs

HTML documents are divided into paragraphs; these paragraphs correspond in a general sense to paragraphs in any document, but they can include more than just words (and need not contain any words). Paragraphs in an HTML document can contain images and links. In general, all information in an HTML document is contained in one paragraph or another. Even when tables are used to organize information, the contents of each table data cell are one or more paragraphs.

Text that is to be placed in a paragraph is simply typed into the paragraph between the starting tag—<P>—and the ending tag—</P>. Other HTML elements (images, formatting elements, etc.) are placed within the paragraph element as well; the delimiters < and > allow browsers to keep HTML elements separate from text.

Carriage returns are normally stripped out by browsers; when it is necessary to insert a blank line, the break element (<BR>) is inserted as at **15**; this causes the two images in the first paragraph to be displayed one below the other. In other cases, it is necessary not to allow browsers to insert a return; at the end of the file, the no break (<NOBR>) element prevents the "FileMaker" graphic and the "4.0" graphic from being separated.

When it is necessary to use the < and > symbols as text (that is, not as delimiters for HTML tags), use the character entity references < (less than, <) and > (greater than, >) instead of the symbols.

The first paragraph in this case starts at **10**. Although no attributes are specified for this paragraph, it is common to specify formatting attributes at the paragraph level.

Anchors

Anchor elements are delimited by the <A> and </A> tags as shown at **11** and **14**. Anchors are often named (using the name attribute); when an anchor is named, it can be used as part of a URL to go to a specific part of an HTML document. If the anchor that starts at 11 were named—

11 `<A name="shopping-cart-anchor" >`

—then you could open this document and cause the browser to position this anchor on the screen by typing in the following:

`default.htm#shopping-cart-anchor`

The name of this file is default.htm; if you are connecting to it over a network or by using TCP/IP on a single machine, the full address would be something like

```
http://www.yourdomain.com/shopping_cart/default.html#shop-
ping-cart-anchor
```

or

```
http://10.10.10.10/shopping_cart/default.html#shopping-cart-
anchor
```

In addition to being used to locate sections of a document, anchors are used to specify links to other documents or to other anchors within the same document. (A named anchor is typically used as the destination of a link *from* somewhere else; an anchor with a link in it is the source of a link *to* somewhere else.)

Hypertext References (Links)	In order to specify a link to another document or anchor, the HREF attribute is placed inside an anchor, as at **12**. The entire anchor (everything from the <A> to the </A>) is "hot"—that is, clicking on any of the contents of the anchor element causes you to jump to the hypertext reference. An HREF attribute is normally a URL, and it may contain any of the optional features of a URL—an anchor, data following the ? character, etc.

In the case given here, the HREF attributes produce valid URLs that are not the locations of static HTML files but that provide a way to send data (the characters following the ?) to the application server. Ignore for now the onmouseover and onmouseout lines; these are discussed in "Scripts and HTML" starting on page 282.

Note that HREF is an attribute of the anchor element—the end of the <A> tag is the > symbol that appears at the end of **12**.

Images

The entire contents of an anchor are "hot." In this case, the contents of the anchor consist of an image—the graphic of the Knitting Factory, which is located in the file images/kf.gif (the file kf.gif in the images folder). An image is placed in an HTML document with the IMG element as shown at **13**. IMG must contain the name of the file; it may also contain an alternate text representation (for browsers with which graphics are not enabled) as well as specifications about the size of the graphic.

Note that images need not be in local files: it is not uncommon to reference an image that exists on a totally different Web site. This is often the case with corporate logos.

Images commonly used on the Web are of two kinds:

1. JPEG—Joint Photographic Experts Group

2. GIF—Graphics Interchange Format

These formats allow images to be compressed and then expanded so that storage space and transmission time are saved. The formats are accepted by various Web browsers, Web authoring tools, and standard graphics software. As the name suggests, JPEG was designed for photographs and other images of that nature. These are characterized by many colors (or shades of gray) and by a lack of sharp lines (faces, trees, and snapshots of birthday parties come to mind). The JPEG format uses the characteristics of such images as well as information about how people perceive images and colors to eliminate picture data that the brain can easily interpolate.

GIF was designed to handle the sorts of images that you create with computers: text, blocks of color, etc. Its compression algorithms work well with the nonrealistic images for which JPEG is less than optimal.

JPEG is a "lossy" format—each time the JPEG image is saved, it is compressed again. Repeatedly saving a JPEG image results in a loss of quality. If you use JPEG images, be certain to keep the original around.

Home Page keeps track of image types and automatically converts other image types to GIFs.

The Basics

From this simple HTML example, these basic points emerge:

- HTML files consist of a single HTML element.

- The HTML element contains a HEAD element and a BODY element.

- Although the HEAD element is technically optional, it should be present and should contain—at the very least—a TITLE element and a comment describing the purpose of the file.

- Everything displayed on the Web page is entered in the BODY element. All information—text and graphics—is displayed in one or more paragraphs (P elements). Paragraphs are drawn on the Web page from top to bottom.

- A paragraph can contain text, which is typed directly into the HTML file. It can also contain an image, which is referred to by an IMG SRC element that specifies the size and location of the image (normally in a disk file).

- All or part of the contents of a paragraph may be placed in an anchor (A). An anchor may have a name; in that case it may be used as the destination of a link such as http://www.abc.com/apage.html#anchor). It may also contain a link to another Web resource; such links are specified by the anchor's HREF attribute. An anchor may have only one name and only one link but need not have either.

- The placement of paragraphs one below the other on the Web page can be altered by using tables. Tables can have rows and columns of varying sizes. For each table row element (TR), you can specify one or more data cells (TD)—one for each column in that row. Within the table data cell, you may place one or more paragraph elements, thus changing the strict top-to-bottom placement of paragraphs in a nontable format.

There is a lot more to HTML than this, but you can go very far (and understand a lot of existing HTML code) if you master these basics. Here are some further points to remember about HTML:

- HTML elements may have contents (as a paragraph does) and an ending tag (such as /P) in addition to their starting tag (such as P). The starting tag is always required.

- When trying to understand an existing HTML file, remember that spaces and blank lines do not matter. Start by lining up start and ending tags so that the structure of the file is clear to you. (Many text and graphical HTML editors do this automatically; they also often use color to highlight tags.)

Learning More HTML

All browsers let you view the raw HTML source code for a page you are looking at. When you see an effect that you particularly like (or don't like), look at the HTML to see how it has been done.

Summary

This chapter has provided an introduction to HTML—what it is and how it works. The easiest way to learn HTML is to read the HTML code for Web pages that you visit. Remember that most people do not write HTML code from scratch: your mission will usually be to modify or extend existing HTML code. In that case, you need to be able to find your way around the code and to figure out what it is doing.

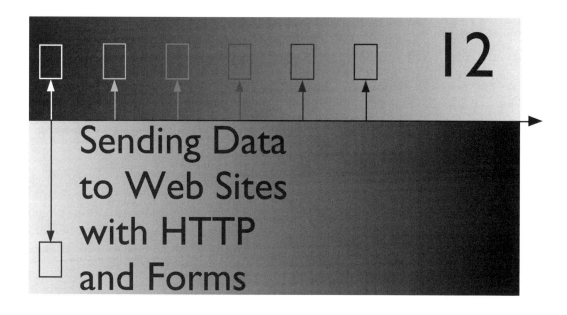

Sending Data
to Web Sites
with HTTP
and Forms

At first glance, this chapter's title may seem backward to you: you get data from Web sites, you don't send data to them. But transmitting data to Web servers (and thence to application servers and databases) is important because it is this data that lets users specify just what they want to see—data on or before a certain date, balances greater than a given amount, or information about a specific subject. Those values—the date, the amount, or the subject—must be sent to the database in order for it to do its work.

First, you will find a discussion of HTTP—the means by which you request resources on the Web. Not only is HTTP the mechanism by which people get to your Web pages, but it also provides for the transmission of data as part of the request.

Following that, you will find a discussion of forms. HTML forms are the very commonly used feature that lets users enter data in a structured manner and send it to a Web server (and thence possibly on to an application server and database). Forms are not just a formatting device—they, too, are an important way to transmit data to Web sites.

Requesting a Resource on the Web

When you type an address into a browser or create a link (technically an HREF attribute of an anchor) on a Web page, you probably think only of the URL you are typing. When the command is executed, a message is sent; that message has two parts—the header and an optional body.

The specification of HTTP states there are actually at least three parts to the message header that is sent. HTTP defines a request-line that contains these three parts:

1. An action that describes what the Web server is supposed to do about the URL.

2. The URL itself.

3. The version of HTTP to which this message conforms. (This allows updates to Web servers to be independent of updates to clients: each knows the most recent version that the other will respond to.)

In addition to the message header (the request-line), the message may contain a message body.

All HTTP requests must receive a response (even if it is an error stating that the address is wrong, the server is busy, etc.). If no response is received, the browser that sent the request gives the user an error message indicating that no response was received. The Web page that you see in your browser is technically the response to the request that you have specified by typing in a URL.

This terminology of request and response is very specific. The words are common English language words, and they are used as people use them in ordinary conversation. Try to get into the habit of using this terminology correctly. If you are sloppy—such as referring to a URL as the address of a Web page—you will confuse yourself and others, particularly when you start dealing with dynamic HTML.

Actions

The most frequently used HTTP action is GET: it requests that the Web server get the resource (usually a Web page) described in the URL. Note the careful phrasing here: it allows the Web server to generate an HTML message that is not a static page. GET is the action that is assumed when you type in a URL or create a link (with HREF).

Another frequently used HTTP action is POST: it is designed specifically to transfer data to the resource named in the URL. That data can be specified using MIME encoding, which means that you can transfer pictures, sounds, etc. to the resource. The POST method is used with forms, which are described in "What Is a Form?" starting on page 272.

Other actions are defined, but these are the two that you deal with in most cases.

URLs

A URL for the Web (HTTP) is specified as having six parts:

1. It starts with the **scheme** followed by a colon and two slashes (http:// for the Web).

2. Next, the **host name** is specified either as four sets of digits separated by periods (such as 192.168.1.3) or as a domain name (such as www.yourdomain.com). If

the host is omitted, it is assumed to be the computer on which the request is being made.

3. Optionally, a colon and a **port number** can be provided. Each scheme has a default port (for HTTP it is 80) that it automatically connects to.

4. A **slash** follows the specification of the host and port. If the local computer is assumed by having a blank host name and if the default port is used, the URL looks like this at this point: `http:///`. For a URL without a port, it looks like this: `http://www.yourdomain.com/`, and for a URL with a port, it looks like this: `http://www.yourdomain.com:80/`.

5. Next, the **path component** is supplied. This is the name of the resource to which the request is directed. Often, it is a Web page with a name that ends in .htm or .html. Thus, the path might be weeklydata.html. If the file is located within a directory on the host computer, that directory and others are specified and separated by slashes as in projectA/webfiles/weeklydata.html.

   In other cases, the path specifies an application to which the request is directed; the application is responsible for replying to the request.

6. If the request contains **data** to be sent to the application server (whether that is Microsoft Internet Information Server, FileMaker Web Companion, Tango Server, or any of the other servers discussed in "Application Servers and Development Tools" starting on page 169) as part of the header, that data (called the searchpart or query) follows the path and is preceded by a question mark. The data format is described in the following section.

| Sending Data as Part of a Request | The simplest HTTP requests simply specify the location of a resource that will provide a response—which is usually a Web page. In order to tell the resource what you want it to do, you must pass additional information as part of the request. |

This is a common need. When you connect to a search engine (such as www.yahoo.com or www.excite.com) you can use it to search for information. If you watch your browser, you will see that when you click on the Search button a URL is constructed that includes your search term. The general syntax for passing information as part of requests is specified as part of HTTP; each search engine uses its own modification of the general syntax.

There are two ways to pass information as part of a request:

1. You can pass the information in the URL as a search-part.

2. You can pass the information in the message body.

Searchparts and Queries

You can include a searchpart in the URL that is part of the request. The searchpart contains text data, each element of which is identified by a descriptive name. The format is

```
descriptorname=textvalue
```

Some elements have no data; their format is

```
descriptorname
```

If more than one element is provided, the elements are separated by ampersands (&). The name of each descriptor is specified by the resource that you are addressing. The data sent in a searchpart must be text data, adhering to Internet standards. The numbers and letters of the alphabet are the most basic text elements; other symbols are represented as described in "Numeric Character References" on page 239.

When you use the GET action (to retrieve a page from a Web location), data is always sent in the searchpart.

"Searchpart" and "query" are interchangeable; "searchpart" is used in the URL specification, and "query" is used in the HTTP specification.

Sending Data in the Message Body

Sending data in the searchpart of the URL has three possible disadvantages:

1. Because it is part of the URL, the data that is being sent may be visible in a browser's location display. (You can verify this by looking at the URL that is generated when you click the Search button in a search engine.) This can pose security issues.

2. Only text data can be sent in a searchpart.

3. Large amounts of data can be unwieldy in a searchpart. Although the searchpart and the URL have been designed to be read by machines, some browsers have difficulty handling long requests, even though they should not.

The POST action is designed to send relatively large amounts of data to a Web resource; the response is often a Web page indicating that the data has been processed. Accordingly, the POST action relies on a message body to pass data. None of the three disadvantages of searchparts exists in a message body:

1. The message body is never shown in a browser's location display.

2. The message body is used for various purposes; browsers and other Web software are used to dealing with multiple-part, multiple-type messages (such as

messages that contain text, sound, video, and custom data types—often all in one message).

3. Message bodies are typically long; unexpected problems with browsers usually do not occur with long messages.

Forms and Tables

The World Wide Web was conceived initially as a way of navigating through information from sites all over the world. It quickly became clear that in addition to being used as a delivery vehicle for information, it could also be used as a simple and easy collection vehicle for data. The form element was devised to make data entry easy.

Both forms and tables are used to structure information. Typically, you use HTML tables to display data that is retrieved, and you use HTML forms to collect data that is being entered. In addition, you can use tables to organize information—whether retrieved or entered—on a single Web page.

A Table Example

For example, Figure 12-1 shows an HTML table that is used to display records retrieved from a database.

The table that is shown here is more complex than some of those shown previously in which a single record is displayed in a single row with one column for each field. The dashed lines that have been superimposed on the screenshot in Figure 12-1 show that for each database record, there are four rows of three cells each:

• The first row contains three cells, each of which contains one field's data.

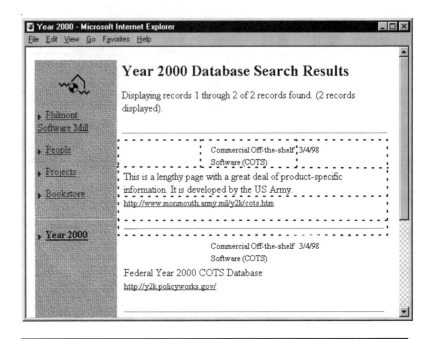

FIGURE 12-1. Table Used to Display Database Data

- The second row contains a single field's data, which spans the three cells.

- The third row contains another field's data which once again spans the three cells. It is an anchor containing a link—an HTML HREF attribute. Note that the database field contains a URL—such as http://www.yourdomain.com. To convert that to a link, you need to generate an anchor with an HREF attribute (for the link) and with text (to identify the link). Thus, the database field is inserted twice into the anchor element—once inside quotation marks as the HREF link and a second time as plain text. You could substitute the second occurrence of the database field for the string "Click here," but that would leave users uncertain of where the link would take them.

- The fourth row contains a carriage return (<BR>) and a horizontal rule (<HR>) spanning the three cells.

HTML for the Table Example

For review, the code is provided here. Note the boldface tags, which delimit a single database record. Everything between them is repeated for each record; thus each retrieved record will generate four table rows. The underlined lines display the data fields for each record that has been retrieved.

Syntax for both Microsoft Access and FileMaker Pro is given. Comparable syntax is used for other databases and development environments—the point is that the structure is the same, and the HTML code is certainly the same in all cases.

```
<P>
<TABLE BORDER=0 WIDTH="100%">
[FMP-RECORD] <!--  Use this for FileMaker Pro -->
<%BeginDetail%> <!-- Use this for Microsoft Access-->
    <!--first row-->
    <TR>
        <TD VALIGN=top WIDTH="31%">
            <P>
            <FONT SIZE="-1">
                [FMP-FIELD: Product] <!-- FileMaker Pro-->
                <%Product%> <!-- Microsoft Access-->
            </FONT>
            </P>
        </TD>

        <TD VALIGN=top WIDTH="31%">
            <P>
            <FONT SIZE="-1">
                [FMP-FIELD: Subject] <!-- FileMaker Pro-->
                <%Subject%> <!-- Microsoft Access-->
            </FONT>
            </P>
        </TD>

        <TD VALIGN=top WIDTH="31%">
            <P>
            <FONT SIZE="-1">
                [FMP-FIELD:Date Entered] <!--FileMaker Pro-->
                <%Date Entered%> <!-- Microsoft Access-->
```

```
                    </FONT>
                    </P>
                </TD>
            </TR>


            <!--second row-->
            <TR>
                <TD COLSPAN=3 WIDTH="93%">
                    <P>
                        [FMP-FIELD:Message] <!--FileMaker Pro-->
                        <%Message%> <!-- Microsoft Access-->
                    </P>
                </TD>
            </TR>
            <!--third row-->
            <TR>
                <TD COLSPAN=3 WIDTH="93%">
                    <P>
                        <A
                            <!-- Microsoft Access-->
                            HREF="<%Reference%>"> <%Reference%>
                            <!--FileMaker Pro-->
                            HREF="[FMP-FIELD: Reference]">
                                [FMP-FIELD: Reference]
                        </A>
                    <P>
                </TD>
            </TR>


            <!--fourth row-->
            <TR>
                <TD COLSPAN=3 WIDTH="93%">
                    <P><BR><HR></P>
                </TD>
            </TR>

[/FMP-RECORD] <!--  Use this for FileMaker Pro -->
<%EndDetail%> <!-- Use this for Microsoft Access -->
</TABLE>
</P>
```

As you can see, a table can be used as a very complex way of displaying formatted data from a database; it need not be evident that it is a table (for example, the table cells in Figure

12-1 have no borders that identify them as being table data cells).

A Form Example

Forms, on the other hand, are usually used for data entry. Figures 12-2 and 12-3 show a data entry form used to enter data to the database shown in Figure 12-1.

By contrast with the table, the form shows a single record at a time. Furthermore, whereas the table suppresses field and record boundaries, the data entry fields in the form are clearly outlined. (This is an option in both designs, but typically forms explicitly show the fields and tables often do not.)

Even more important, the form is designed for user interaction: note the New Record and Clear Form buttons at the bottom of Figure 12-3.

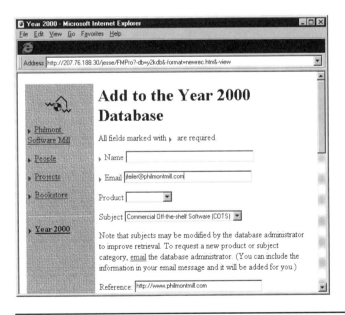

FIGURE 12-2. Form for Data Entry (1)

You can combine tables and forms. In addition to being used to display data with the [FMP-Record] or <%BeginDetail%> tag, tables can be used to position objects on a page. (The data entry screens shown in Figures 12-2 and 12-3 actually show a table—the left-hand navigational panel is a single data cell of the table and the right-hand cell contains the data entry form.)

Frames let you do something similar. However, with frames each section of the screen can come from a different URL. This can be a very effective way of combining database data with static data from two different servers.

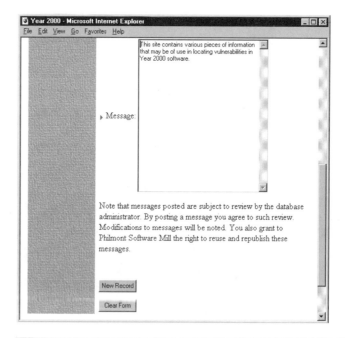

FIGURE 12-3. Form for Data Entry (2)

| Example Code for a Form within a Table | Here is the HTML code for the page shown in Figures 12-2 and 12-3. It is a one-row table that has two cells: the first contains the navigation bar at the left of the window, and the second contains the body of the page. (You will recognize this layout as a very common Web page design, which is why it is given in its totality here.) It is important to note how you can combine the physical structuring of tables with the functionality of forms for data entry. |

| *Page Header* | First, here is the typical header for the page: |

```
<HTML>
<HEAD>
   <TITLE>Year 2000</TITLE>
</HEAD>
<BODY BGCOLOR="#FFFFFF" LINK="#000099"
   ALINK="#3DC7FF" VLINK="#003366">
```

Next, inside a paragraph, a table is created, and its first (and only) row is specified.

```
<P>
<TABLE BORDER=0 CELLSPACING=4 CELLPADDING=4 WIDTH="100%">

   <TR>
```

| *The Navigation Bar* | The first table data cell consists of the graphics and links at the left of Figure 12-2. A background image is set for the table data cell, and the logo is set using an IMG element. |

```
        <TD VALIGN=top BACKGROUND="images/bg.gif" WIDTH=132>
        <CENTER>
           <IMG SRC="images/PSMLogo.gif"
              WIDTH=57 HEIGHT=43 ALIGN=bottom>
        </CENTER>
```

Now, for each of the links in this navigation bar, the same code is repeated. A small image (the blue arrow) is inserted; next, an anchor element is created that links to another page on this site. The anchor element contains the link (the HREF attribute) as well as a meaningful description of what is located there. Thus, in the first example, "Philmont Software Mill" is a link to http://www.philmontmill.com/index.html.

```
<P>
    <IMG SRC="images/bluarrow.gif"
        WIDTH=8 HEIGHT=11 ALIGN=bottom>
    <A HREF=
        "http://www.philmontmill.com/index.html">
            Philmont Software Mill</A>
</P>

<P>
    <IMG SRC="images/bluarrow.gif"
        WIDTH=8 HEIGHT=11 ALIGN=bottom>
    <A HREF=
        "http://www.philmontmill.com/people
            index.html"
        People</A>
</P>
```

Links to Projects and Bookstore use comparable code; they are omitted here. For reference, the code to insert the horizontal rule is shown:

```
<P>
    <HR>
</P>
```

Below the horizontal rule, there is a boldface link. This is typical in Web site construction; it is the area of the site in which this page is located. Note that the text for Year 2000 has part of a bold element (delimited by <B> and </B>).

```
<P>
    <IMG SRC="images/bluarrow.gif"
        WIDTH=8 HEIGHT=11 ALIGN=bottom>
    <A HREF="http://www.philmontmill.com/year2000/
        index.html">
        <B>Year 2000</B>
    </A>
```

```
    </P>
  </TD>
```

The Data Entry
Form

The next table data cell contains the data entry form. The form syntax is provided in more detail later, but you can safely follow this template, adjusting it for your own purposes.

```
<TD VALIGN=top>
  <H1>Add to the Year 2000 Database</H1>
```

A form action specifies how the data will be sent and to what destination. In the case of FileMaker Pro, the action is always FMPro, and the method is always post.

```
<P>
<FORM ACTION="FMPro" METHOD="post">
```

In the case of Microsoft Access, the method is also post, but the destination is an IDC file that contains the query to be executed (in this case, an INSERT). If that query were in newrec.idc, the syntax would be

```
<FORM ACTION="newrec.idc" METHOD="post">
```

The values to be passed to the database server are passed in fields of the form. Some of those fields may be hidden from the user, as is the case with the following three hidden fields that would be used with FileMaker Pro. In Microsoft Access, their information (the name of the database, for example) is contained in the IDC file.

```
<P><INPUT TYPE="hidden" NAME="-DB" VALUE="y2kdb"></P>
<P><INPUT TYPE="hidden" NAME="-LAY" VALUE=""></P>
<P><INPUT TYPE="hidden" NAME="-FORMAT"
    VALUE="newreply.htm"></P>
```

Now comes the data entry form. By comparing the HTML with the screenshots shown in Figures 12-2 and 12-3, you can see how the form data is collected. (See "Controls" on page 273 for more information.)

```
<P>All fields marked with
    <IMG SRC="images/arrow_gold.gif"
```

```
                  WIDTH=7 HEIGHT=11 ALIGN=bottom> are required.</P>

<P><IMG SRC="images/arrow_gold.gif"
     WIDTH=7 HEIGHT=11 ALIGN=bottom>
Name <INPUT TYPE=text NAME=From
     VALUE="" SIZE=45></P>

<P><IMG SRC="images/arrow_gold.gif"
     WIDTH=7 HEIGHT=11 ALIGN=bottom>
Email <INPUT TYPE=text NAME=Email VALUE="" SIZE=45></P>
```

A selection menu (such as the product and subject selections shown in Figure 12-2) is a common part of forms. Microsoft Access and FileMaker Pro provide an easy mechanism for creating such selections where the choices are drawn from database data. For FileMaker Pro, the code is as follows:

```
<P>Product <SELECT NAME=Product>
     [FMP-Option: Product, list=Products]
</SELECT></P>

<P>Subject <SELECT NAME=Subject>
     [FMP-Option: Subject, list=Subjects]
</SELECT></P>
```

For Microsoft Access, the code is remarkably similar:

```
<P>Product <SELECT NAME=Product>
     <%BeginDetail%>
     <OPTION><%Product%>
     <%EndDetail%>
</SELECT></P>

<P>Subject <SELECT NAME=Subject>
     <%BeginDetail%>
     <OPTION><%Subject%>
     <%EndDetail%>
</SELECT></P>
```

The form then continues with standard text. (Note that the anchor within this section contains a link to an e-mail address—it is underlined.)

```
<P>Note that subjects may be modified by the database
    administrator to improve retrieval. To request a
    new product or subject category,
    <A HREF="mailto:info@philmontmill.com">email</A>
    the database administrator. (You can include the
    information in your email message and it will be
    added for you.)</P>

<P>Reference: <INPUT TYPE=text NAME=Reference
    VALUE="" SIZE=45></P>

<P>Where you find the information--a URL, publication,
    testing, etc. Not required, but very helpful.
    (Entries without references may be deleted.)</P>

<P><IMG SRC="images/arrow_gold.gif" WIDTH=7 HEIGHT=11
    ALIGN=bottom>
Message: <TEXTAREA NAME=Message ROWS=20 COLS=50
    WRAP=virtual></TEXTAREA></P>

<P>Note that messages posted are subject to review by
    the database administrator. By posting a message you
    agree to such review. Modifications to messages will
    be noted. You also grant to Philmont Software Mill
    the right to reuse and republish these messages.</P>
```

Forms end with two buttons—a Submit button and a Clear
button. Note that you can name them anything you want (in
this case, the Submit button is named "New Record").

```
<P><INPUT TYPE="submit" NAME="-NEW"
    VALUE="New Record"></P>
<P><INPUT TYPE=reset VALUE="Clear Form"></P>

</FORM></P>
</TD>
</TR>
</TABLE>
</P>
</BODY>
</HTML>
```

And that is the data entry form; it is placed inside a two-cell table that helps to structure the page. Now it is time to look more closely at forms.

What Is a Form?

A form is a container for controls. Controls are normally the data entry elements with which users interact. In addition to being a container for controls, forms have attributes that enable them to interact with programs on a remote computer:

- Forms have a **method**. The method instructs the browser how to transmit the data from the form to the action program. GET and POST are the most commonly used methods; they are discussed in "Actions" on page 257.

- Forms have an **action** associated with them. The action is the name of a program (and the path to get to it); the program is executed when the user submits the form. (See "Actions" on page 257.)

Other characteristics of a form are usually less important to you. They include the following:

- Forms may be named.

- A form's character encoding determines what characters it will accept and how they will be transmitted.

- The content type of a form specifies how data submitted with the POST method is transmitted. (If you are transmitting graphics and other nontext material, you must use the content type attribute.)

Form Tags

The starting tag for a form element must contain the form's method and action. Here are typical starting tags:

```
<FORM METHOD="POST" ACTION="NewRec.idc">
<FORM METHOD="POST" ACTION="FMPro">
```

If you are sending a form from a Web page on a different computer, you must include the address—as in

```
ACTION="http://192.168.1.1/NewRec.idc"
```

Everything after the starting tag until the ending tag (</FORM>) is part of the form. Like most HTML elements, forms may also be named. Naming your forms makes the code more readable and can allow you to manipulate them using controls located outside the form on the same Web page (see "Controlling Forms and URL Requests with Scripts" starting on page 304).

Controls

Controls are the elements of a form with which a user interacts. Most of them are coded in HTML using the INPUT element. The types of controls and their attributes are described in this section.

Types of Controls

Controls are familiar to users of any graphical interface.

- Buttons may be general or the submit and reset buttons that have special meanings within a form. Other buttons may be used to launch scripts.

- Checkboxes allow yes/no choices.

- Radio buttons can be grouped (by giving several of them the same name). Only one of a group of radio buttons can be on at one time.

- Menus provide single and multiple selections from a designated list of options.

- Text controls (such as the Name field in Figure 12-2) allow entry onto a single line.

- Text areas (such as the Message field in Figure 12-3) allow entry into a larger multiline area.

- Special text fields for passwords are defined; typing in them does not display the characters that you type.

- Image controls display an image.

- Hidden controls have no visible representation, but they can contain data that is submitted with the form. The code snippet shown in the previous section uses a number of hidden controls. (They will be explained in "Hidden Controls" on page 275.)

- Object and file select controls are also part of the HTML specification. Consult an HTML reference for more details about them.

Attributes of Controls

Control attributes let you manipulate your form's controls. The attributes that matter most to you are these:

- Type. You must specify a type (such as radio, text, text area, or hidden) for the control so that the user's browser knows how to display it.

- Name. Each control has a name. It is used to identify the control within the form and the control's data within the message that is transmitted to the action program. When you are collecting data within a form that will be sent to a CDML action, the control names are normally the names either of database fields or of requests (such as -db or -lay). (An enhancement to HTML lets you associate an ID attribute with a control and add a LABEL element that places a label on that ID.)

- Value. Each control has a value. You specify an initial value (often blank as in VALUE=""), but normally users can enter new values. (Buttons, which cause actions, have no data values in this sense; the value of a button is the text that is displayed on it.) The data transmission when the user submits the form includes pairs of NAME=VALUE. Thus, your form may combine control names and values to transmit data such as

```
firstname=John
-db=students.fp3
```

Other attributes let you specify the size (width) of the control, the maximum number of characters for a text or password control, whether or not a radio button or checkbox is checked, etc.

Note that controls flow down the page just as all other data elements do. To position them from side to side or in more complex manners, place them within a table. Note also that controls can be commingled with other HTML elements within a form—as the instructions in Figures 12-2 and 12-3 are.

This basic code snippet—

```
<INPUT TYPE=x NAME=y VALUE=z>
```

—will work its way into your fingers very quickly.

Hidden Controls

Hidden controls are used frequently in forms that update databases. A hidden control has the same three attributes that all other controls do—its type ("hidden"), a name, and a value. Just as with other controls, a hidden control is transmitted as part of the data when a form is submitted. Its transmission is exactly the same as that of other controls—

```
controlname=controlvalue
```

This is the way in which data can be transmitted to the database without having been entered by the user. You can create hidden fields and set their values to the values of fields in the current or other databases (using the FMP-Field element); you can also set the values of hidden fields to dates, times, or other items that you construct or calculate when the Web page is displayed.

Hidden controls are a specified type of control: you cannot hide radio buttons, text fields, or menus. A hidden control has no visual representation, and so only its name and value matter. There is a distinction between a hidden control and a control of another type which is placed so that it is not visible.

Submitting a Form

Any of three things can be done with a form:

1. It can be submitted—the content of its controls are sent using the specified method to the action program.

2. It can be reset—all entered values are replaced with the values specified in the VALUE= attribute of each control.

3. It can be ignored—the user can move on to another page or another activity.

The SUBMIT input type (<INPUT TYPE=SUBMIT>) is used for a button that submits the form. The value of this control is used as the name for the button.

Likewise, a RESET input type is used for the button that will reset the form's values. Its value is used for the button name.

In the example given previously in this chapter ("Example Code for a Form within a Table" on page 267) you will notice that no SUBMIT or RESET input types are present. This will be explained in the following chapter ("Scripting for Database Applications" starting on page 281).

Form Design Issues

As soon as a form gets larger than a few fields, design issues come into play. There are many references about the design of graphical user interfaces. Perhaps the most important point to note is that there is no substitute for usability testing: not everyone follows directions, and not everyone behaves the way you do. Furthermore, telephone calls interrupt people while they are working, cats stretch out on computer keyboards, and a host of other events happen that may interfere with filling in your form.

Size of Forms

In general, forms should be as small as possible. The complexity of a large form is daunting, whether it be on the computer or on paper.

Scrolling and Screen Size

When possible, a form should be able to be seen with as little scrolling as possible. Although this is hard to do when you are designing forms for devices ranging from desktop computers to palm-size products, try to keep as much information visible as possible. Often, you can do this by using a table within your form so that the various data entry fields are arrayed across the page as well as down.

Logical Size

Try to keep your form to the smallest part of your Web page. In general, a form that consists of an entire Web page is too big. Forms can contain text, graphics, and other HTML elements, but if they are not to be submitted as data, it is best to keep them out of the form. Lay out your page—with its graphics, links, etc.—and place the form within a small section of it. The examples that ship with FileMaker Pro and Claris Home Page adhere to this practice. It makes the code easy to maintain and read.

One trick for accomplishing this is to create the page without the form. Lay everything out and preview it with something like "here is a form" instead of the actual form. When you are happy with its layout, replace "here is a form" with the <FORM> element.

Managing Large Forms

Sometimes, you simply do need to have a lot of data on a form. One way to do this is to split the form into several separate screens. On the first screen, place the first batch of data fields. Using the GET method, send those fields and their data to the next screen. Place them in hidden fields on that screen, and let users enter the visible fields.

In this way, you can have a reasonable number of entry fields on each screen (perhaps 10), and accumulate the entries from prior screens into hidden fields on each current screen. The final submission will send all data from both hidden and visible fields for processing.

Help and Assistance

Do not forget the need for help and assistance with the forms that you create. You can integrate instructions (both graphical and textual) with the form elements, but this can take up valuable space. One way to solve the problem is to place links on the names of the various fields, linking to definitions of the fields.

Place the links on the field names, not on the fields themselves.

Automating Forms

You can automate many aspects of forms—from computing values for fields, to performing edit checks, and to submitting forms without a Submit button. These are covered in the next chapter, "Scripting for Database Applications" starting on page 281.

Summary

Forms are the easiest way to collect data to be sent to databases. They can combine hidden fields with user-entered data that you generate in any of a number of ways, sending everything to be processed when it is complete.

You can further extend the power of forms by providing scripts that perform error checking, validation, and automatic submission. The next chapter deals with some of those issues.

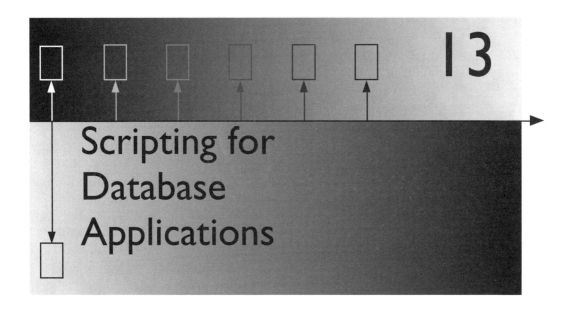

Scripting for Database Applications

Scripts extend HTML, allowing Web pages to do more than just sit there in a browser where they are statically displayed. There is a scripting interface to HTML that is language independent; you can use the standard HTML scripting syntax to integrate scripts written in JavaScript, Visual Basic, Tcl, or other scripting languages (including those that you create).

This chapter provides an overview of HTML scripting in general as well as a guide to some specific uses of JavaScript.

You can use scripts for many purposes. The three most basic ones for which scripts are used in conjunction with database-driven Web sites are:

- *Scripts can be used to manipulate data that users enter into forms; it can be edited, copied to hidden fields, etc.*

- *Scripts can be used to enhance the interface, highlighting objects as the mouse moves over them, changing colors of buttons, etc.*

- *Scripts can be used to control the submission of forms and to generate complex URL requests.*

Examples of each of these three types of scripts are given later in this chapter.

This is not a complete guide to HTML scripting. It is designed to give you a feel for some of the things that you can do with scripts as well as to give you an overview of the logic behind scripts. As with so much of HTML, a lot of your work will consist of modifying existing code written by other people to do what you need it to do. Such work is much easier than starting with an empty piece of paper (or computer screen) and writing a script from scratch.

Scripts and HTML

Scripts are downloaded with Web pages—just as text or graphics are. They are written in a scripting language of your choice and are designed to be executed by your browser, which reads the script and carries out its actions as needed.

Scripts provide a way to enhance significantly the user experience of Web pages; much of the development work that is going on today is devoted to these kinds of enhancements. Specifications (usually in the form of draft specifications) are proliferating; if you are planning to work on the cutting edge of this technology, make certain that you have the latest information. However, the techniques that are described in this chapter are among the most basic; you can use them without looking over your shoulder to see if the specifications have changed since yesterday.

Scripts differ from applets (such as those written in Java); applets are not interpreted in this way by the browser; their code is read and processed before they are attached to Web pages; what is downloaded to the browser is the machine instructions to be executed.

The process of changing a human-readable scripting or programming language into computer code is thereby done once, rather than each time the page is displayed. This means that applets can run faster (there is less work for the browser to do); it also means that they are somewhat more complex than scripts.

The processed code that is downloaded to a browser may be actual executable code, generated by a compiler. In the case of Java, it is an intermediate route: the preliminary compilation produces something called byte code, which is interpreted by a Java Virtual Machine that your browser contacts as needed.

This section describes the basic object model that underlies HTML scripting as well as the syntax for the HTML script element.

The Object Model

Scripts designed to work with HTML are much less complex than programming languages, which are usually designed to work in many different environments with many types of data. Thus, HTML scripts need not start at a primitive level of defining variables for you to use (those pesky things that are often called i or x or temp); instead, they start at the more sophisticated level of HTML objects. They recognize concepts such as documents, windows, forms, and HTML control. Scripting languages do let you create variables like i or x or temp, but you use them in addition to the more sophisticated constructs.

Furthermore, they come complete with simple mechanisms for asking a question of a user ("Are you sure you want to continue?") as well as for posing alerts or warnings ("Beware—this action may cause serious problems."). They also often incorporate fairly sophisticated tools for manipulating the user's browser environment.

Using HTML Objects

Modern scripting languages build on the concepts of object-oriented design. In this type of structure, the data and procedures or functions of old-fashioned languages are linked to objects that are recognizable—documents, windows, forms, buttons, etc.

Scripting languages usually let you refer to HTML objects by using their HTML NAME attribute. (If an ID attribute has also been provided, you can use it, but the NAME attribute takes precedence over the ID when both exist.) This, then, is the reason why it was suggested in the previous chapter that you name forms—when a form is named, a script can then refer to it. (See "What Is a Form?" on page 272.)

Objects at Rest

Each object that you deal with has a number of attributes; you can think of attributes as adjectives that refer to nouns—the objects. Attributes are sometimes called fields or properties. Not surprisingly, the attributes of a named HTML object (such as a form, a button, or an input control) can be accessed by scripting languages. In addition, other attributes may be defined by the scripting language—or by you—and you can access these as well.

One of the most frequently accessed attributes is the VALUE attribute of input controls. As noted in the previous chapter, you frequently write HTML code like this to create an input control and to set its initial value:

```
<INPUT TYPE=TEXT NAME=City VALUE="">
```

Once the user has entered a value to the `City` text field, it is automatically submitted as part of the form that it is on when the user clicks the Submit button. However, before submitting the data, you can use a scripting language to manipulate the entered data in some way. For example, you can test to see that it is not blank, that it contains at least a certain number of characters (useful for checking passwords), that it differs from or matches some other field's value, or any of a host of other operations.

Some attributes and properties can be read and changed; others can only be read.

Objects in Action　　In addition to their attributes and properties (the "adjectives" of objects), objects can participate in actions ("verbs"). Just as in life (and language), they can act and be acted upon.

Functions and Methods　Scripting languages let you define functions (sometimes called procedures or subroutines) that can be executed in different cases. (These are the actions that objects perform.) For example, any of the data manipulation functions described previously could be written as a function. The advantage of doing so is that the function—such as determining that a field is not blank—can then be used for many different fields.

Sometimes, you create such functions, procedures, or subroutines and place them in the <HEAD> element of an HTML page: any script on that page can then use those functions. In other cases, you may want to tie a function closely to an object; in those cases, you can create a function that is a **method** of an object—it is callable only by that input control, form, etc.

Do not worry too much about how to create functions, procedures, subroutines, or methods. In most cases, you take an example of the scripting language that you are working with and modify existing code. Knowing the broadest outlines of the architecture is sufficient to let you cut out the one line of code that obviously counts the number of characters in a field and replace it with another line of code that checks that no blanks appear in the field.

Event Handlers In addition to performing actions themselves, objects can be acted upon—that is, events can occur to them. Events are defined in HTML for many types of actions that can occur to an HTML element. Note that these definitions are not specific to individual scripting languages; these are part of the HTML standard and should be supported regardless of the scripting language that you use.

Because they are general, the basic events defined in HTML 4.0 are provided in Table 13-1. They are the glue that causes scripts to be executed (although scripts can be executed in other circumstances, this is the most common case). Often, they are user events—mouse clicks, for example. For events that apply only to certain HTML elements, those elements are listed in the third column; a blank means that the event applies to most HTML elements.

Event Name	When the Event Occurs	Elements to Which It Applies
onload	On completion of loading a page or all frames in a frameset.	BODY FRAMESET
onunload	On unloading a page or all frames of a frameset.	BODY FRAMESET
onclick	When the mouse is clicked over the element.	
ondblclick	Same, but for a double click.	
onmousedown	The first half of a mouse click event.	
onmouseup	The reverse of onmousedown; the same note applies with regard to mouse click speed.	
onmouseover	As the mouse moves over an element if no clicking occurs.	

TABLE 13-1. HTML Events Designed for the Scripting Interface

Event Name	When the Event Occurs	Elements to Which It Applies
onmouseout	When the mouse moves out of the bounds of an element.	
onmousemove	When the mouse is moved while over an object (not necessarily entering or leaving the object).	
onfocus	When the element is focused—for text, that is available for data entry (the cursor is blinking).	LABEL INPUT SELECT TEXTAREA BUTTON
onblur	When focus is lost to another element (as when tabbing to another field).	LABEL INPUT SELECT TEXTAREA BUTTON
onkeypress	When a key is pressed and released over an element that has focus.	
onkeydown	When the key is depressed (and held) over an element.	
onkeyup	When the key is released over an element.	
onsubmit	When a form is submitted.	FORM
onreset	When a form is reset.	FORM
onselect	When any text is selected (using the mouse or the Select All menu item within a field).	INPUT TEXTAREA
onchange	When data is changed and focus is subsequently lost (compare to onkey... events, which track changes while the focus remains on the control).	INPUT SELECT TEXTAREA

TABLE 13-1. HTML Events Designed for the Scripting Interface (Continued)

Script Elements

You can type script commands into your HTML file in many places. The most convenient way to use scripts is to place them within a script element.

The HTML script element contains a starting tag (<SCRIPT>), content (the script), and an ending tag (</SCRIPT>). The starting tag can take several attributes:

- As in other elements (such as IMG), you can specify the SRC attribute as the location of the script's content. In such a case, the ending script tag immediately follows the starting script tag.

- The type attribute specifies the content type of the script as a MIME type such as text/javascript, text/tcl, or text/vbscript. This is a new feature of HTML; it supplants the language attribute. Either attribute may be used, but type is preferred.

- The defer attribute can be set to true or false indicating whether or not this script will modify the document. If it will modify the document as it executes, the browser must stop its imaging in order to execute the script and incorporate its content into the page. If defer is true, the browser has an indication that no content will be modified or generated and imaging of the page can continue, leaving the execution of the script until after it is complete. This attribute is provided for optimization purposes, and you need not worry about it.

The content of the script is placed between the starting and ending tags (or is incorporated from the location specified by the SRC attribute). This script must adhere to the standards of whatever language is specified in the type or language attribute. A script can contain a single line of code or a number of functions.

Comments within JavaScript are limited to a single line that starts with //. The entire script can be placed within an HTML comment (starting with <!-- and ending with -->), This hides it from browsers that might be tempted to display the script on the page that they are imaging (a common problem with older browsers or those that do not recognize the scripting language that you use).

Manipulating Data with Scripts

There are many reasons to manipulate data with scripts, but most of them fall into these two categories:

1. You can automatically copy data from one field into another as it is entered.

2. You can analyze data as it is entered, possibly modifying it as a result of your analysis.

Copying Data

There are many cases in which you want to copy data automatically. One of the most frequent involves a page like that shown in Figure 13-1.

This shows a page with three forms. The first, at the top, contains fields for first and last names. The second lets you enter billing information and subscribe to a periodical. The third lets you simply browse one issue for free. Both the subscribe and browse forms need the name information; rather than repeat those fields several times on the page, the common information can be placed at the top and automatically filled in as needed.

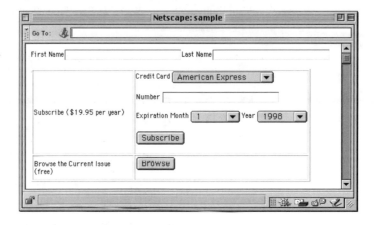

FIGURE 13-1. Subscription Form

How to Do It with Script Commands

This is done by creating hidden fields within the subscribe and browse forms and filling them with scripts from the fields at the top of the page. For each field, you need to specify its type, a name, and an initial value. The code for the First Name field is this:

```
First Name <INPUT TYPE=text NAME=firstnm VALUE="" SIZE=30 >
```

In the subscribe form, the FORM tag and the hidden first name field in the subscribe form are:

```
<FORM name = "subfrm" ACTION="FMPro" METHOD=POST>
<INPUT TYPE=HIDDEN NAME=firstnmsubscribe VALUE="" SIZE=30>
```

After data entry, the value of the firstnm field will be whatever the user has typed in. You can access the value attribute from a script. Armed with the full name of the hidden field, you can add the following code to those two lines (additions are shown in boldface type):

```
First Name
<INPUT TYPE=text NAME=firstnm VALUE="" SIZE=30
    onchange="subfrm.firstnmsubscribe.value=this.value">

<<FORM name = "subfrm" ACTION="FMPro" METHOD=POST>
<INPUT TYPE=HIDDEN NAME=firstnmsubscribe VALUE="" SIZE=30>
```

This example shows the syntax for using FileMaker Pro; for other databases, different actions are used. In the case of Microsoft Access, the ACTION attribute is often set to the name of an IDC file—as in ACTION="subentry.idc".

In order to reference the input element that is inside the subscription form, you need to be able to identify it by its name and the name of the form in which it is located. This is why you have to start to get used to naming forms (which is normally optional). In using this recipe, add the boldface lines of code and modify the underlined words to reflect the names you give your forms and input fields.

You do not have to name the input field from which data will be taken; the event handler can simply refer to it as "this" as in the code here.

How to Do It with a Script Element

The onchange event handler can easily be added to the input field as shown in the previous section. However, when you have a longer script, it is easier to use the script element.

Here is the same code implemented as a script element with a function:

```
<SCRIPT NAME=changer type=text/javascript>
    function changer (theField1, thefield2)
    {
        thefield2.value=theField1.value
    }
</SCRIPT>
```

It is invoked by the onchange event handler just as before; this time, though, the function is called to do the work. This can make the code more readable, and it also means that you can use and reuse the function with many fields, calling changer (name2,name1), changer (firstname, hiddenfirstname), etc., as you see fit.

Here is the changed event handler code:

```
<INPUT TYPE=text NAME=name1 VALUE="" SIZE=30
    onchange=changer(name2,name1)>
<INPUT TYPE=text NAME=name2 VALUE="" SIZE=30>
```

To make the script itself into a comment so that it is not inadvertently displayed by browsers that do not support JavaScript, you can bracket it with comments as shown here:

```
<SCRIPT NAME=changer type=text/javascript>
    <!--
    function changer (theField, thefield2)
    {
        thefield2.value=theField.value
    }
    //-->
</SCRIPT>
```

This is unnecessary if you are certain that people will not be using old browsers; however, adding those two lines is not a problem for most people and it can forestall problems.

Analyzing and Editing Data

Although your database may have excellent data validation routines, it is much more efficient to use a script for validation if you can. In practice, this means relying on your database for edits that require database accesses but relying on scripts for such things as determining that a field on a form contains a certain number of digits of is not blank—which requires no database access.

You can make a distinction between **validity edits** (those that can be done based simply on the characteristics of the data that is entered—such as a minimum number of characters) and **quality edits** (those that involve comparison with data in the database). Note that validity edits may involve data comparisons—they just don't involve comparisons with data in the database. Checking to make certain that the total field on a form is actually the sum of its elements is a validity edit. Checking to see that the total amount purchased by the customer is within a specified credit limit is a quality edit and requires a database access. A further distinction is that validity edits normally cannot be overridden, whereas quality edits are the sorts of edits that can be overridden by a manager or supervisor.

You may need to build on the example given previously if you need to compare the contents of a field with the contents of another field. As long as the fields are named (and their forms are named if they are not in the same form), you can use the value attribute to test them. JavaScript provides a number of operators and functions that let you compare values.

How to Do It

Here is a simple example of a JavaScript edit. A text input field (field1) is compared with another field (called field2). If the value of field2 is greater than the value of field1, field1's value is changed to the value of field2. (In other words, field1 will wind up with the larger number.)

Here is the code. It is implemented as an onchange event handler:

```
<INPUT TYPE=text VALUE="" SIZE=30
    onchange="if (field2.value > this.value)
        this.value=theform.field2.value">
```

Just as in the previous example, you use the name of the other field and the word this for the field that you are working from (the field to which the event handler is attached).

You can go very far with this line of code. You can even do some edits that you might normally think required database accesses. For example, you might download a limit for purchase amounts and store it in a hidden field; you can then let someone know that a proposed purchase is over the limit without making that limit obvious. (Hidden fields can be seen by sophisticated users, so you should not consider this to be a secure solution.)

Of course, if you are going to reject data or change it in any way, it is appropriate to let the user know. You can enhance the previous code by adding an alert:

```
<INPUT TYPE=text NAME=name1 VALUE="" SIZE=30
   onchange="if (field2.value > this.value)
      {
      alert ('The value is automatically being changed');
      this.value=nafield2me2.value
      }">
```

The alert function is built into JavaScript; it poses an alert dialog that the user must dismiss by clicking an OK button. The text that you enter is displayed in that dialog. Note that when an if statement contains multiple statements (in this case the alert and setting of this.value), they must be bracketed as shown here with { and } and separated by a semicolon between them (only between—it is not required after the final statement).

Enhancing the Interface with Scripts

Perhaps the most common use of scripts is to enhance the interface. As you move the mouse over a button, you can change its image or display a paragraph that describes what the button does. Or both.

As you look at various Web pages, you can see what techniques are most useful and attractive to you. Get in the habit of critiquing the pages you look at. And watch out for overuse of these techniques. For example, it is all well and good to display information only when the mouse is moved over an area of the page, but can you be certain that the user will move the mouse over that area?

Decide What to Do

This section uses one of the FileMaker Pro samples (Shopping Cart); it is shown for reference in Figure 13-2. (Although this is an example from FileMaker Pro, it is purely HTML—there are no database references in the code in this section. You can use the same code with any Web server or database.)

There are two sections of the page that are hot—that cause visible changes when the mouse is moved over them. They are outlined with dashed lines in Figure 13-2.

FIGURE 13-2. Shopping Cart Default Page

The visible change is the Enter button at the bottom of the page—it changes from green to red when the mouse is moved either over it or over the Knitting Factory graphic outlined above it. When the mouse is moved out of either outlined area, the Enter button reverts to green. This is an interesting example of the use of interface-enhancing scripts: actions in two separate areas of the page have the same effect on one object (the Enter button).

How to Do It

Once you have decided what you want to do, you need to plan how to implement it. Most interface enhancement scripts start from the onmouseover and onmouseout events—the first is triggered when you move the mouse into a control's area, and the second is triggered when the mouse leaves. Remember, there is no guarantee that a user will move the mouse over the area in question; there is also no guarantee that onmouseout will be triggered (the user can go to another page without moving the mouse from the area).

Onfocus and onblur are another pair of events that are prime candidates for interface-enhancing scripts. You can also use a single event as a trigger for your script, modifying the page when the user moves the mouse over an area and leaving that modification in place. (This can make for an interesting game that will make those idle Web-browsing hours pass quickly.)

Here are the steps to take:

1. Locate the object that will be hot.

2. Identify the object that will be changed.

3. Write the script(s) that will be triggered.

4. Associate the script(s) with the hot object.

Locate the Object That Causes Script Activity

In this case, there are two objects that need to cause script activities. The first one is the Enter button itself. Here is an excerpt of the code from this page:

```
<A HREF="http://www.knittingfactory.com/entry.htm">
<IMG SRC="images/enter1.gif" ALT="Enter"
    WIDTH=75 HEIGHT=41 BORDER=0 ALIGN=bottom name=enter>
</A>
```

This is the code that creates the anchor for the Enter button. Inside the anchor element the HREF attribute is set to a URL request. If you click on the Enter button (the anchor), this link will be requested. The content of the anchor is an image, whose source is images/enter1.gif.

So the first step is done—the object that will be hot is this anchor.

The object that will start the script executing must be an HTML object such as an anchor. If you want an area of the page to be hot that is not an object, you will need to create an object (perhaps one with no content) so that you can make it hot. This situation rarely occurs, however, because it is generally poor interface design to surprise the user—which is what making an invisible object hot does.

Identify the Object That Will Be Changed

The script will need to change the image of the Enter button from a green button to a red one. The only way that a script can do such a thing is for the object that will be changed to be identifiable. Note in the code shown previously that the name attribute has been supplied for the IMG element; images are not normally named, but there is no harm in doing so and it will be necessary to have a name (or ID) in order to carry out the script.

In the code shown previously, the object that will be changed (the image) is named "enter" with the line that is underlined.

Write the Script(s) That Will Be Triggered

For this step, you need to know something about the scripting language you are using. For many people, it is quite sufficient to have a few simple recipes on hand to do what you need to do. Here is the recipe for changing an image. It is one of the most frequently used pieces of JavaScript.

```
active_button=new Image;
active_button.src = 'images/enter2.gif';
document['enter'].src = 'active_button.src';
```

You can use it without understanding how it works. All you need to do is to customize two sections:

1. The underlined text should be the location of the image to which you want to change the object. It can be a complete URL (perhaps even on another site—although that will degrade performance). In this case, it is a file called enter2.gif that is located in the images folder on the site (a common location).

2. The italicized word should be changed to whatever the name of the object to be changed is. That is, it should be the name that you have set in the previous step.

You can use this code snippet over and over. All that you need to do is to attach it to a specific event on the object that will start the process, as detailed in the next step.

If you are curious, the code works in this way. First, a new image object is created; it is placed in a variable location called active_button (it could be called anything). In the second line, the src attribute of that object is set to the file name. In the third line, the object named "enter" on the current document has its src attribute set to the evaluated value of "active_button.src."

Associate the Script(s) with the Hot Object

This is the final step in the process. The code shown previously is enhanced by adding an onmouseover event handler to the anchor. The added code is italicized in the following snippet:

```
<A HREF="http://www.knittingfactory.com/entry.htm"
   onmouseover="
        active_button=new Image;
        active_button.src = 'images/enter2.gif';
        document['enter'].src = eval('active_button.src');"
   >
```

```
<IMG SRC="images/enter1.gif" ALT="Enter"
    WIDTH=75 HEIGHT=41 BORDER=0 ALIGN=bottom name=enter>
</A>
```

To change the image back, you can add an onmouseout handler. The code is identical, but you need to use a different image (the green Enter button in the Shopping Cart example is images/enter1.gif, in case you want to use it).

Example: **Animating a** **Button**	You can repeat the steps shown here whenever you want to change an image. In the Shopping Cart example, the scripts are more sophisticated. Rather than repeat the code each time, several functions are created that make it even easier to manage this sort of interface change.

This is actually the most complex example in this chapter. If it frightens you, feel free to stick with the recipe shown previously. You may type more lines of code, and you may increase the time it takes to test and troubleshoot your pages, but it may be worth it if this section scares you.

As you can imagine, things can get complicated fairly quickly when you are dealing with multiple images for interface elements. To make it simpler, the Shopping Cart example creates a few rules:

- Each image has two versions—the highlighted (or active) one and the normal one. They are in files with identical names except for the digit 1 or 2 at the end. Thus, the green (unactivated) Enter button is in the file enter1.gif, and the red (activated) Enter button is in the file enter2.gif. There also are two Browse buttons— browse1.gif (unactivated) and browse2.gif (activated). This makes keeping track of files easier.

- Rather than repeat the lines of code shown previously, a function is created that does the generic work. It is called setimg, and it takes two arguments—the basic name of the image and true/false indicating whether or not the active version is required. If you call setimg with the parameters enter and true, it will look for a file called enter2.gif; if you call it with the parameters browse and false, it will look for a file that is called browse1.gif. This enables you to write the event handlers as follows:

```
onmouseover="setimg('enter',true)"
onmouseout="setimg('enter',false)"
```

- The script is placed in the HEAD element of the page. Its functions execute only when called; however, it has some statements that execute automatically when the page is loaded. They are italicized in the code that follows. They check to see that an appropriate version of the browser is running (one that can interpret the Java-Script); after that, in the italicized lines, new images are created and their src attributes are set to the appropriate URLs; they are ready for use whenever one of the script's functions is called. And this is the final rule that is established: within the script, the image containing the appropriate image for each button is identified with the _active suffix for the active version.

- A text string is associated with each object (in either the active or inactive form). In the code shown later in this section, it is identified as a localization section— that is because you can often change the language of a script (as from French to German) only by changing these lines of text.

Combining these rules, you get names for the Browse button as shown in Table 13-2.

All that you need to do is to set up your files with the naming convention of …1.gif and …2.gif and to add code as necessary to associate those file names with variables of the form … and …_active (in the two lines of code that are both italicized and boldfaced). Then, to use the script, replace the boldfaced code

Names of files	images/browse1.gif (inactive)
	images/browse2.gif (active)
Names of variables that reference those files	browse (inactive)
	browse_active (active)
Name of variable with descriptive text	browse_txt

TABLE 9-2. Browse Button Naming Conventions

to associate the setimg function with the appropriate event handler and to name the object whose image is to be changed.

You also need to add a variable like enter_txt in the style ..._txt; it should be set to the text that you want associated with the object—as in "Enter the Knitting Factory" in this example (it is shown in bold).

In the following code, the underlined text is used for FileMaker Pro; the italicized text is used for Microsoft Access. You can see that the bulk of the page is not specific to any given database. Remember that Microsoft Access IDC files and ActiveX pages (ASP files) contain the database commands and controls that are passed as parameters in FileMaker Pro URLs.

```html
<HTML>
<HEAD>
    <TITLE>Welcome to the Knitting Factory</TITLE>
    <!--This is the main entry point for the Knitting
        Factory shopping cart solution. This page simply
        contains 4 images. When two of the images are
        clicked, they'll create a new record and take you
        to the search page.

        The JavaScript™ below is used to animate the entry
        button. This script is very similar to the nav.js
        script in the includes folder. Since this page is
        returned directly to the client and not processed
        (STATIC), it was necessary to place it here. In the
        remainder of the solution, the FMP-include tag is
        used to automatically insert the script.-->

    <SCRIPT LANGUAGE="JavaScript">
```

```
<!--Hide from older browsers
    var app;
    ((navigator.appName == "Netscape") &&
        (parseInt(navigator.appVersion) >= 3)) ?
        versionOK=true : versionOK=false;

    // Localize here...
    enter_txt = "Enter the Knitting Factory.";
    // ...end localize

    if (versionOK)
    {
        enter = new Image();
        enter_active = new Image();

        enter.src = "images/enter1.gif";
        enter_active.src = "images/enter2.gif";
    }

    function helptxt ( name )
    {
        self.status = eval(name + "_txt");
        return true;
    }

    function setimg ( name, activate )
    {
        if (versionOK)
        {
        if (activate)
                document[name].src =
                    eval(name + "_active" + ".src");
            else
                document[name].src = eval(name + ".src");
        }
        return helptxt ( name );
    }
    //End hiding-->
    </SCRIPT>
</HEAD>

<BODY BGCOLOR="#6666CC" BACKGROUND="images/headerbg.gif">
<CENTER>
<TABLE BORDER=0 CELLSPACING=0 CELLPADDING=10 WIDTH="100%">
    <TR>
        ... comment removed ≥
        <TD ALIGN=center VALIGN=top BGCOLOR="#FFFFFF">
        <P>
            <A HREF="FMPro?-db=Orders.fp3&
                -format=search.htm&
```

```
                    -new"
                    HREF="OrderEnt.idc?"
                    onmouseover="return setimg('enter',true)"
                    onmouseout="return setimg('enter',false)">
              <IMG SRC="images/kf.gif"
                    ALT="The Knitting Factory"
                    WIDTH=341 HEIGHT=250 BORDER=0
                    ALIGN=bottom>
              </A>
              <BR>

              <A HREF="FMPro?-db=Orders.fp3&
                    -format=search.htm&
                    -new"
                    HREF="OrderEnt.idc?"
                    onmouseover="return setimg('enter',true)"
                    onmouseout="return setimg('enter',false)">
              <IMG SRC="images/enter1.gif"
                    ALT="Enter"
                    WIDTH=75 HEIGHT=41 BORDER=0
                    ALIGN=bottom name=enter>
              </A>
          </P>
          </TD>
      </TR>
      <TR>
          <TD ALIGN=center VALIGN=top>
          <P>
              <NOBR>
              <IMG SRC="images/BannerAnim.gif"
                    ALT="Powered by FileMaker Pro"
                    WIDTH=230 HEIGHT=90 BORDER=0 ALIGN=top>
              <IMG SRC="images/header.gif" ALT="4.0"
                    WIDTH=99 HEIGHT=67 BORDER=0 ALIGN=top>
              </NOBR>
          </P>
          </TD>
      </TR>
</TABLE>
</CENTER>
</BODY>
</HTML>
```

Controlling Forms and URL Requests with Scripts

Figure 13-3 shows a common example of a page on a Web site: it contains a list of items for sale (in this case items that are specials); users can order any of those items by entering a quantity to be ordered and then clicking the Buy It button at the right of the page.

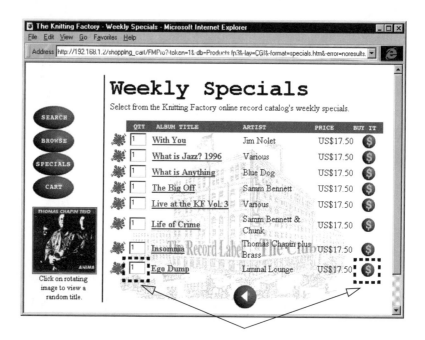

FIGURE 13-3. Weekly Specials

This type of page is normally built dynamically—a database query retrieves all items that are on sale in a given category (such as specials). You need only write the code for a single row of the table and enclose it within your database's record delimiters (<%BeginDetail%> and <%EndDetail%> for Microsoft Access; [FMP-Record] and [/FMP-Record] for File-Maker Pro).

Each row of the table is its own form, and the Buy It button could be a Submit button; however, this example builds on the previous section of the chapter, and instead of a Submit button, a Buy It icon is displayed. The Buy It icon has two different GIFs associated with it—as you move the mouse over it, it changes color. Furthermore, a line of JavaScript code submits the form for that line.

How to Do It

The form for each line consists of hidden fields (product ID and order ID) and the visible field Quantity that are submitted when the form is submitted. Other information on the line (the price, name of the item, etc.) is not submitted as part of the form. Thus, the contents of the form are located at the left of each line (in the area surrounded by the dashed line at the left of Figure 13-3). The icon at the right of each line (surrounded by the dashed line at the right of Figure 13-3) must be able to submit that form—even though it is not within the form as a submit button would be.

Naming the Form

The way to do this is to name each form (that is, the form on each line of the page). Your only difficulty is that you do not know how many lines there will be. By using the <%BeginDetail%> or [FMP-Record] tag (or whatever your database uses), you can create dynamic names that incorporate unique identifiers. Thus, you can create a form that is named prodform102 for product 102, prodform103 for product 103, and so on. Assuming that the product ID is in a field called ID, you can use the following templates.

Naming a Form with FileMaker Pro You do that within the [FMP-Record] element of FileMaker Pro as follows:

```
<FORM METHOD="POST" ACTION="FMPro"
   NAME="prodform[FMP-field:ID]">
```

Naming a Form with Microsoft Access   With Microsoft Access, you do that within the <%BeginDetail%> element as follows:

```
<FORM METHOD="POST" ACTION="yourfile.idc"
    NAME="<%ID%>">
```

Submitting a Form with JavaScript

Later—beyond the bounds of the dynamically created form—you can submit that form. Here is that code, with the line for FileMaker Pro in bold and the corresponding line for Microsoft Access shown in italics.

```
<A HREF=
    "javascript:document.prodform[FMP-field:ID].submit()"
    "javascript:document.prodform<%ID%>.submit()"
    onMouseOver="return setimg('buy.[FMP-field:ID]',true)"
    onMouseOut="return setimg('buy.[FMP-field:ID]',false)">
<IMG SRC="images/buy1.gif"
    NAME="buy.[FMP-field:ID]" ALT="Buy"
    WIDTH="24" HEIGHT="24" BORDER="0">
```

What happens here is that an anchor is created; clicking on it submits the form that is identified by this name. You as the Web page designer do not know what the form's name will be: all you have to do is make certain that the naming of the form and the naming in the submit statement match.

Note the onMouseOver and onMouseOut code: as noted previously, that code will change the GIF as users move the mouse over the icon.

You can use this code safely without knowing any more than this. Just make certain that the underlined words match in the form name and in the submit statement.

Summary

Scripting is built into current versions of HTML. It relies on an object model that lets you access HTML elements and their attributes. Scripting languages like JavaScript implement functionality that may be specific to individual browsers.

This chapter has provided an overview of the sorts of things that you are likely to do with scripts and FileMaker Pro databases. It is only a start, but the examples shown here can be used as templates for a great deal of productive work.

How to Do It: Using Your Database on the Web

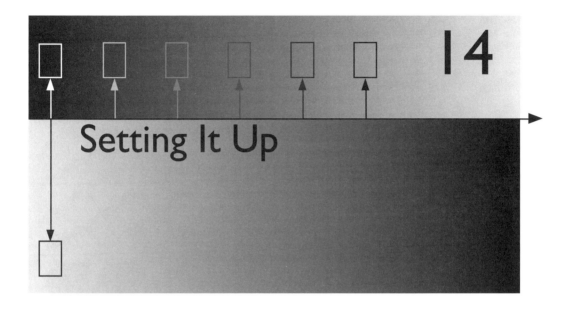

14

Setting It Up

This part of the book may be the most difficult: it deals with issues that you normally need to deal with only when you set up your Web site. Any task that is done infrequently is hard to master. Unfortunately, these are the issues that you need to address at the beginning of your project. Do not be discouraged: once you have set up your database-driven Web site, it is much easier to manage and maintain than a traditional Web site.

One way to make life easier for yourself is to hire a consultant to do the setup work for you; you will also find many Internet service providers who will include these services as part of a bundle. Even if you do not do all the work yourself, you should read the chapters in this *part of the book in order to see what is being done for you and to un-derstand how to answer some of the questions that you will be asked.*

This chapter is about the details of setting up your database-driven Web site. You may be starting from scratch, or you may be starting from an existing Web site, building on a corporate intranet, or inte-grating several sites and databases. Database-driven Web sites are easier to maintain than traditional Web sites, but they are usually more complex and require more attention to their design and setup than other sites. This added complexity is outweighed by the ease of maintenance, but it does mean that you have to pay more attention to your site's design than you might be used to.

The sections of this chapter cover

- *Tools and resources for your database-driven Web site*

- *Organizing the Web site structure*

- *Managing the site: interacting with users, management, content providers, and database administrators*

- *Promoting the site*

- *Managing the site in the public world of a network*

Tools and Resources for Your Database-Driven Web Site

This is a checklist of the tools that you need. Most have been discussed at length in previous sections of the book; you should now have enough information to make your choices. These steps need to be done both sequentially and simulta-neously—almost everything depends on everything else. For-tunately, you do it only once.

| ISP and Web Server | Whether it is a commercial Internet service provider, an in-house intranet, or some combination, you need a basic Web site and the means to get to it. If you are setting up your own Web server, you need to select the software (and hardware) to run the Web site; for most people, the choice of Web server hardware and software does not matter—whatever your ISP offers is what you get. |

For more details, refer to "Choosing Your Internet Service Provider" on page 69.

| *Compatibility* | Remember, however, that your database must be able to interact properly with the Web server hardware and software. If the database is to run on the Web server (rather than on another machine), it must run on the hardware and software involved: Microsoft Access runs only on Windows platforms, FileMaker Pro does not run on Unix platforms, and so forth. |

By the same token, if you rely on application server software to run on your Web server (either as a plug-in or as an extension), make certain that it can run and that it does run—the fact that an ISP can run a product like Tango does not mean that they will do so for one customer.

Often it is for reasons of compatibility that people choose a second ISP (or DSP—database service provider) to support the database pages on their site. Also, it is a good idea to stick to standard software in all cases. The market for Internet software is large, and every component has at least two significant products. It will always be much easier to locate an ISP running basic Internet Web-hosting software than to find one that is running a particular version of a particular server (supporting particular plug-ins).

| *Domain Name* | This is also the time to get your domain name resolved. If you do not have one, obtain one now from the appropriate agency |

(in the United States that is Internic—www.internic.net). If you do not use a domain name, you leave yourself open to having to reprint stationery and business cards as well as to change Web pages whenever your location changes. This may be due to your changing ISPs—or even to the ISP changing part of its configuration. Your domain name is yours and you can rely on it staying unchanged.

Although the registration process is simple, allow at least a week for it to be completed. The Internet tables need to be updated, and your ISP needs to install your domain appropriately.

Application Server

Your application server—the interface between the Web server and your database—can be part of the Web server (as is the case with Microsoft Internet Information Server or FileMaker Web Companion), a plug-in to that server (as can be the case with Tango), or a separate application that is called by the Web server as needed (as with a Perl script or other installations of Tango).

For more details, refer to "Application Servers and Development Tools" starting on on page 169.

The application server needs to be compatible with everything: your choice here may limit your choices with regard to ISP or database—in some cases to one option. Because this choice can be so limiting, make certain that you understand your options. If you are selecting a package that includes a database and application server, understand that that combination may be yours forever: you may be able to change your database only if you change your application server (and vice versa).

In practical terms, the application server is often the first choice that you make.

Database

Your database must run on the hardware available and must interact correctly with your application server (which is why so many application server/database combinations are available). Most databases today are based on SQL, and for that reason your database design will probably be transportable to another database (together with all of your data); however, your scripts, transactions, and processes defined in your application server may not be transportable.

In fact, this can be a blessing. If you find that you have made the wrong choice of application server (too complicated, not well supported, or not reliable enough), you can pick another one and move your data—if necessary—to another database. Rewriting your application server scripts, processes, and transactions is much less of a problem than redesigning a database.

Your database may not be your choice: in a large organization, there may be an enterprise-wide database (or database standards) to which you must adhere. In all other cases, however, it is a good idea to keep up with at least one database other than the one you use. You do not have to duplicate your work—or even do any work in the other database, but you should spend a little time thinking about how you would use another database to accomplish your goals. As noted previously, databases today are remarkably similar (despite a certain amount of puffery in their promotional materials). If you find something that you are doing that really is possible only with one database, make a note of it, and remember that you are sowing the seeds of nonportable solutions.

For more details, refer to "Database Software" on page 93.

Web Authoring Tools

With your ISP, Web server, application server, and database in place, you can start to actually develop your Web site. Again, you have a variety of choices, and prudence suggests that you try to avoid tying yourself to a single product that may in turn tie you to a specific database, Web server, or application server—or even to particular versions of those products.

In addition to those products, remember that you are normally designing Web pages to be used by people who use different browsers and different versions of those browsers. Even within a private intranet, it is rarely the case that every user uses the same version of the same browser.

When it comes to authoring tools, the situation is the reverse of that with application servers and databases: you do not have to make a choice. Remember that the benefits of the Web derive in large part from reliance on the international HTML standard. Whether you create HTML with a text-based editor or with a product such as Microsoft Front Page, Home Page, or Page Mill, you are creating the same material. You will increase your options if you do not tie yourself to a single product. (Furthermore, you may decrease your costs if you need to hire temporary or full-time HTML authors and you can let them use whatever authoring tools they choose.)

If you do make deliberate choices that limit your other options, make certain to document them for future reference.

Obviously, these recommendations fly in the face of companies that bundle products—their own or those of others. You should simply be aware of your choices and the consequences of your decisions. There may be an enormous advantage in buying a single-vendor turnkey solution that locks you into proprietary products for ever and ever: that advantage may be expressed in terms of cost, training, maintainability, or particular functionalities.

FTP

Your database, Web pages, scripts, and other files need to get onto your Web and application servers: the tool that you use for this is FTP (the Internet file transfer protocol). FTP is one of the oldest protocols, and it is a very simple and stable one. FTP consists of two basic connections: a control connection and a data transfer connection. There are programs that implement FTP by itself (such as Archie and Anarchie); in addition, Web authoring tools and Web site management tools often include FTP functionality so that you can manage a site.

Be careful of such integrated tools: they often assume that you are working with a simple site located on a single Web server—and that often is not the case with database-driven Web sites. Some of your site's files may need to be uploaded to different directories or different servers, and the complexity of that structure may best be handled by an FTP program that lets you manipulate files and directories explicitly.

Because FTP is such an ancient and simple protocol, it does not change very often: you do not have to worry about updating your FTP tool or about its compatibility with your server: just about everything is compatible with everything else. Furthermore, since you use the tool relatively infrequently (except in a very aggressively managed site), choose the tool that you are most comfortable with—one whose operation is most intuitive. You may well forget special tricks between maintenance sessions. Your FTP tool may be bundled as part of your HTML page creation software; if it is, you may not be particularly aware of its existence. Note also that changes to your

Web pages can frequently be made without reuploading the pages: that is one of the benefits of creating Web pages from database data.

HTML files that are uploaded to your site are normally given read-only access automatically by your FTP software (there are options and preferences for this choice, but you may never have noticed them). Some of the files in your database-driven Web site may need to have execute permission set for them. If you experience strange problems involving files that appear to be missing but that you are certain are on your Web site, check to see if their permission is set correctly. If you are not dealing with critically secure files, you may just want to change the file's permission to execute temporarily just to see if it solves the problem.

E-Mail

E-mail software is not actually part of your Web site, but you need a good e-mail program to manage your site. You may generate e-mail messages automatically when things happen (this involves the mail server at your ISP, not an e-mail program on your computer). In order to deal with the e-mail that you receive from your site, you need a program with which you are comfortable; it should also be able to filter messages based on subject and address fields. That way, messages to info@yourdomain.com can wind up in a different folder on your personal computer than messages sent to you@yourdomain.com—even though both are delivered to your e-mail account (which might be something like t12345@isp.net).

Some older e-mail software does not handle multiple mail accounts easily. Make certain that yours does, because you will probably be sending and receiving e-mail from multiple accounts.

Organizing the Web Site Structure

There are two structures to your database-driven Web site: the structure that is apparent to users as they move from one area to another and the structure that you use to implement it. You need to know what is where and how to keep track of everything: a database-driven Web site is almost always more complex than a traditional Web site.

This section provides tips with regard to these important aspects of your Web site:

- The site structure that your users see

- The site structure that you manage

- File naming tips

- Version control

The Site Structure That Your Users See	Your site might have areas (subsites) for different parts of your organization: customer service, product information, employment opportunities, and general information. That is the organization that your users see.

Users don't see the actual file locations (unless they look closely). They simply click on links—or go to URLs that they have been given. On any site—and particularly a database-driven Web site—you need to make your site easily understood.

These are the critical issues:

- You need to consider how people view and navigate your site as a whole.

- You must realize that sections of the site will be virtual—that they may exist on a variety of computers and in a number of locations.

- Not all pages on the site will exist at all times.

- Pages on the site may well contain different content at different times (after all, one of the reasons for creating a database-driven Web site is so that you can automate the process of updating the site).

What Does the Site Look Like?

Your site is very special to you—you know it and understand it, and you probably know your way around it better than anyone else in the world. Although it may shock you to think about it, some people who use your site will care only about a small section of it—perhaps only a single page. People need to be able to maneuver through your site to the information that they want without undue difficulty.

It is very hard to redesign an entire site after it has been put up—you may need to make changes on every single page. Before you set your first page in HTML (a less mutable medium than you might think), consider what your site should look like. There are three structures in common use (and many combinations of them are used, too):

1. Unified sites, where each page has a guide to the entire site

2. Distributed sites, where each page follows certain design standards but where the navigation is facilitated within each subsite rather than across the site as a whole

3. Fragmented sites, where each page or subsite obeys its own rules

Designing a Unified Site   A unified site has its entire structure visible on every page: from every page you can go to every section or subsite of the main site. Figure 14-1 shows the home page of such a site.

The implementation of this particular site relies on frames: there are actually two separate HTML pages shown here— one is the page with the navigation buttons at the left (with its own scrollbar) and the other is in the center and right of the screen (it, too, has a scrollbar). (This type of site can also be implemented without using frames: in such a case, the navigation buttons on the left are repeated on each of the site's pages.)

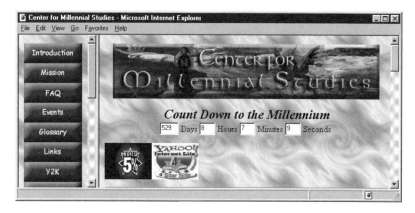

FIGURE 14-1. Center for Millennial Studies Home Page

If you click on the Events button, you go to the page shown in Figure 14-2. That page is also actually two HTML pages—the frame at the left contains the same HTML page as in Figure 14-1; the frame in the center contains new content for this page. (Again, although this implementation uses frames, the design can be carried out without using frames.)

Remember that the HTML pages that are combined in frames can be located on different servers: one can be a database server and the other can be a standard Web server. If you design the two pages with the same background and graphics, few people will notice that the page is assembled from two separate locations.

FIGURE 14-2. Events Page at the Center for Millennial Studies

At first glance, a unified site might appear to be the ne plus ultra in site design—until you start to think about the mechanics of designing, implementing, and using it. That unchanging set of buttons at the left of each page takes up precious space, and for someone who is interested only in one area (or even one page of the site) they are a distraction. Furthermore, their space could be used for navigation within a subsite, and that is not possible.

A unified design works best when the number of navigation buttons (subsites) is relatively small—under 10, at most—and when the subsites are not complex. If the Events of Y2K subsites in this example were to need their own set of navigation buttons, you would quickly have a page with more navigation tools than content. (The page shown in Figure 14-2 is a good example of the type of subsite that works with this design: the subsite page has a number of links to its individual pages, and they have no further links within the site.)

Another difficulty of using a unified site is that the navigation buttons need to appear on all pages. If you use frames, you actually use the same navigation page in all cases, so you do not have to worry about that. If you do not use frames, you have to repeat the navigation buttons on each site page—and if you rename the Events button to Goings-On, that can entail renaming navigation tools on many, many pages.

Designing a Distributed Site   A distributed site keeps certain design and navigation elements constant across all pages, but it takes liberties with them—the most common being to use the navigation tools to apply to each subsite rather than to the site as a whole. In Figure 14-3, you see another home page, that of the Mid-Hudson Library System: it uses this technique.

This site does not use frames, but it is similar to the page shown in Figure 14-1: the sections of the site are shown in the navigation bar at the left. (This page uses tables, rather than frames.)

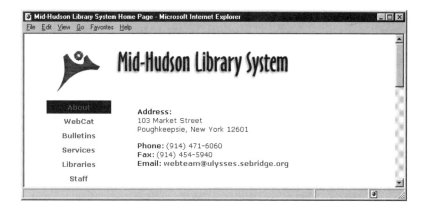

FIGURE 14-3. Mid-Hudson Library System Home Page

If you click on the WebCat link, you can go to the page shown in Figure 14-4, which lets you choose from a variety of catalog searching tools. Note that this page uses the same logical layout as the home page of Figure 14-3, but its navigation bar reflects options for this section of the main site rather than for the site as a whole.

A site such as this that allows each of its subsites to set its own design and navigation rules can be considered a distributed rather than a unified site.

Distributed sites avoid many of the problems with unified sites: changes to the layout of the site affect navigation tools only within the affected subsite, and there is more space on each page for customized navigation tools. In designing such a site, it should be clear what design and navigation elements are required to be used on all pages, which elements are required on all subsite main pages, and what (if any) design navigation elements may not be used (for example, a site as a whole may have a rule against using frames, or a certain palette of colors may be enforced).

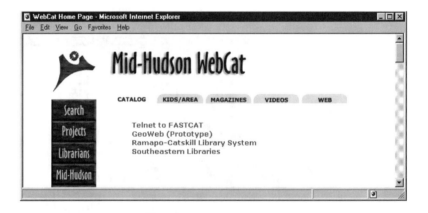

FIGURE 14-4. Subsite Main Page for Mid-Hudson Library System

If the pages inside a site are totally unrelated graphically to the main site, the site is more fragmented than distributed.

Using Fragmented Sites   The rules for subsites can be very loose: they can copy the general style and navigation rules (as the page in Figure 14-4 does from the page in Figure 14-3), or the subsite pages can be totally unrelated to the main site—as shown in Figure 14-5, the page that appears if you click the GeoWeb link in Figure 14-4.

You would not know that this page is part of the same site, and it is not surprising to learn that it is located on a different computer and that it uses totally different software from that used in Figures 14-3 and 14-4. It is the search page for a library catalog that uses a database (Informix) to store its data. It is integrated with the previous pages because you arrive at it through their links, but it looks totally different.

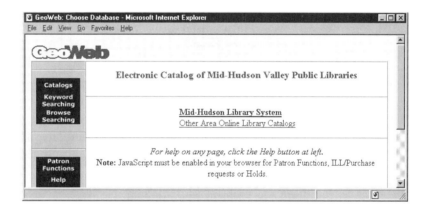

FIGURE 14-5. GeoWeb Search Page

Making Your Choice   Many people think that a unified site structure is the most elegant and efficient until they consider these points:

- It may be impossible to decide on what the overall site structure—which appears on every page—should be. Whether this is because a multinational enterprise has trouble reaching consensus or because you keep changing your mind about how to present your personal Web site, the problem is essentially the same.

- The unified structure is actually quite un-Web-like. The essence of the Web is that people can jump around from place to place, clicking on links or entering URLs. Most people do not stay within a single site. (Exceptions to this are corporate intranet sites that are designed to allow no access to the outside or to make a very clear distinction between inside—the unified corporate site—and the Web in general.)

- Most important for database-driven Web sites, you may not be able to modify pages that are generated dynamically to match a predetermined template. Often the use of frames can solve this problem, but in many cases (such as Figure 14-5), a prepackaged design comes along with a commercial database.

What It Means to You In practical terms, you should think about what options you have. In the realm of issues related to your organization, your experience should help you decide whether a centralized and unified site is feasible. On the technical side, look for the pages that have the greatest constraints and work from there.

If you are using an application server (either integrated with a database like Microsoft Access or FileMaker Pro or a separate product), it may not allow you to customize the dynamically created Web pages as much as you would like. (In practical terms, it may actually allow someone who knows more than you do to customize those pages, but you may not care to spend your time doing more than using the default pages.)

It is much better to plan for a site with some design constraints than to get into the middle of your project and discover that one crucial page doesn't fit into the pattern. Although individual Web pages are very easy to create and modify, rearranging and redesigning a Web site are about as easy as remodeling an office with a number of very large and heavy pieces of furniture.

Virtual Subsites

Sections of your site (as well as the site itself) may be virtual in the sense that the single site lies across many different computers. Its structure from your point of view is very different from the structure that is visible to users.

Use Graphics to Identify Virtual Sites   What brings coherence to the site from a user's point of view are the graphics and navigation tools: they should make it clear where (in the virtual site) the user is.

Use Links, Not URLS   Avoid exposing URLs: it is very easy for people get confused as to whether your catalog is at sales.yourdomain.com or products.yourdomain.com. In most cases, it is easier to change the URL behind a link icon (the HREF attribute in the anchor element) than to retype a URL— and get people to notice it.

Your Physical Site Layout Is Your Business   Resist the temptation to explain to visitors how your site is laid out physically. In the first place, this can pose security problems; but in the second, it is just one more piece of information on your Web site that needs to be changed if you do normal maintenance and rearrangement. On the other hand, do make it very clear what the logical (virtual) arrangement of the site is.

Pages May Not Exist

The issue of virtual subsites arises in particular with database-driven Web sites because they so often involve more than one Web server. Adding to the complexity is the fact that many of the pages on a database-driven Web site may be created dynamically: that means that they do not exist at all times.

A user cannot bookmark a page that represents the results of a database search in many cases. If it is the result of a POST operation for a form, the URL does not contain all the needed information to regenerate the page. If it is the result of a GET operation (with the search parameters included in the URL), the page can be regenerated, but it need not be the same.

You need to choose whether or not to emphasize this to people who view your pages. You can place a message saying "Do Not Bookmark This Page" on the page—but then you may wind up having to explain so much about why users should not bookmark the page (including how your site is constructed) that it may not be worth it. Consider posting a prominent notice on the appropriate page saying, "Bookmark This Page to Return," which requires no additional explanation and will (presumably) encourage users to bookmark a page that always exists rather than one that is transient. You can also consider using cookies (see "Cookies" on page 374) to store user choices automatically.

Pages May Be Different at Different Times

Because pages may differ from time to time, it is hard to make reference to them. You need to remember which of your pages have dynamic data on them and the ways in which they may appear. For example, results pages may be a single page or they may be a set of dynamically created pages, each of which contains ten items retrieved from the database.

In an enterprise environment, you may have to make this very clear to people who are creating documentation or manuals of procedures for using your Web sites. They must very clearly indicate which illustrations are dynamic and which are not—otherwise, people will wonder why the results they get are different from those in their manual.

Managing Complexity

The fact that database-driven Web sites are often more complex than other Web sites should not discourage you. You need to spend a little more time designing the site and deciding what it will look like to users; however, you save a great deal of time by not having to create so many Web pages (the database creates them for you).

The Site Structure That You Manage

Beneath the logical and well-organized site that the user sees, you may need to manage a site that is organized according to a very different logic: pages requiring the services of your database or application server may be on one (or more) servers—regardless of the section of the site that they are in—while static HTML pages may be on different servers. As noted previously, each of these servers may be located at a different physical location; one or more of them may be under the control of your organization, and one or more of them may be managed by an ISP or DSP.

As if that were not complex enough, you need to establish a way to develop, test, and use your static and dynamic HTML pages. In traditional Web sites, you may establish different environments—each is a complete copy of your Web site, and each represents a different version of the site. Environments vary, but these are typical ones:

Production/Server Ultimately, your files must be placed on a Web server where people can access them. You typically do not have control over the directory in which these files are placed, but you do have control over the subdirectories.

These files are the ones that people access. No files other than your finished files should be in this directory. You may think that a file called private.htm will be invisible to everyone if you do not have a link to it, but it is very easy to list the files in a directory on a Web server.

All of these files should be backed up as part of the Web server's routine maintenance. Unless you are the administrator, you should not be responsible for backing up the files that you have placed on the server.

Production/Mirror This is an identical copy of your production/server environment. You may set up your Web server to distribute user requests among the production/server and production/mirror environments. Frequently, a number of production/mirror environments are set up—often at various locations. It is usually cheaper to have a number of mirror servers set up than to have one massive server that can fulfill all of your users' needs. In addition, it is more reliable to have a number of re-dundant systems than to have one critical system. Of course, as with all aspects of complex Web sites, mirroring adds to complexity at the same time that it reduces operational costs.

Production/
Backup

If it is at all possible, you should have a complete copy of the files and folders on your Web site on a single computer that is not the Web server. This is your production/backup site— the site that you can use for final testing.

This site is on your computer and is under your control. You should be responsible for backing it up whenever changes are made; you should also be responsible for moving files from it to the Web server.

Do not allow your production/backup site to differ from the production/server site. Sometimes a few files accumulate on one site that are not duplicated on the other one. Deal with these either by deleting them or by duplicating them to the site from which they are missing. Keep these two sites identical.

When a file needs to be modified or added to your site, you move that file into the production/backup environment. You should run through your test procedures there; when you are satisfied, move the file onto your Web server.

Note that you *move* files into your production/backup environment: you do not create them or make changes to them there.

If you have multiple servers, your production/backup environment will also have multiple servers.

Test Environment

A test environment lets you experiment with Web pages and your databases. It differs from the production/backup environment in that it may not have your entire site on it but only the files on which you are working.

Depending on your security needs and the nature of your site, you may or may not allow modifications to files directly in the test environment. You certainly should never allow such modifications directly in either the production/backup or production/server environment, and you always allow that behavior in your development environments.

Your test environment, may need to have multiple servers if your production environment has multiple servers. If it does not, you will wind up with different file naming conventions in the two environments; things will work in one case but not in the other. (Typically they will work in test and fail in production—see standard references on Luck and Fate for further information.)

Development Environments

A development environment is just that—an area where you and your colleagues can work on databases and Web pages. All bets are off in these environments: you can rename files, you can move them, and you can change the structure of the site as your ideas evolve. This is the only way to be productive in developing a Web site.

Because you need this kind of freedom, you will need to establish a development environment where this can happen: you cannot do these things in the production or test environment. If you make exceptions (even for yourself), before you know it you will have different file structures in each environment and you will not know what files belong where.

Archives

Another common environment that you may have consists of archives. You should have regular backups of all of the files on your computer, but you may want to make special backups (perhaps on removable media) of your production/mirror environment every time you change it.

Why It Matters

If you have not worked in a controlled environment before, this may seem like a lot of overhead to you. In fact, it is the standard way to control large systems involving multiple files. Before long it will become second nature to you.

If you cut corners, you will soon find yourself with incompatible versions of files all over the place; even worse, you will not know what is the correct combination of files to make your Web site function. Unfortunately, as with disk backups, it usually takes an accident to convince people of the need for such preventive actions. Remember that your Web site—even if on an intranet—is a very public area. Do you really want your boss to ask you why the site is all messed up?

It is rare that you can establish a full panoply of environments such as these when you are dealing with database-driven Web sites: the number of servers involved in each of the major environments is large, and items such as the cost of additional licenses for test versions of databases can quickly add up. Figure out what you need, what you can afford, and what you can maintain.

This last point is very important: a series of environments that is so complex that only you (or someone else) can manage them will fail: problems always occur during vacations, holidays, and when someone is sick. The least technically adept member of your team must be able to understand and manage the various environments.

File Naming Tips

It should come as no great surprise that Internet service providers and Web site management tools make it very easy to create a site quickly. The day-to-day maintenance of that site for years to come is a lower priority. The tips in this section make it easier for you to manage the site in perpetuity (which, on the Web, is likely to be a few weeks). Since your database-driven Web site is likely to be more complex than a simple site, these tips are all the more important.

Do Not Rename Files

The cardinal rule is never to rename a file. Once you have given it a name, that is its name forever and ever. Adhering to this rule will prevent the broken links that are generated when you rename a file and leave HTML pages pointing to the old name.

Renaming a file includes moving it to a new folder or directory: that changes its name for some purposes. Thus, this rule means that you must put the file wherever it is going to be with the name it is going to carry—forever.

File Structures for Easy Maintenance

Managing a Web site quickly becomes a difficult task as files are modified, added, and removed. Managing a Web site that also involves databases is even more complex.

On your desktop, you can pretty much put files anywhere you want and call them anything you want. To a large extent that is true on the Web, but in practical terms you will find substantial limits on the freedom you may be used to.

Naming conventions and filing strategies differ from computer to computer—as they do from person to person and from organization to organization. Using a very standard structure will often make it easier for other people to access your files (either for maintenance or with Internet browsers).

"Folder" and "directory" are used interchangeably. In general, "directory" is the name that is used in character-based environments, and "folder" is the name that is used in graphical user interfaces.

Eight Dot Three

The most restrictive naming convention is that used in DOS (and later in the first versions of Windows)—an eight-character filename followed by a three-character suffix that identifies the file. Examples are schedule.doc, program.exe, and autoexec.bat.

Some operating systems (Mac OS, for instance) incorporate the information from the suffix in the file itself; thus, the file-name is not used to identify the kind of file it is. Other operating systems (Windows 95, for instance) use the suffix to help identify the file type and determine the kind of icon to represent it with, but they normally do not display the suffix. Other operating systems (Unix, for example) allow multiple suffixes that can be interpreted in various ways.

Of all of these, the eight-dot-three convention is the most restrictive and therefore will work on most platforms. Although you need only a naming convention that will work on your Web server, adhering to this convention will ultimately make it easier to support your files.

The only exception to this is Web servers—often those running Unix—that allow four-character suffixes and require .html rather than .htm as the suffix for HTML files.

Capitalization

Some systems (like Unix) distinguish between upper- and lowercase characters: the file schedule.doc is not the same as Schedule.doc. Others (like Windows and Mac OS) do not make this distinction. For this reason, it is best not to rely on capitalization to distinguish between files.

Whatever conventions you use, remember that capitalization should be used only to provide extra information to people and not as a distinguishing characteristic of files.

Keep Track of Files and Folders

Because you are not going to be moving or renaming folders, it makes sense to keep track of what you have. Files and folders have been known to disappear from Web servers: you need to be able to restore what should be there.

The easiest way to keep track of your Web site is to keep an updated list of each file, together with its contents, its update date, and the folder in which it belongs. You can create a small database with this information and publish it on your Web site (or on a section of your site that is available only to your project team).

Note the distinction between a database listing the files that you think should be on your Web site and the directory listing of your Web site, which is a listing of what is actually there. If you have a housekeeping accident and accidentally delete files or move them to the wrong directory, the database will help you reconstruct what should be where.

Establishing Directories

The principle of not renaming files extends to directories. As a consequence, it will not do to name a directory ClientTst and another one ClientPrd (for test and production environments). Create your directories at a higher level—such as Test and Production—and then place all of the files and folders for your Web site in each folder. That way, nothing will ever have to be renamed. Within the Test, Production, and other folders, you may have duplicate files and duplicated directory structures, but since they are in separate environments, nothing should be confused.

Web servers are very good at accessing other files within the same directory as the file that they are currently processing. Most people get into trouble when they try to mix files from other directories.

If you think of each site and area of your site as its own site and place it within its own directory, all will be well. Within each directory, place a default file—called default.htm, index.html, or home.htm according to your Web server's standards.

Special-Purpose Folders

Within your Web site, you can have any number of subfolders. As noted previously, you can use such subfolders (or subdirectories) for self-contained portions of your site—subsites, in fact. Within each site (or subsite), there are often special folders.

Images   This folder typically contains all of the graphics used in your site. If you use other types of files such as sound files or video, you may place them in the Images folder or in separate folders named Sound and Video. Try to avoid having a folder with one file in it. If you have one video clip and 14 images, stick the video clip in the Images folder even though technically it is not an image.

Databases   You may also create a Databases folder. This is a common solution for databases such as Microsoft Access and FileMaker Pro; for databases such as Oracle, DB2, Informix, or Microsoft SQL Server, you may not have a choice of where to place the database (your ISP or DSP will tell you where it is).

Special Files   Your application servers, development tools, and databases may have special files that are used to construct your dynamic Web pages. Some may be named as if they were static Web pages (with a suffix of .htm or .html); putting them in their own folder will help you keep track of these files and prevent you (or someone else) from accidentally modifying them when sitewide changes are made.

Version Control

Even if you properly maintain separate environments for production, test, and development, you still need to provide some kind of version control so that you know which pages and databases work together. The easiest way to provide version control is to provide a version explicitly for every item on your Web site. (If you are using a database to keep track of them, this makes your life even easier.)

Do not waste time trying to provide a unified version scheme across all files: making certain that database version 1.4 matches HTML version 1.4 will soon drive you over the brink. You can provide a general version system in which version 1.x is the same for all files and version 2.x is the same for all files, but leave incremental revision numbers to fluctuate separately for each file.

Versioning the Web Pages

It is normally a good idea to place a version number at the bottom of each Web page. You may also place a date there, but for infrequently updated pages that may suggest to users that the site is getting a bit old to be relied on (even though with dynamic HTML that displays data from a database the content of the page may be much more recent than the date that is displayed).

You may want to consider placing the modification date of each Web page as a hidden field that you can view but that is not shown to users. (You can place a version number as part of the text to be placed in the HEAD element of each page on your site.)

Versioning the Databases

Many databases allow you to set a version explicitly or to set a global field for a table or database into which you can place a version number.

Note that a database version typically applies to the database format—its fields and layouts. A database timestamp shows the date and time of last update.

Why Not Just Use Dates?

Your database, HTML, and other files may be on different computers—they certainly will be as you move them from the production/mirror site to the production site on the server. Each machine will have its own date and time. The use of an explicit version identifier provides you with a tool that is independent of each machine's clock.

Managing the Site

Managing a database-driven Web site is often much easier than managing a traditional Web site: once it has been set up, it chugs along by itself, and the Webmaster or other coordinator often has less work to do. This is because pages do not need to be updated whenever any piece of information on the site changes: the underlying databases are updated, and the revised data automatically flows onto Web pages as necessary.

Nevertheless, you have to set up the site properly to make this dream of simple management a reality. This section covers the major issues:

- Managing databases from afar

- Database housekeeping

- Scheduling maintenance and updates

- Managing change (testing)

Maintaining Your Databases on the Web from Afar	What actually happens when you have a database-driven site?

Although some people maintain their own Web server and application server, for many people it is an Internet service provider (ISP) that maintains these computers and keeps the Internet and database software running. In real life, only a few people have access to their Web server (which provides all Internet services), their application server (which may be the same computer or may provide only database services), and all aspects of their databases (with maximum access privileges).

If you do have access to the Web server, the application server, and privileged passwords, your life may be easier…for the moment. Except in very rare cases, that is a security disaster waiting to happen. If you go on vacation, does that mean the site and the database have no one to maintain them? Or does that mean that all of your security chores are delegated to someone else? Who? Just as is the case with backups of your hard disk, for most people the only way to learn the importance of security is to discover what happens when you don't have proper procedures in place.

Databases That Move and Those That Do Not

There are two basic scenarios for managing a database on the Web: you can move the database to and from your Web site as you do your HTML pages or you can move data to and from the database on your database service provider's computer. In the first case, you have a great deal of control; in the second, the database service provider maintains the database and you work within it. Typically, personal computer–based databases (such as Microsoft Access and FileMaker Pro) are managed in the first way, databases such as Oracle, DB2, and Informix in the second.

Even personal computer–based databases can quickly grow too large to be reasonably moved back and forth; you (or your DSP) may decide to treat them as immovable, with the information within the database being imported and exported but the database itself remaining on the server.

All databases provide for high-speed import and export (sometimes referred to as batch loads and unloads). These procedures are suitable for large groups of records; they are supposed to implement the same data security and editing rules that are used for record-by-record updates, but experience has shown that batch loads often allow invalid data to be entered to databases. In particular, be aware that if you have changed editing rules, you may have to make those modifications to a batch load program as well.

Database Directories

For databases that move, your DSP will typically provide you with a specific directory in which to place them; you must use this directory. The DSP must know about the databases and where to find them so that the database software can open the databases automatically as needed.

Typically three folders will be prepared for you. Their names may differ from DSP to DSP, but their functions are generally the same. Also, the names are usually established by the DSP: use them, but do not rename them.

Incoming Databases   This is a holding directory into which you place your databases. You move them into this directory using your favorite FTP application (Archie, Anarchie, Fetch, etc.).

Live Databases   At a certain moment, the manager of the database computer will move your database from Incoming Databases to the Live Databases directory. This may be done manually, but often it is done by a script that runs on the application server. It may run periodically—once a day, once an hour, or at some other interval—scanning all Incoming Databases folders and moving their contents to Live Databases. It may also run in response to explicit commands—either from the database administrator or from you.

Figure 14-6 shows the interface to Digital Forest's Alder database manager, which performs this task for you. There are many other such tools available: the process is the same, however, in all cases.

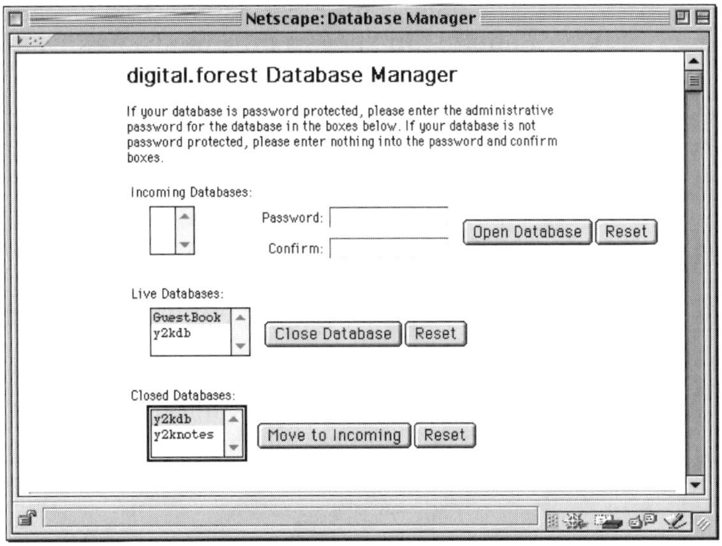

FIGURE 14-6. Digital Forest Database Manager

You can select one or more databases in the Incoming Databases list to be opened by using the Open Database button. When you click that button, the databases you have selected are moved to the Live Databases folder and are shown in that list.

When a database is moved to the Live Databases folder, it is also opened by the database software as part of this script or procedure. Remember that users cannot access a database that is not open. At the end of this process, all of the databases in Live Databases will be opened and made ready for use.

If the application server ever needs to be restarted, all of the databases in the Live Databases folder will automatically be reopened.

Closed Databases   As you can see from Figure 14-6, you can also select databases in the Live Databases list and click the Close Database button. This does the reverse of the Open

Database button: it closes the database and moves it to another folder—in this case Closed Databases.

When a file is in use, you normally cannot copy it. You need to be able to close a database in order to copy it back down to your own computer. If you are allowing updates over the Web to your databases, you periodically need to do this so that you have local copies of your databases. You may also find it easier to do maintenance (see "Database Housekeeping" on page 343) on your own computer.

In this case, a shortcut is available to move a database from Closed Databases back into Incoming Databases. You would use this button to close a database briefly to allow its copying and then to move it back into production.

In most cases, if you move a new version of a database into the Live Databases folder (via the Incoming Databases folder), the previous version is automatically moved into the Closed Databases folder.

Variations   There may be different names for these folders and a different process involved, but this is the process that needs to be in place for you to manage your databases from a remote location (your home, office, or boat). When you are discussing establishing an account with an DSP (whether a commercial service provider or someone within your organization), make certain that you understand their terminology and procedures in this area.

Some installations may have automatic updates from a folder such as Incoming Databases; others may not have the ability to let you manually close databases or copy old versions to your computer.

Database Housekeeping	Once you can move databases to and from your Web site, you can start to think about the housekeeping that you need to do.
Backups	Your DSP should provide you with backup as part of the service. These backups are done routinely (at least daily) for all files on the database and Web servers. They are normally not done by site or directory. In other words, the ISP takes the precautions necessary to make certain that in the case of catastrophic failure the files on a given computer can be restored from a reasonable point in time.

This backup may not be appropriate for you. There are several reasons why you might want your own backup schedule:

- You may want to keep backups from specific points in time: ends of months, years, semesters, etc.

- You may want more than one previous backup.

- You may want more frequent backups—if you have a class registration database, you may want to back it up hourly during the days of semester registration.

- You may need to place backups at a certain location for security purposes.

Know what your DSP's backup schedule is and determine whether you need additional backups.

Related to backups is the question of archiving and partial archiving of data. You may want to remove old records from your online database but keep them in a backup. In the case of a guest book, you might want to upload a totally empty database periodically and retrieve the previous one for integration with your master database on your local computer.

It is faster to do wholesale deletions of records on your local computer rather than on the application server. In doing this, however, remember not to leave a window of vulnerability in which updates to the online database are lost while you manipulate a copy of the database. That is why it is safest to upload the new database first (to Incoming Databases) and then to download the old database (from Closed Databases).

Offline Databases

If you are going to be conducting database maintenance in this way, remember that you will temporarily be causing links to fail. The best way to manage this is to have an alternate home page that announces that the site is undergoing maintenance. Start by replacing your normal home page with this page, and then move databases back and forth. When you are done, restore the original home page.

Thinking that you can just slip a database in or out of the server is wishful thinking. Something will always go wrong (if only that in reaching for the telephone you knock over a cup of tea and wind up forgetting that you forgot to reupload a database). One of the signs of a well-run Web site is that it is not always a mess. A Web site is not your closet: it is a public area.

Scheduling
Maintenance
and Updates

Many people do not spend much time browsing their own Web sites: they know them well. As a result, it is not uncommon to get a telephone call or e-mail message remarking that your site (or part of it) has been in disrepair for some time. Make certain that you have a routine schedule to check the site

Furthermore, you need a schedule for database maintenance. This may take the form of a wholesale database cleaning and reorganization or just a relatively minor check that everything looks OK.

A database-driven Web site should take care of itself to a large extent; however, you cannot wait until a disaster has happened to implement a maintenance schedule. Be particularly sensitive to the fact that such a site often involves a variety of people: at least one Internet service provider, a database administrator, Web designers, authors, editors, and testers. You can implement a relatively permanent schedule of maintenance (such as database maintenance on the first of the month, Web page maintenance on the fifth, and so on); alternatively, you can schedule a wholesale maintenance effort on a certain routine basis (such as database, Web page, and content updates all during the last week of the month).

Whatever you do, do not think that this is a maintenance-free effort. The results will show!

Managing Change	Many are the tales of minor changes to computer programs that have brought down major systems—for hours or days. There is no such thing as a minor change in an integrated digital world.

There is also no such thing as a Web site that does not change. You need procedures to manage change—and those procedures must include testing. Depending on the nature of your site, you may need several sets of procedures for managing change: if you may have emergency changes, you need a streamlined procedure that saves time but does not bypass security and other restrictions. (Many security breaches come in the aftermath of emergencies.)

In general, the person who has made a change is not the best person to conduct final testing. The person making a change should do preliminary testing to make certain that everything is working properly, and in fact everyone should assume that there will be no further testing—do not rely on someone else catching problems.

Promoting the Site

Whether it is on the Internet, an intranet, or a local area network, your database is now public. The typos and misspellings in the data records are visible; the incorrect information is published. The interface to your data becomes part of your data both explicitly (if you switch the "Length" and "Width" data field labels, people will receive invalid information) and implicitly (as the quality of your data is judged based on the quality of your interface).

Not only are the contents of your database and Web site public: your maintenance of them is also public. "Temporarily unavailable" is not the best response to a search request from a user.

The principal issues to consider are as follows:

- What are you doing on the Web?

- What your site says about you

- Letting people know about your site

- Managing problems in the public world of a network

- Handling feedback

- Dealing with registration, guest books, and gatekeepers

What Are You Doing on the Web?

The Internet is a mass medium in terms of its reach (scores of millions of people); however, its performance from moment to moment as an individual user clicks from link to link is less that of a mass medium than that of a highly personalized and individual communications medium. What an individual sees—the links traversed—is almost always a unique sequence. Indeed, with dynamically built Web pages based on database searches, the very pages that a user sees are unreproducible and ephemeral.

In addition to being simultaneously a mass and a personal medium, the Internet (as is true of all networks to a greater or lesser extent) brings together people from a wide variety of backgrounds and areas. Your site will most likely be used by people who share certain interests (mountain trekking, for example) that are relevant to your site; at the same time, these people will bring different regional, cultural, linguistic, and social perspectives to your site.

What Your Site Says about You	The look and feel of a site often betray unwanted and unnecessary information about its developers and sponsors. In an international context, references to "abroad" are ambiguous or insulting. It is not a matter of political correctness to make certain that the manner in which you present your site and its information does not make people feel unwelcome: it is a matter of good manners (and often good business).

By the same token, the look and feel of a site can provide a vast array of desirable information about its developers and sponsors. A database of movies is perceived very differently if it is encountered on a site sponsored by a church, by a women's group, by a school, or by a gay and lesbian association—even if the database contains exactly the same information in each context.

It is a mistake to believe that your site's information is unaffected by its context; it is an even bigger mistake to believe that you have somehow or other managed to construct a neutral environment for your information. Its mere presence on a network makes a statement about the potential users and the information: the users are computer literate (or semiliterate) and the information is more or less public.

What Is Your Objective?

Make certain that your site's purpose is clear. That may seem self-evident, but all too often sites are jumbles of unrelated information. Use tools such as site maps and subsites to keep different parts of your site in different locations; use backgrounds and other graphics to create a common look for pages (or subsites) that have common purposes.

Design Concerns

New design concerns crop up every day—particularly on the Web. One of the latest involves set-top boxes—the devices that sit on top of TV sets and let you surf the Web on your TV screen. This technology is available now and may become very common in the near future.

Meanwhile, back at the TV factories, a new television technology—high-definition TV (HDTV)—is marching forward. In the United States, all television stations will be broadcasting a new HDTV signal within a period of not too many years. (For the next few years, both traditional and HDTV signals will be transmitted by various stations as this transition occurs.)

What matters to you is that someone looking at the Internet on an HDTV set with a set-top surfing device is going to be looking at a very different screen than the current computer monitor or television set. The HDTV screen has a different aspect ratio: it is much wider in relation to its height than a typical TV screen (much as the shape of a movie screen is wider than the shape of a TV screen).

For some purposes, people may start to design Web pages that are much wider than those in use today, so as not to waste the new HDTV screen space. Particularly if you are publishing your database on an intranet or extranet that you know to be populated with HDTV screens, you may want to think about new designs.

Another area to watch is that of color. Originally, the mantra was quite simple: use color, but not as a distinguishing feature. This allowed people with black-and-white monitors to appreciate computer graphics just as well as those with color monitors. Today, color monitors are ubiquitous, and many designers are working only with a color design rather than starting from a black-and-white design and adding color.

Furthermore, many designers are now working solely on the screen: more and more corporate logos require not just color but also animation for their full display.

Of course, the rise of handheld devices that do not have high-resolution color screens adds uncertainty to this area. Again, if you are certain that your users will be using a certain type of device, optimize your design for it.

When it comes to design, the principles of design, aesthetics, and communication are centuries old; the details of implementation change by the minute.

Not only do design details change by the minute, they also go out of date by the minute. Experienced designers and computer users can date a computer interface just by looking at it. If your site's overall design is to last for a long time (perhaps a year), avoid the widget-du-jour syndrome.

Letting People Know about Your Site

There are two ways of publicizing your site:

1. You can place references to it on other Internet resources; people can place links to your site on their sites.

2. You can place these references in other media—magazine articles, corporate newsletters, books, etc. This is the best way to reach people who do not normally use the Internet.

In either case, you should try to achieve one goal: do not change your address. This will invalidate many Internet links and make printed references out of date.

The easiest way to avoid changing your address is to follow as many of the following guidelines as possible.

Do Not Change Your Address

Make certain that your site is (or is part of) a named domain that you control. For a modest fee, your Internet service provider (ISP) can help you obtain an address such as mycompany.com. It is a simple matter to change the Internet routing tables if you should move mycompany.com to another Internet service provider. What is particularly important is that these changes are made by you and not by people who visit your site. All links and printed references remain intact.

In order to make this most effective, make certain that you are named as one of the contacts for your site. In most cases your Internet service provider will be named as a technical contact for the site; you should be named as the business contact. That way, you can move the site if it is necessary to move to another ISP.

Identify the Site in Relation to a Known Address

If you do not have a domain of your own (for example, if you are a department of a corporation), give out your site's address in a context that will not change. It is easy to place a button on a corporation's home page that links to your site. Then, give out mycorporation.com as your address (if necessary, telling people to click on Division X). If you give out an address like mycorporation.com/~divisions/manufacturing, people may get confused.

The Site Is Part of Your Address

Once you are satisfied that you have a site address that will not change, make certain that it is part of your return address in e-mail, regular mail, and on letterheads. Although your data may be the most important data in the world, in practical terms people may consider your shakes and shingles to be interchangeable with those from another company whose Web address they happen to have in a catalog ad.

| Managing Problems in the Public World of a Network | You are not alone anymore. Problems—network problems, application server problems, database problems, Web server problems—can stand between your information and your users. It must be very clear who is responsible for support. It is not sufficient for users to be told that the person they have managed to reach is not responsible: a clear path of problem management must exist. |

Usually your Internet service provider or network administrator will be happy to sit down and discuss these issues with you. After all, it is typically the ISP or network administrator who first gets the irate telephone calls. Both of you should know what problems are likely to occur and how each of you should manage complaints about the other's problems.

You should know one another's schedules. Often, a DSP is located far away from you; it may be in another time zone. The time that is convenient for you to do wholesale site maintenance might just be a time when there is no one on site who can help if a problem occurs. Plan for such maintenance (copying of databases, opening and closing databases on the server, etc.) at a time when you know support staff is available—at least at the beginning.

Finally, prepare a short but thorough manual of procedures to follow when problems do occur. The first step in every procedure should be a clear description of when it should be invoked. It is human nature to think that the solution to a problem is just one more try away. The best network and database administrators have hard-and-fast rules about the amount of time that passes after a problem is noticed before contingency procedures must be put into place.

It is wise to have an alternate home page that says the database is temporarily unavailable. This is much better than letting users get an error message. Replace your standard home page with this one if you know that the database has been unavailable for a period of time—such as 15 minutes. You may have every assurance that the database will be back after 16 minutes, but it just might be 2 more hours.

Handling Feedback	In the networked world, people quickly become used to immediate feedback and response. If you have mail links on your Web pages, make certain that those messages go to an address that is monitored. The explanation that "it was Easter Sunday" won't cut the mustard when the message is from Jakarta (capital of the largest Muslim country in the world). There are problems with monitoring mail accounts from several locations. One way is to remove your mailto links and to replace them with form-based messages that are stored in one of your databases. That way you can format the message appropriately, capture the date and time, make certain the user has provided all necessary information, and otherwise clean up the message before it is even sent. You can then provide limited access to that database to yourself and members of your project team. This will eliminate the problem of one person retrieving a message that no one else knows about.
Dealing with Registration, Guest Books, and Gatekeepers	Databases that contain information for which a fee is charged need to have a registration screen or gatekeeper that can collect the fee or handle password information. Other databases often have such gatekeepers. There are arguments pro and con. The most important argument in favor of such a gatekeeper is that you know who is getting to the database (more or less—people tend to type in gibberish like sdsdsddsd for their name) as well as the date, time, and number of such accesses. The biggest argument against such a scheme is that it is one more roadblock (albeit a minor one) between the user and the information. It will certainly cut down access to your site; this may or may not be a good thing.

If you have some kind of registration screen, you can use hidden fields to pass a session ID or user ID along as the user browses your site and your databases. You can log this information—down to the mouse click. Although many people are aware that such information can easily be collected over the Web, some do not like you to do so (particularly if you sell or give the information to others). In most cases, the best approach is not to attempt to follow each mouse click; if you decide that you need that information to improve your site, a message on the registration screen that you would like to monitor activity as a way of improving the site in the future is appropriate. (If you make it an option that can be turned off, that is even better—although your statistical results will not be a random sample.)

Summary

Setting up your database-driven Web site involves choosing your tools and vendors as well as designing and implementing the initial site. Once it is up, you need to have procedures in place to manage it so that updates to both databases and Web pages are moved into production appropriately (and with adequate testing). In the public world of the Internet, your site says a lot about you: its design and layout no less than its implementation and maintenance are your face before the world (or at least your coworkers on an intranet).

And yet that is not all: having made your site easy to understand and use and having promoted it appropriately, you have to think about how to keep people out and how to restrict your information. This is a different mindset from that involved in the topics covered in this chapter, and so security is discussed in the next one.

Security

Security is an issue that most people would just as soon ignore— whether it is on the Web, in your car, at home, or anywhere else. The essence of security is keeping things safe: in the case of the Web, that means information. Safety is defined as many things: keeping the wrong people out, letting the right people in, allowing only certain people to enter or modify certain data elements, determining conditions under which security procedures can be modified, and on and on and on. In practical terms, security often seems to be a barrier or roadblock erected between the user who wants information and the information provider who wants people to have information.

Security on the Internet is a topic that is being widely addressed in many venues, from government agencies and international groups

to corporations and citizens' groups. The details of security imple-
mentation are changing rapidly, but the essential issues are constant
(and have been for ages—"Open Sesame" is as much a security fea-
ture as was Jack Benny's carefully guarded combination to his safe).

This chapter covers the major issues involved with security as it af-
fects information: they include the security of your servers and soft-
ware (needed to prevent people from stealing or damaging your
hardware, software, or Web site), the security that you put in place
to limit access to your site and information on the part of people us-
ing browsers, and the security that you put in place to maintain the
confidentiality of your data. It also describes in detail the implemen-
tation of password-protected directories and cookies.

When You Do Not Have to Worry about Security

Most experienced computer managers would say that "Never" is the only proper response: you always need to worry
about security. Web sites are prone to all sorts of problems.
Even if you are posting information that is in the public domain (the Bible, for instance), you—along with everyone else
on the Web—run the risk of having hackers invade your Web
site and replace Genesis with "Madame Tedra's Night of Or-
gies." Some people think this is funny, although it is not—and
is usually illegal.

There is no Web site that does not have some part that is secure and confidential (the password you use to upload files to
your Web site is an example of a confidential piece of information for everyone).

There can be very nasty consequences to not keeping your site
secure. Allowing access to the Internet through your account
to unauthorized users can be grounds for canceling your account—or for your Internet service provider suing you for
theft of services! If hackers replace your Web pages with their

own, you may find yourself responsible for the information that they have posted. And if your Web site includes computers within your organization (as often happens with database-driven Web sites), you may be responsible for the damage that people do when they infiltrate other computers and databases.

This is a serious issue, and you cannot ignore it. Fortunately, it is not hard to implement a reasonable level of security that protects you and your site and makes it easy for you to do your work and for your users to do what they want to do. But first, there are several myths about security that need to be demolished.

Myth: Ignorance Is Security	A remarkable number of people rely on ignorance and naivete as security. "No one around here would know how to do that" is the mantra of this crowd. This is a very foolish approach: it insults the people about whom you are speaking, and it presumes that dangerous books such as the one you have in your hands now do not exist. Particularly at a time when so many people are working to make computers and the Internet easier to use, it is not safe to rely on this myth.
Myth: No One Would Care	Although it is true that you should carefully appraise the value of your information, you cannot assume that it has no value to anyone. Certain information—trade secrets, confidential correspondence—obviously needs to be treated more carefully than other information, but even such seemingly innocuous information as the day's menu for a resort needs to be safeguarded (if only from pranksters intent on replacing "Cherries Jubilee" with "Eye of Newt Surprise").

Myth: We Can Fix It Later	Security is one of two major system elements that cannot be retrofitted (the other is networking). You must plan for them from the start of a project, even if you do not implement them until later. For any security measures to be effective, they must be complete and consistent, and retrofitting security almost always means that it is incomplete and inconsistent.
Myth: You Can Never Have Too Much Security	Finally, you should realize that more security is not always better: in fact, after a certain point, adding security is counter-productive. While you may have several security mechanisms in place, the first one is usually the most effective: each additional security measure adds less and less. At a certain point, the nuisance of your security measures exceeds the point at which people are willing to put up with them, and they break. You will find passwords taped to the side of computer terminals, combinations for locks written in "safe" places (on the back of a poster on the wall nearby), and so forth. Put in as much security as you need…and then stop.

Physical Security

When it comes to security, nothing is more effective than physical security. In the case of objects (diamonds, gold, people, or chocolate cakes), physical security is the only realistic choice. Information, however, can move through the air and over wires, and it needs different types of security.

Nevertheless, do not ignore physical security. The only safe computer is one that is not connected to a network and that is locked in a windowless room. (Of course, it is not particularly easy to run a database-driven Web site on such a computer.)

Your server clearly needs to be connected to a network, but there is no reason for it to be accessible to many people. If it is located at an Internet service provider, security is one of the features that you are paying for: you have every right to ask what precautions are taken.

Physical security extends beyond the equipment to the data that you use: careful backups of data can be a vulnerability if they are stored in a less secure location than your server itself. (Many people keep offsite backups in their homes: this is not a particularly safe practice unless your home has security devices that exceed those normally found in residences.)

Security at Your ISP

One of the services that your ISP or DSP is providing is security: in some cases, that is one of the most important selling points for a company. (Typically, companies providing high levels of security also provide redundancy and emergency power and communications. They may have originally been set up to handle the needs of major corporations, but some of them now see the value of these services even to small businesses.)

If security is any kind of a concern to you (and it should be), discuss with your ISP what procedures are in place. Be prepared for incomplete information: revealing security procedures tends to lessen their effectiveness. You should look for a sense of seriousness with regard to security (it is not a joking matter) as well as a knowledge of the issues. A responsible ISP will be forthcoming in describing the broad outlines of its security: employee standards, written procedures, and periodic warnings to users to change passwords and otherwise attend to security concerns. If you hear something like, "Our consultant set it up and we don't know how it works," run to another provider.

Unless you are the provider. In that case, you need to bring yourself up to speed on security issues quickly. The best way to do so is to spend several days at an installation similar to yours that has good security: you can see how new users are added to the system, how backups are done, and how procedures are implemented. Of course, not many organizations are willing to give such tours (they are obviously high security risks).

Failing that, a good three- to five-day course on computer security can provide you with a good overview as well as the chance to ask questions about the specific products that you use. And, of course, books and manuals will help you to use the hardware and software that you have on hand.

Remember that if you are going to be responsible for a Web site (whether traditional or database driven), you are responsible for its security.

The Password Issue

Many people today are starting to suffer from password overload: there are simply too many different passwords required for Web sites, e-mail, ATM cards, and the other accounts and situations that require them. As a result, many people are starting to adopt one of three strategies:

1. They are simply writing down their passwords and keeping the list in a (presumably) safe place.

2. They are using the same password for many different purposes.

3. They are disabling password security where possible and are visiting Web sites that do not require passwords and registration.

Obviously, these strategies are dangerous and defeat the purposes of passwords; they may also be violations of policies set by employers, Internet service providers, and others. Nevertheless, unless you want to go into the password remembering business, it has become impossible to keep track of the number of different passwords you need to manage.

To head off these problems, security implementors have a number of their own strategies; these two often deal with the breaches caused by users' shortcuts:

1. Instead of allowing users to select a password (which can be easily remembered but could also be used for many accounts), a password is given to the user.

2. Users are required to change passwords on a regular basis (in many organizations, this is handled automatically once a week).

In implementing your security, you need to be aware of these concerns; you also need to distinguish between the different types of passwords that are in use.

Authentication and Identification	Passwords are used for authentication and identification: stating and proving an individual's identity. In the nonelectronic world, photographs and signatures are often used for this purpose: some documents (such as passports) combine a number of authentication mechanisms—the signatures of the individual as well as a government official as well as a photograph of the person. In the electronic world, "secret" passwords known only to the individual in question (hah!) are typically used.

Many people are working on authentication schemes today that do not rely on passwords: fingerprints, voice recognition systems, cards with embedded microprocessors, and other mechanisms are being developed, tested, and deployed. Although physical recognition mechanisms can be expensive, they hold the promise of working easily and not requiring a user to memorize a password. (They also cannot be easily by-passed.)

For most Web sites, however, you are limited to passwords. Before you blithely set up a password on your Web site or your database, consider whether you really need a password for authentication and identification—that is, a password that identifies a particular individual. Sometimes it is sufficient to use a password to identify someone as a member of a group.

Access Control

You use a password to identify someone as a member of a group when you want to limit access to a group such as employees, students, residents, or others who can be treated collectively. These passwords are typically not secure—too many people know them, but they are useful for limited periods of time. On an intranet, it may be sufficient to send out an e-mail message once a week with the week's password for medium-security sites. This will keep nonemployees out (probably), and in most organizations it will take several days for people to spread the "secret" password around.

You cannot use access control passwords to monitor who has been accessing your data—you cannot break events down below the group level.

Passwords Everywhere

With a database-driven Web site, you are often dealing with three levels of passwords: they are often three completely different passwords, and they are managed separately.

Internet Access Passwords

Most people need to enter a password to connect to their network. It may be embedded in a modem's connection script, but it is there somewhere. This consists of the password and account name that are assigned to you by an ISP or a network coordinator.

If the access password is embedded in a modem script that runs automatically when you connect to the Internet, anyone who uses your computer can use your password. They cannot necessarily read the password (it is usually encrypted in one way or another), but letting someone use your computer means letting them use your Internet account.

Web Page Access Passwords

A Web site designer can associate a password (and user name) with an individual page or a directory. (See "Passwording a Section of Your Site" on page 364.) These passwords can be unique for individuals, or they can be access control passwords that are shared among groups. They are controlled by the Web site designer or Webmaster.

These passwords may be stored in cookies (see "Cookies" on page 373); if they are, once again you have the case that letting others use your computer means letting them use your access to Web pages. That is why the Cookies option in many browsers is disabled on public access Internet terminals such as the ones in public libraries.

Database Passwords

Passwords can be assigned to databases or to tables within them; in the case of many database-driven Web sites, these passwords are implemented from the application server that is actually interacting with the database. All individuals accessing the database may be using the same password (the one assigned to the application server). The application server itself may implement a level of security that reimplements this database level. This varies from product to product, but be aware that you may have to set a level of access for your application server that is much less restrictive than the access you would normally grant to individual users.

Passwording a Section of Your Site

Several mechanisms are available to let you password a section of your Web site. All work in much the same way. You can use them to implement passwords at an individual level (for identification and authentication) as well as for access control at the group level.

As with all security procedures, start small and build up to prevent locking yourself (and your users) out of the site.

Overview

Protecting directories or files is a procedure that is done at the transmission level—that is, as part of an HTTP (hypertext transmission protocol) scheme. Most browsers support basic procedures, as do most Web servers. There are many new schemes being presented today; some work only on certain servers and some work only with certain versions of browsers.

Because protection is implemented at the transmission protocol level, it stands to reason that HTML pages (whether static or dynamic) are unaffected by it; you can implement or remove protection from a directory or file without touching the file itself. This means, too, that you can practice implementing security in a test directory on your Web site with fake files in it (finally a use for those "Hello World" Web pages from beginning HTML class). Once security works for the test directory, you can simply move your security files to the directory you actually want to protect, and all should work properly. You do not have to test security with the actual Web pages that will be protected.

What Should Be Protected?

The simplest form of protection is provided with a user name and password such as are shown in Figure 15-1.

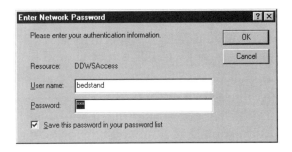

FIGURE 15-1. Enter Password Browser Alert

If the authentication fails, the browser displays a message such as that shown in Figure 15-2. Both of these screens are generated automatically for you: you do not have to code either the password entry or the error screen.

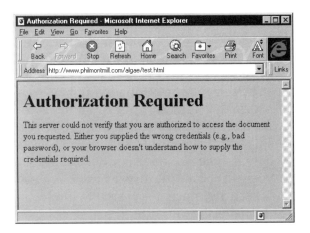

FIGURE 1-2. Authorization Failure

The files in a directory that has been protected cannot be accessed by a browser that does not successfully return an appropriate user name and password. (Note that the Web server must support this, but most do.) If the authentication fails, the Web server returns a messages such as that shown in Figure 15-2.

This very basic level of security is sufficient for many, many purposes, but what directory should be protected?

- You can protect your entire site in this manner, but that is usually overkill. You probably want one page that contains basic information—including the person to contact if someone has forgotten a password. If a user cannot get past this alert, there is no way of getting any information from your site.

- You often want to protect a directory that contains queries: these are the static pages that will in turn generate dynamic HTML with data from your database.

- The data from the database usually does not need to be protected: it is shown in dynamically created pages, and if they are created only from queries that themselves are protected, you do not have to worry about the end result. (With traditional Web sites, static pages with data do need to be protected in many cases.)

As soon as you start to think about what parts of your site need security and what parts do not, you may decide to restructure your directories; you may even decide that there are several levels of security to implement. For example, all employees may have access to a broad part of your site using a single access control password; a selected few may have update privileges using individual passwords. In such cases, your physical directory layout may reflect the different levels of security, since it is easiest to implement security at a directory level.

Note also that these security mechanisms allow for implementation based on IP addresses as well as passwords. You may want to make update access to your database restricted to people using devices that are physically within your office—another example of physical security at work.

Basic authentication was implemented in 1995 in NCSA Mosaic (the earliest browser) and NCSA HTTPd. Since then, additional implementations have been developed. The W3C (World Wide Web Consortium) has done further work on HTTPd, as have vendors ranging from Microsoft (with support in Microsoft Front Page for their security mechanism) to Netscape.

Two basic structures are in place:

1. A special file can be placed in a directory that needs to be authenticated. The name of this file is set by the installation (the ISP or network administrator). If a file with such a name is found, its commands are used to control access. In this case, the setup involves identifying the file at the server level; creating and maintaining these files can easily be left to individual Web site managers (they either create such files or do not).

2. Alternatively, server configuration or setup files can identify the security rules and the files or directories to which they apply. These files may need to be created and maintained by the ISP or network administrator because they may be located in directories to which individual Web site administrators do not have access.

Your network administrator or ISP can tell you what type(s) of security access is available on the servers that you use and can provide you with the names of installation-specific files you need to know about. A number of ISPs that have particularly well-implemented security systems have tutorial Web pages (including interactive forms) that will help you implement security.

Some ISPs discourage users from implementing security on their Web sites. Although it is true that security implemented incorrectly can cause grief, that grief should be limited to the Web site in question: it should be very difficult for a Web site administrator to bring down an entire Web server.

HTTP Basic Authentication

The original implementation is based on a pair of files: one contains access rules, and the other contains user names and encrypted passwords. These files are briefly described here, because the logic is used in other schemes as well. (This actual syntax is used in the Apache Web server.)

Specifying Access Control— .htaccess

The first file involved is normally called .htaccess; it is placed in the directory to be protected. It is a text file that looks like this one:

```
AuthUserFile /moss/.htpasswd
AuthGroupFile /dev/null
AuthName "DDWSAccess"
AuthType Basic

<LIMIT GET POST PUT>
require user bedstand
</LIMIT>
```

Each of the first four lines consists of a keyword followed by specific data. The keywords are unchanged; you use the appropriate filenames and text strings for your situation. They can be in any order. The meanings of these keywords are as follows:

AuthUserFile This is the name of the file that contains passwords and user names (it is discussed in the next section, "Specifying User Names and Passwords—.htpasswd" on page 371). The file is identified fully within the domain: that is to say, starting from the root of your Web site's directory, the name contains any appropriate directory. In this case, the user name file is in another directory called moss, and the file itself is named .htpasswd. It is normally a good idea to place the user name file in a directory by itself; your ISP can help you set the access for that directory so that only you—via FTP and the Web server itself—can access it.

AuthDBMUserFile can be used instead of AuthUserFile; its contents are the same, but it is a Unix database file and is much more efficient when large numbers of user names are in it.

AuthGroupFile   This is the name of the file that specifies groups—collections of user names that can be granted the same access privileges. The /dev/null name is a standard Unix way to say that there is no file associated with this keyword. Basic security often does not implement groups.

AuthName   This keyword introduces the string that browsers will display in their dialog box. Note in Figure 15-1 that Microsoft Internet Explorer displays DDWSAccess as the "Resource:" entry (that figure reflects the code shown here). Other browsers display it as a realm or simply construct a sentence. The AuthName string may include spaces; if it does, it must be enclosed in straight quotation marks.

AuthType   This keyword lets you select the authentication to be used; choices may include such schemes as PGP, Kerberos, or Digest. Basic is the string to use to implement the basic user name/password authentication described here.

LIMIT   Next is an SGML element—note the <LIMIT> and </LIMIT> tags. The introductory tag specifies the methods that are limited by this file. In this example, the most common HTTP methods are affected; you may want to limit only the GET method, allowing POST to proceed without security constraints. That would allow people to access files in the directory through a form, but not simply by typing in a URL.

Within the LIMIT element you enter your security rules. Here, only the user bedstand is allowed access via the GET, POST, and PUT methods.

```
<LIMIT>
require user bedstand
</LIMIT>
```

You can have many lines within the LIMIT element; each one corresponds to a rule. Require lets you specify the name of a user that must be authenticated before access is provided.

Other rules let you implement different types of access based on domain names. For example, you can enter a limit rule that says

```
allow from .mydomain.com
```

That allows anyone from your own domain access to the protected files. That is fine, but you also need to keep other people out, and you can do that with the line

```
deny from all
```

which allows no access whatsoever. Obviously, you need a way to combine such rules, and the order rule does that. It simply states the order in which to apply the rules. Thus this LIMIT element denies access to everyone except people from .mydomain.com.

```
<LIMIT GET>
order deny, allow
deny from all
allow from .mydomain.com
</LIMIT>
```

And this LIMIT element does the reverse: it allows access to anyone except people within mydomain.com.

```
<LIMIT GET>
order allow, deny
allow from all
deny from .mydomain.com
</LIMIT>
```

Specifying User Names and Passwords— .htpasswd

The user name and password file (which is identified in the AuthUserFile keyword) contains user names and passwords in the following format:

```
bedstand:HxUDWDFItN65Q
```

The password is stored in an encrypted form; this is not totally safe for high-security cases, but it is sufficient for many purposes. The password's encryption is specified as part of the rules. You can find a number of tools on the Internet (perhaps even on your ISP's own site) that will help you create passwords. In Figure 15-3, for example, you see ComputerLand's tool to generate passwords.

FIGURE 1-3. Generating Passwords

Figure 15-4 shows the response: you simply copy and paste the text into your AuthUserFile. (The actual algorithms used to create these passwords can be found in references on security. Someone who knows the algorithm can reverse engineer an encrypted password given enough time and computer resources. However, as noted previously, these passwords are quite sufficient for most purposes.)

Notes on Files and Filenames

Netscape's server can use an .htaccess file; however, its default is .nsaccess. Note also that on Unix, filenames starting with a period are hidden from normal view: they can be found be people and applications looking for them, but they are not normally displayed in directories. Furthermore, the restrictions to a directory in which an .htaccess or .nsaccess file is placed are for HTTP access: FTP access (the method you normally use to browse, upload, and download files) is not restricted in this way—it is restricted by the server's standard security procedures (which you normally set for your own files).

FIGURE 1-4. Generated Password

Finally, it is important to note that in a configuration file, you can create a <DIRECTORY> element—and you can place these commands within that element rather than within an .htaccess file inside the directory affected. This allows security to be controlled at a higher level than at the individual Web site manager.

W3C Authentication	The other form of access control lets you specify somewhat more sophisticated rules in protection setups that can then be applied to specific cases. A protection setup is named, and it contains the same information as used in the basic method of the previous section—with some more added in.

A typical protection setup is

```
Protection demosetup {
    UserID          marcus
    GroupID         nogroup
    AuthType        Basic
    ServerID        DDWSAccess
    PasswordFile    /moss/.htpasswd
    GroupFile       /device/null
    GetMask         group, user, group@address, …
}
```

Within a configuration file, you can then apply that setup to a specific directory:

```
Protect /algae/* demosetup
```

Cookies

One of the problems with passwords is that people have to remember them and reenter them each time they visit the page or directory that is protected. Cookies provide a way of storing information on a user's computer between sessions—even without the user explicitly doing anything.

Using cookies almost always involves writing code—in C, C++, Java, or JavaScript. (The exceptions are when you use application servers that provide explicit cookie support.) Thus, this section includes code with which you may not be familiar. If that is the case, focus on the concepts; if you need to use cookies, show this section to your favorite programmer and ask/plead/beg for assistance.

How Cookies Work

Cookies are used most often to store information that is needed to display a Web page properly. This can range from a user name and password to an option for the layout or color of the page. A cookie can contain almost anything. Cookies are stored on a user's hard disk and retrieved from it by the browser; the browser stores them in response to a request in the header of an HTTP request. This request is normally generated in the header that accompanies an HTML page, and it is generated by either a script or a program. Languages such as Perl and JavaScript make it easy to do this; in addition, many application servers provide simple cookie implementations.

The data to be stored in the cookie can be static—such as the name of a Web page that has been visited—or it can be data that a user has entered onto an HTML form. In the latter case, a script is used to collect data from form elements and copy that data into cookies, which are then stored on the user's disk. (This is the way in which a password can be stored.)

Cookies contain a single named data value; they may also contain six attributes. Elements of the cookie are separated by a semicolon.

Cookie Data

Like the parameters in an HTTP searchpart, cookies contain a named data value such as the following:

```
password=bedstand;
username=charles;
backgroundcolor=blue;
lastvisit=19990529;
```

The entire string can include no blanks, commas, or semicolons; if they are necessary, they must be encoded with an escape character (%XX). The format is totally under the control of the person who sets up the cookie: presumably, that person will also be responsible for retrieving the cookie at a later date.

Nothing prevents you from encrypting the data in the cookie: just as passwords for access to files are encrypted, you can encrypt any of the values shown here. (A good argument can be made for encrypting all cookies. Be very leery of storing passwords without encrypting them.)

Expiration

When a cookie is set, you can specify an expiration date for it. The date must adhere to the Internet standard date format (specified in RFCs 822, 850, 1036, and 1123); it is expressed in Greenwich mean time. The format is

```
expires=Wdy, DD-Mon-YYYY HH:MM:SS GMT;
```

as in

```
expires=Monday, 03-January-2000 10:00:00 GMT;
```

(The time is always expressed in GMT so that there is no ambiguity when people transport computers and cookies across time zones.)

Browsers are responsible for destroying cookies that have expired. It is a good idea to set an expiration date for the cookies that you set: it helps avoid disk clutter and can prevent performance degradation from large numbers of cookies. When you choose an expiration date, choose the earliest one that makes sense: an hour, a day, or a week is usually sufficient. The default value of the expires attribute is when you quit the browser application.

Note that the actual standard specifies a Max-Age attribute that is expressed in seconds. Browsers convert your date to the Max-Age attribute if needed. Expires is not part of RFC 2109.

Domain

The domain attribute specifies a domain to which the cookie applies, as in

```
domain=yourcompany.com;
```

Domains can be fully or partially qualified, as in

```
domain=www.yourcompany.com;
domain=sales.yourcompany.com;
```

The domain attribute cannot be set to a top-level domain (such as com or edu) or to a high-level domain (such as ca.us—California). The default value for the domain attribute is the domain from which the cookie is being set.

Cookies are retrieved only for the appropriate domain: in other words, a browser should not return a cookie to a domain other than that which set it.

Path
Within a domain, you can specify a path to which the cookie applies. By default, the path is the same as the document that set the cookie. The syntax for the path attribute is

```
path=/;
path=/customers;
```

Secure
The secure attribute requires the cookie to be sent over a secure connection (see "Secure Servers" on page 379). This is independent of any encryption that you may have done to the data that you store in the cookie.

Comment
You can include a comment about the cookie; some browsers have an option that allows users to decide on a case-by-case basis whether to allow a cookie to be set. In such cases, the comment is displayed to help the user decide what to do.

Version
This is the version of the cookie specification to which the cookie conforms. It is not the version of your software or browser. (You can omit it and the default value will be used.)

Cookie Syntax
In the HTTP header, you simply add the text Set-Cookie: followed by the named value and any attributes that you want to set. Multiple cookies can be set with one Set-Cookie header:

if you do so, the cookies are separated by commas. Each cookie must start with the name=value pair.

Here are some examples:

```
Set-Cookie: userid=153356
Set-Cookie: userid=645234; domain=yourcompany.com
Set-Cookie: userid=6453, password=abdc, preference=green
```

(The last Set-Cookie statement contains three cookies.)

Creating a Cookie

Because cookies often contain dynamic data (such as information that someone has entered into a form), they need to be created dynamically. Here are two samples.

JavaScript

In JavaScript, you can use the cookie attribute of the document to access a cookie. To set a cookie, you set that attribute. The examples shown previously are shown here in JavaScript:

```
document.cookie="userid=153356"
document.cookie="userid=645234; domain=yourcompany.com"
document.cookie="userid=6453, password=abdc;,
    preference=green"
```

The keyword document refers to the current HTML document; do not replace it with a specific name.

Perl

You can use Perl to generate a dynamic HTML page complete with its HTTP header, which may contain a cookie. Here is a sample Perl script that generates a page saying "Thank you" and that also sets a cookie.

```
print "HTTP/1.0 Content-type: text/html\n\n";
print "Set-Cookie: userid=153356\n";
print "<html>\n";
print "<head>\n";
print "</head>\n";
print "<body>\n";
print "Thank you"\n";
print "</body>\n";
print "</html>\n";
```

This type of script would normally be run using a variable rather than the constant for the userid. That variable would be retrieved from a form.

Retrieving a Cookie

Cookies are automatically sent by a browser when a URL matches the domain and path attributes of a previously set cookie that has not expired. That part of the retrieval is automatic (from the Web page's point of view). It is up to the Web page author to examine a cookie that has been returned.

JavaScript

In JavaScript, you access the same document attribute: document.cookie. You should check whether a cookie exists by looking at its length:

```
if document.cookie.length > 0
```

You can then use standard JavaScript code to parse the cookie looking for specific names (userid, for example).

Perl

In Perl, you extract cookies from the HTTP_COOKIE environment:

```
%thecookies = split('[;=] *',$ENV{'HTTP_COOKIE'});
```

This gives you an array of cookies through which you can then iterate.

Cookies and Security

Like authentication, cookies are part of the HTTP protocol.[1] They are supported in most of today's browsers, but users can generally control whether they are used or not. Since cookies allow data to be stored on (and retrieved from) a user's hard disk, there are security issues that arise.

---

1. See *HTTP State Management Mechanism*, RFC 2109; it is available with other RFCs on many Internet Web sites. You can use a search engine to search for RFC 2109 to locate it.

Cookies are specific to the computer on which they are stored; they can be used to identify that computer and the preferences that people using it have chosen. This is an important distinction between the use of passwords and the use of cookies: passwords can be used to identify individual users, whereas cookies can identify the computer. If several people use a single computer, cookies stored on it can represent a variety of their choices and information; likewise, a single person who uses several computers (perhaps a laptop as well as a desktop computer) will have cookie information scattered around.

You can avoid some of these issues by storing this information in a centralized location: your database. As a rule of thumb, if you are going to ask people to identify themselves before they can access your database, you might as well store information in the database rather than in cookies: this eliminates any difficulties with multiple computers, multiple users, and so forth.

Secure Servers

The closer you can get to physical security, the better off you are. That means protecting access to your computers as well as trying to make your network connections secure. Securing network connections can be done in a number of ways:

- You can use your own cabling (rather than the public telecommunications network or a building's shared network) and run it through spaces that you own or control (such as your building, suite, or apartment).

- You can encrypt the communications over a network if you control both ends of it; this can be done with a physical device at each end. (Many banks use just such a mechanism to communicate with their branches and ATMs.)

- You can use software to secure connections: this also requires the use of devices at each end of the connection. Many browsers and Web servers provide such security today.

The use of software to secure connections is usually easier and less expensive to implement than solutions involving hardware. However, software security implementations can often be broken more easily than physical security implementations. Furthermore, software implementations of security use machine resources, and this can slow down communication.

Today's personal computers are fast enough to be able to implement very sophisticated security mechanisms; they can encrypt and decrypt messages quickly enough so that the degradation in performance is not particularly noticeable. This is one of the most rapidly growing areas of Internet development today; new products are being developed that provide higher levels of security with less delay.

Secure servers are implemented at the protocol level: a secure version of HTTP replaces the standard HTTP protocol. HTML pages (whether static or dynamic) function in exactly the same way in a secure environment. You may wonder why everyone doesn't just convert to using secure servers. The answer is cost: running a secure server requires more resources (both managerial and computer) than running a nonsecure server; in addition, the communications burden for secure servers is higher, because authentication messages need to be exchanged along with content messages. If the past is any indication, it will not be long before these costs have dropped below their current levels, and the use of secure servers for all data transfer will probably become commonplace.

Until that happens, secure servers are used only where needed: on e-commerce sites, they are used to process credit card information, but catalog browsing is usually done on nonsecure servers. Even shopping carts are normally not handled on secure servers: only the checkout process is secured.

Setting up a secure server is not a simple task: there are many steps involved, and any incorrect installation can cancel all of the security procedures. This is a very good opportunity for those ISPs that do have secure servers, and many of them have taken advantage of it. If you need a secure server, you can either choose an ISP that offers that service or place your critical pages on an ISP with that service and leave your other pages elsewhere (even on an internal server).

Nonclick and Automated Access

Before leaving the topic of security, think about automated access to Web pages and data. Most people think of the Web as a highly interactive medium (which it is). But even on a good day, it can take you a significant amount of time to log on to a site, search for what you want, deal with the data, and then go on to something else. Increasingly, people are trying to script the Web; it is not unreasonable for people to expect to be able to speak or type the following commands:

```
log on to www.nytimes.com
download today's crossword puzzle
    (my password is 12345)
print the puzzle
print the first page
```

Most of this is feasible today; what gums up the works, though, is the need to enter variable data (the password, in this case). The user name and password alert shown previously in Figure 15-1 assumes that a live person is sitting at the computer waiting to type it in. Messages that are shown as HTML pages (such as that shown in Figure 15-2) are compatible with an automated and scripted world, but those in alert boxes that require you to click an OK button are problems.

As you build Web sites that require interaction of this sort, remember that the interaction may exclude certain types of access. This is going to be an increasing problem as people demand more and more from the Web. If you are writing scripts and applets, resist the temptation to display information in alerts that need to be clicked to dismiss them.

Handling Security Problems

Part of your security mechanism is developing a procedure for handling problems. Your security is supposed to be productive and preventive, but it is also supposed to help you identify and deal with breaches.

One of the worst cases arises when a valid user is locked out (particularly if that user is you!). This often happens when someone reformats a hard disk or otherwise inadvertently destroys cookies with passwords embedded in them or logon scripts used by modem software. You may not even know that you have a password that lets you access the daily paper that you read on line: you may have registered several years ago, and a password-equipped cookie does its work each morning.

There are two alternatives when a valid user is locked out:

1. You can destroy the old account and create a new account with a new password.

2. You may be able to create a new password for the existing account (if you have that type of security authorization).

There are two other alternatives, neither of which is acceptable:

1. You should not be able to look up anyone's password on a master list of all passwords: such a list should not

exist. Some office managers like to have a list of all the passwords for all the computer accounts in their offices: this is very dangerous.

2. You should not "temporarily" give anyone your own or another account and password. (However, a legitimate variation of this is to have a standard Guest account with a changeable password; if such an account has limited access, it can be given—in a controlled manner—to anyone who needs temporary access.)

Many severe security problems arise out of minor breaches.

Digital Signatures and Authorial Authentication

Finally, you should consider the issues of digital signatures and authorial authentication. These are the reverse of user identification: they let users know that the information they are viewing on the Web is from the source they think it is from.

Many techniques are being developed in these areas: digital watermarks can be inserted into documents and images so that their provenance can be determined; this is designed to cut down on copyright infringement. The ease with which Web pages can be developed means that someone who wants to spoof your site can do so without much effort. Depending on the information that you provide and who you are, you may need to consider using electronic tools to convince visitors that they have really reached the site that is yours.

Summary

Security is—and should be—an obstacle to people who want to access your site; however, it should be the smallest hurdle possible to protect you and your site and to minimize irritation on the part of your visitors. Security is not an add-on: it works only when it is integrated into a site from the beginning. You have many choices when it comes to security, and you should understand them before you decide which combination to use in any given situation (almost all good security is a combination of elements).

Security on the Internet is an area of great interest today: were it totally resolved, the Internet would probably be used much more extensively for transactions than it already is. The interest and amounts of money involved are both high: there is no reason to doubt that security will increase and become cheaper very quickly.

Nonetheless, the basic issues of this chapter—physical security, user authentication, the use of cookies, secure servers, and procedures for handling problems—are likely to be constant.

Copyright, Pornography, and Treason

16

This chapter provides a very brief snapshot of three critical issues on the Internet today. They are alike in that they cause many people to distrust the Internet. They are also similar in that they are topics that many people are uncomfortable discussing. If you are among those people, feel free to skim the chapter—but remember that you may find yourself addressing these issues suddenly and without preparation.

You may argue that you have no intention of infringing on anyone's copyright, of publishing pornography, or of encouraging sedition; unfortunately, your actions—as documented by your Web site— may belie your words. The technology has outstripped much of the legal system; in the United States, the ordinary act of taking a laptop

computer with an Internet browser installed on it overseas may con-
stitute exportation of a controlled munition (the encryption technol-
ogy in the browser).

Being a Publisher

You are a publisher, and just as a book publisher is concerned about the look of a book's cover as well as what is
inside, you need to be concerned about your site's appear-
ance.

In addition to considering the look of your site, you have to
think about some issues you may never have considered
before.

Who Owns the Material You Are Publishing?	You must consider whether you are publishing information that you do not own. Where did your database come from, and under what circumstances was its information collected? The data that you legitimately can collect, index, and store may not be yours to publish electronically (even if you have the right to publish it on paper).

Publishing a database can compromise copyrights that you
own. The law is still evolving in this area, but there are some
rulings that say that even public information can be copyrighted in a database form: in other words, even though each
item is public information, the database compendium is
copyrighted.

If you feel that your project may fall into these areas, consider
what precautions you need to take to avoid losing your copyright on your database when you publish it on line. (A legal
warning may be sufficient—consult an attorney for guidance.)

What Is the Nature of the Material You Are Publishing?	This is a very tricky area. The Internet is an international medium, and laws vary from country to country with regard to issues such as pornography, violence, and other hot topics. What might be a database of chemical formulas to you could be a bomb maker's guide to someone else. Personal information is another area that requires careful thought. The convenience of using the Web to publish the names and addresses of all students in a school may be out-weighed by the problems that such publication might cause.
Are You Delegating Your Publishing Power?	Databases that allow online access permit users to publish in-formation. If you are hosting a database of messages, what happens if a user pastes copyrighted material into a message? The greater your control over the data, the more liable you are for the actions of others. It is unclear whether maintaining a database (as opposed to hosting an online chat room) crosses the line to make you liable for any information posted in it, but it is likely that you do have greater liability in the case of the database. You may be able to reduce your liability by including a care-fully written warning on the page that users use to enter data. In this as in other cases, you must consult an attorney to know what your rights and responsibilities are.
Is It Worth It?	With these cautions and concerns, you might wonder if it is worth publishing your databases on a Web site. The answer is almost always a resounding Yes. The fact that you can get a very nasty paper cut by slitting open an envelope doesn't mean that you should leave your billets-doux unopened in the letterbox. But there is no excuse not to be aware of these issues—just as you must be aware of security on your site.

Rating the Web

Sometime in the 1990s, people were shocked to discover pornography on the Internet. It would be extremely cynical to suggest that this story garnered so much interest because it combined a simple concept (sex) with an intriguing and little understand one (the Internet). Somehow, the presence of sex made the Internet understandable to many people: it was a sewer of smut that poured out of every modem in the world.

Soon people were demanding controls on the Internet's content; the basic nature of the Internet (both the spirit of its developers and users and its actual implementation) makes such controls extraordinarily difficult to implement.

Managing the Internet's content can be done in two ways:

1. The receiver of Internet services (a user) can in some way limit what is received.

2. The provider of Internet content (a Web site designer) can identify what is posted using certain standards.

Screening software is available to help people implement the first type of management; it lets certain sites be blocked from access or it may act positively and allow access only to known sites. Some screening software also uses advanced techniques to try to evaluate the contents of a site automatically.

The World Wide Web Consortium's Platform for Internet Content Selection (PICS) has proposed a system of document labels that can be incorporated into the META tag of an HTML document or into HTTP headers; the labels are generated by a rating service, and they contain information about the document.

In an interesting way, this is somewhat similar to certain aspects of XML; both try to describe the content of a document.

If you are publishing innocuous data (at least from the pornographic point of view), you may think that you do not need to worry about ratings. However, you may need to rate your pages (or have them rated by a rating service) to show that they are suitable for children. Since the vast majority of information on the Web is not rated, screening software needs to know how to handle unrated pages; the most conservative approach is to block anything that is not explicitly marked as OK.

International Relations

Finally, consider treason. Information is often very dangerous. The amount of information on the Web is mind-boggling. You can learn how to make a bomb and how to make your own wedding dress; the text of the Koran is posted—as is the text of the Unabomber's manifesto, the Domesday book, and *Moby Dick*.

Since the Internet reaches almost every country in the world, your audience may consist of people who have very different views from those that you hold. The information that you provide may compromise people who receive it. From time immemorial, governments have tried to control information; in most cases it is a futile effort, but that has not stopped people from trying.

If you require people to register before accessing your site, that information may be interesting to many people: commercial competitors as well as others ranging from e-mail spam artists to investigators. Guard your guestbook or registration database carefully; do not inadvertently publish it on your Web site (you can do so if you do it deliberately).

Summary

These issues are age old, but they have gained new urgency with the development of the Internet. Because database-driven Web sites by their very nature tend to contain more information than traditional Web sites, and because they often allow people to browse through information resources that would otherwise be unavailable to them, they can easily run afoul of common practices and laws in some areas.

This in no way should discourage you; in fact, it should spur you on as you realize that you are in the vanguard of a new information age that the world has never before seen. The final section of this book looks at several database-driven Web sites: you can see how the tools and techniques discussed so far are brought together to produce very impressive results.

Doing It: Case Studies

VI

Publishing Data on the Web

The chapters in this part of the book detail five different database-driven Web sites. You can see how people have actually used the techniques outlined in this book to create Web sites that provide and share information, support e-commerce, automatically update a Web site, and even invent a new business. The people and organizations that have done this range from large to small—but most are relatively small. If they can do it, so can you.

The resources of the library at the Museum of Modern Art in New York are available to scholars and researchers by appointment. As is true of many private libraries and information resources, its primary purpose is to serve the needs of its organization; its secondary *purpose is to provide access to members of the public who may be working on projects unrelated to those of the institution itself.*

In this case, the library is located in mid-Manhattan, and that fact alone makes it relatively inaccessible to many people who would like to take advantage of its resources. In 1997, when the library purchased an automated cataloguing system, one of its objectives was to provide access over the Web to information that people around the world had heretofore been unable to use. Voyager software from Endeavor Information Systems is built around an Oracle database; the software is available in a number of versions, providing a variety of different interfaces.

The design and evolution of the MoMA library Web site provides a good case study in how you can integrate a database—and, in particular, an existing application built around a database—into your Web site.

DADABASE

The Museum of Modern Art is one of the most important collections of modern art in the world; it will soon occupy a large part of a block in midtown Manhattan. Its influence on the worlds of art and design has been enormous; its Web site provides information about the museum and its services as well as a gateway to its library catalog. Figure 17-1 shows the home page of the Museum of Modern Art with its traditional (for it) and distinctive typeface.

Some people come to grief when it comes to using distinctive typefaces on their Web pages. The problem is that you can specify a given font in HTML (or via an authoring tool like Microsoft Front Page or Home Page from FileMaker), and that font will be used—if available—for the text that you have selected. On your own computer (and possibly on all of the computers in your organization), that font will be available, and everything will look fine. On other computers, however, another font will be substituted.

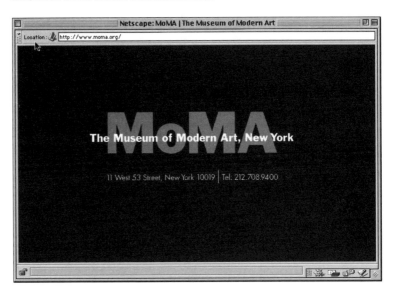

FIGURE 17-1. MoMA Home Page

Avoid this problem by creating a GIF graphic of the text you want in the font you desire. Insert the graphic—rather than formatted text—onto your Web page. GIF graphics are typically small, and this will usually not substantially increase download time for your Web page.

Once you have entered the site, you can go to the library catalog, which is shown in Figure 17-2. (The distinctive type for the title—DADABASE—is a graphic, not formatted text.)

This page presents a typical library catalog searching interface, but its layout and the design of its title and buttons reflect the style of other Museum of Modern Art pages and publications. This page is actually generated dynamically by Web Voyáge product (based on an Oracle database). The product is designed for customization and integration into a

Web site; this is a task that you may be asked to perform with a database product in your organization. Here are some of the issues involved.

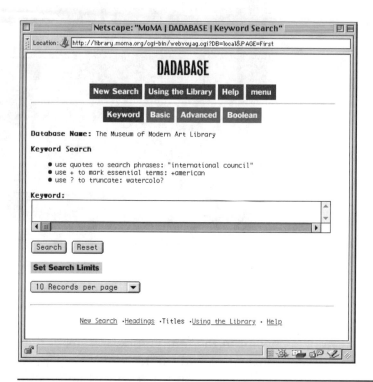

FIGURE 17-2. DADABASE Web Page

How to Get Started

There are many products that incorporate a database (such as Oracle, DB2, FileMaker Pro, or Microsoft Access) along with specially written tools and reports; these products may be developed for an individual organization, or they may be developed for a vertical market such as real estate sales, dentistry, education, or construction. Sometimes these products are brand new, but often they are old; some date from the mainframe era, and others date from the earliest days of personal computers. If you are presented with the task of placing such a product and its database on a Web site, you need to know what you are dealing with.

This chapter addresses the particular case of presenting information from an existing database or application. In this case, you do not have control over the database design and you may not have much control over the page designs. This section shows how you work in an environment with those constraints. For the case in which you do have control over the database and/or the page designs, you can follow the steps in the "How to Get Started" sections of the following chapters, which all address the situation where you have more control.

Character-Based Interfaces

The earliest interfaces to many of these products were used on dumb terminals rather than personal computers, and they had no graphics. Figure 17-3 shows one such interface.

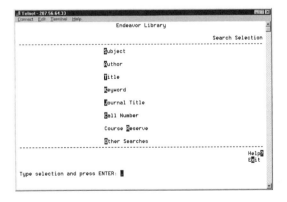

FIGURE 17-3. Character-Based Interface

You type the underlined letter of your choice, and the software does whatever you have requested. Often, all that consists of is to show you another character-based screen (such as that shown in Figure 17-4) on which you can enter more data.

You often have to go through several screens of this sort in order to get the program to do anything. As illustrated in these two figures, you choose what you want to do (Figure 17-3), and then you provide more details about that particular choice (Figure 17-4). Because this type of interface was originally designed to run on dumb terminals that have no memory or computing facilities, it relies on the software at the other end to keep track of where you are. That software has to build up your request in screen after screen: it is a classic example of stateful software (as opposed to HTTP, which is stateless, where every request has all of the information needed for the software to carry out the entire action).

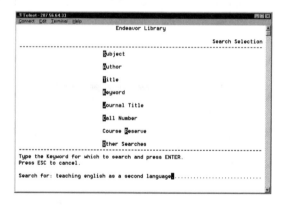

FIGURE 17-4. Second Data Entry Screen for Character-Based Interface

What It Means to You

If you are asked to integrate a product with this type of interface into a Web site, you should realize that you are probably dealing with old software and that somewhere the software is storing each terminal's state. In some cases, that may make it difficult to convert to a Web-based system, but that is not always the case. Here, the same product shown previously (Web Voyáge) has implemented a character-based interface that is totally separate from its Web-based interface.

Graphical User Interfaces

Graphical user interfaces are generally associated with smart terminals or personal computers. The terminal or personal computer can actually run a program and manage the interaction with the user for many cases. For example, in Figure 17-5, you see a screen that allows the user to select many of the choices shown in the character-based interface of Figure 17-3.

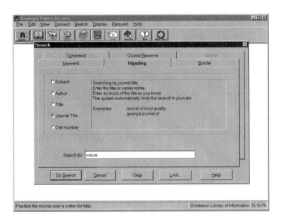

FIGURE 17-5. Graphical User Interface

This screen is part of a program that runs on a personal computer (or a smart terminal—the difference is not important in this case). The program may include the entire system—database, application, and reports as well as data entry—or it may handle just the data entry processing. In the latter case, it is called a client, and the program that handles everything else is called the server (as in client/server systems). Often, the client and server are on different machines (a server may run on a mainframe and interact with scores—or thousands—of clients on personal computers all over the world).

Unlike the case of a character-based interface, there need be no interaction with the computer at the other end of the network cable until all the data has been entered—even if it involves several screens' worth.

Thus, the terminal can display and process the data entry screens shown in Figure 17-5 and 17-6 without any communications; only when you click the Do Search button is any data sent to the server (or to that part of the program that is handling server operations).

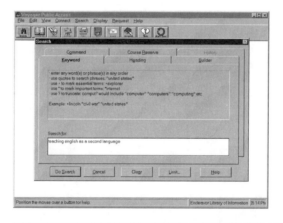

FIGURE 17-6. Second Data Entry Screen for Graphical User Interface

What This Means to You

A database application with this sort of interface may be easier to adapt to a Web site than a character-based one. You need to reimplement the graphical user interface using HTML forms; then you send the same stream of data when the user clicks the Do Search button as the terminal program would have done.

Fortunately, you often do not have to do any implementation—a vendor can do it for you fairly easily. This is the case here, as you will see in the next section.

Web Interfaces

More and more applications are coming with Web interfaces built into them. The use of standard communications (TCP/IP and HTTP) and of HTML makes it easier to develop and maintain such systems—both for vendors and for users. If you have such a system, you may be called upon to integrate it with your own Web site. Here is the basic scenario.

The Basic Interface

The product is typically shipped with a basic interface—Figure 17-7 shows the "out-of-the-box" interface to Web Voyáge.

FIGURE 17-7. Default Interface to Web Voyáge

These systems are usually installed either as a complete Web site or as a subsite within a larger site; in either case, the default home page shares the features shown in Figure 17-7:

* It identifies the site; by default it identifies the vendor of the product, not the owner of the information (you).

- Several options are provided; each is identified with a default icon.

- This is a static HTML page: it requires no database access. (For more on this topic, see "Some Notes on Performance" on page 451.)

Customizing the Basic Interface

The first step for most people is to customize the basic interface by adding their own logo and text. Figure 17-8 shows the Syracuse University Library's page: it is actually almost identical to the default page shown in Figure 17-7, but it clearly is Syracuse's page.

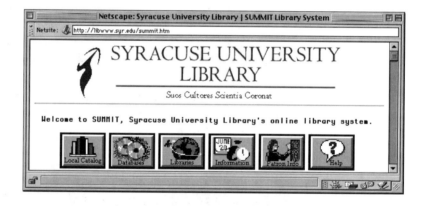

FIGURE 17-8. Partially Customized Interface

Integrating the Customized Interface

Figure 17-8 still uses the default icons and the navigational structure of the default page. There is nothing wrong with this, but it may not be what you want. If it is to be part of your site, you need to integrate it in a way that makes sense.

Integrating with the Main Site   On the Web site of the Museum of Modern Art, the page shown in Figure 17-8 is quite different; it performs the same functions, but it looks like the rest of the MoMA site.

FIGURE 17-9. Museum of Modern Art Library Interface

What is important to note here is that the site is identified (further identification is at the bottom of page, out of view in the figure), it provides links to other parts of the site, and it is a static page.

Practicing, Experimenting, and Testing Although the page shown in Figure 17-9 is static, the link to the DADABASE is a link to a dynamic page. The default Web Voyáge page is shown in Figure 17-10.

Like the first default page, it, too, identifies the software more prominently than the owner of the site. A little experimentation and testing can help you to evolve the page. After just such a process, the MoMA DADABASE page evolved into Figure 17-2.

If you compare the two pages, you will see that they are actually very similar. Some changes to graphics, a reorganization of buttons, and the removal of the pencil icon are apparently superficial—but they make the difference between a jerky transition between apparently unrelated pages and an integrated Web site.

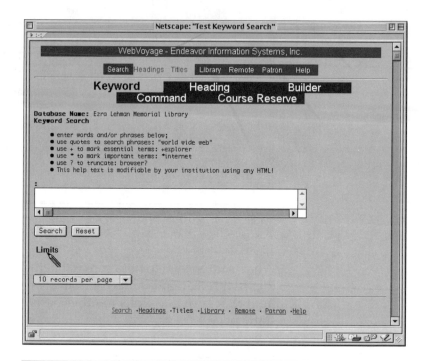

FIGURE 17-10. Default Web Voyáge Search Page

One of the hallmarks of a successful project is the involvement of different people with different ideas in a collaborative manner. In addition to soliciting feedback from a variety of people both within and without the Museum of Modern Art, the staff at the library held a contest for all museum employees to choose a name for the database.

Dealing with Vendors

Some vendors are still not comfortable with this paradigm: they want to control everything. If your vendor tells you that you cannot customize your own Web pages or that only they can do it for you, consider whether you have the best product available. Remember, it is your data and your Web site: your name should be on it and it should look like you want it to;

and if you need a stronger argument, remember that you are the customer—and it is your money.

The example shown here is a product that encourages customer experimentation and customization.

Summary

This chapter has focused on the basics of publishing information on the Web. In the next chapter, that process is expanded into sharing data—a two-way street.

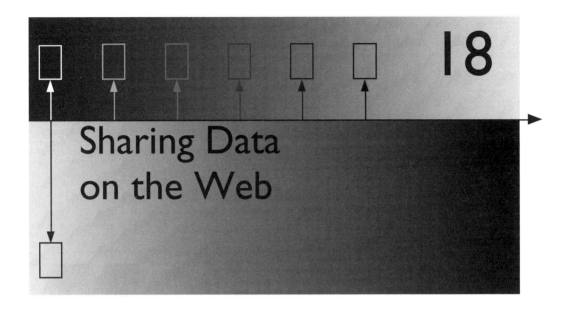

18

Sharing Data on the Web

There are many ways to share information on the Web: you can use Usenet newsgroups, which emulate bulletin boards; you can use mailing lists in which a message to the list is manually or automatically sent on to all subscribers; or you can use a database-driven Web page.

The problem with newsgroups is that it can become hard to follow a thread—a given conversation; each message is part of a single thread, and sometimes they are posted to the wrong thread or apply to several threads. You also need software to read newsgroups (although such support is built into most modern browsers). More seriously, not all Internet service providers carry all newsgroups—and many are behind firewalls of individual organizations.

Mailing lists are simpler, since they are based just on e-mail. The biggest disadvantage of mailing lists is that you get messages when someone sends them—not when you feel like looking at them.

A database is an ideal tool for managing a discussion group. That discussion can be of any nature: it might be messages sent back and forth between individuals (messages as simple as to-do notes or telephone messages), or it might be messages that form the basis of an extended electronic conversation over time. In yet other cases—such as the example shown here—the discussion is a classic bulletin board topic of trying to find homes for unwanted goods that would otherwise be thrown out.

Upper Valley Materials Exchange

UVME—the Upper Valley Materials Exchange (in the Upper Connecticut Valley of New Hampshire)—has a simple objective:

> [It] links businesses and community members who have surplus furniture, supplies, materials, equipment, etc. with schools (and other non-profits) in the Upper Valley that have a use for them. By giving away what they would normally throw away, businesses and individuals can save disposal costs while reducing their impact on the environment and benefit Upper Valley Schools (and other non-profit organizations) at the same time!

This is a typical example of the sort of thing that can be done well with the Internet: it requires some initial setup, but after that, it chugs along under its own steam. People post listings of goods they will donate; people who can use the goods contact the listers directly. No money changes hands, and the Exchange stresses that all logistics are up to the parties involved.

UVME Home
Page

Figure 18-1 shows the UVME home page.

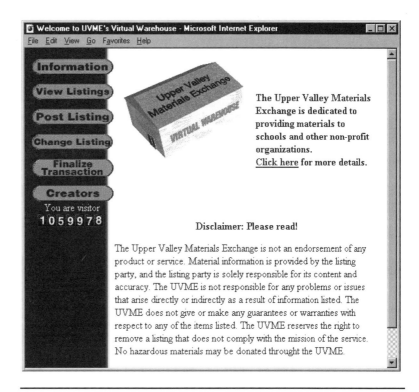

FIGURE 18-1. UVME Home Page

It is a static home page; some of the links—Information and Creators—go to static, text-based pages. The others go to a FileMaker Pro database that uses FileMaker Web Companion to support database-driven Web pages.

Retrieval Page

If you click on the View Listings button, the page shown in Figure 18-2 is displayed. This type of page is very important for sites that share data: unless you want to see all messages (or all messages within a certain time period) you need to select the messages based on certain criteria—in this case categories.

As a designer of a site like this, you need to decide whether the categories will be static or dynamic; the advantage of using a fixed set of categories is that it forces people to file their listings appropriately. If you let people add categories, you often wind up with many overlapping categories; in addition, people may have to check several categories to find the information that they want.

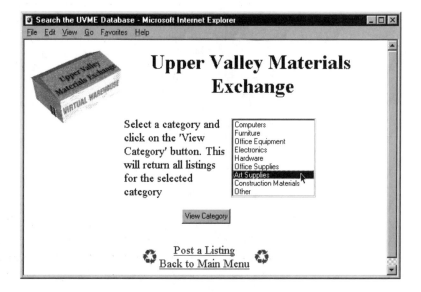

FIGURE 18-2. UVME Categories

Most databases and application servers let you construct scrolling lists and pop-up menus either statically or dynamically based on database contents.

Summary Display	Figure 18-3 shows the results of a query (for the category art supplies).

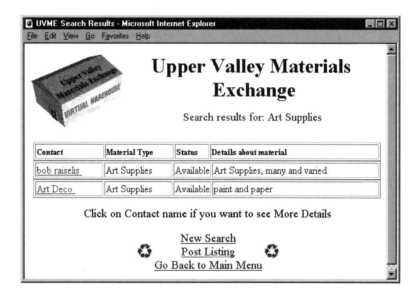

FIGURE 18-3. UVME Search Results Page

This, too, is a typical type of display for a Web site like this: it contains summary information about the data; you can click on an icon or field (the contact, in this case) to see a full record display—such as that shown in Figure 18-4.

This page has a design pitfall waiting for you. It is supposed to be a summary, and its usefulness is in displaying as many records as possible in the smallest amount of space. As you go through the database fields, you must be very hard-nosed about which fields belong on the summary. Before you know it, you may have created a summary with every database field.

Full Record Display

Figure 18-4 shows the display of a full record, with most of the database fields shown. Note that this is a display of data—it does not allow data entry.

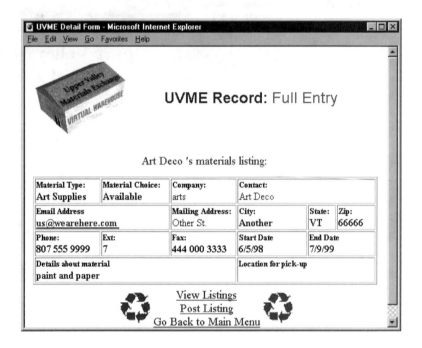

FIGURE 18-4. UVME Full Record Page

Data Entry

If you want to enter data, you use the screen shown in Figure 18-5. If you compare the data entry form in Figure 18-5 with the full record display in Figure 18-4, you will note that some fields (such as Password) are not shown even in the full record display: they are displayed (and relevant) only for data entry.

This page may contain instructions and indications as to which fields are required. It may also contain a legal disclaimer that allows you to republish the information. (Such a disclaimer belongs here rather than on the home page; it needs to be visible at the moment when someone actually submits the data.)

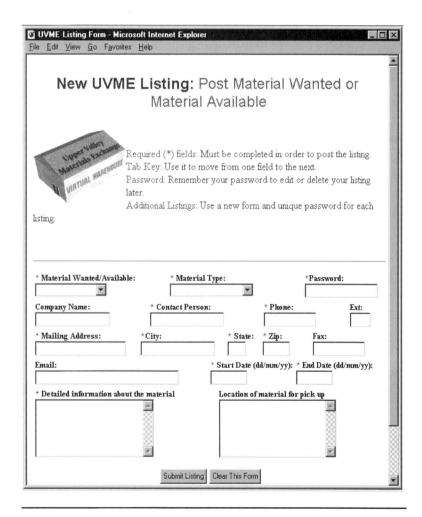

FIGURE 18-5. UVME Data Entry Page

Confirmation Page	After someone has entered data, it is usual to display a confirmation page; it may be a static page with a simple "Thank you" on it, or it may contain the entered data (or a summary of the data or a link to the fill record display for that data).
	This page should be designed to display as quickly as possible: do not include a query on it that is going to tie up the database for some time. The reason for the need for speed here is that if people do not see a confirmation page quickly, they may take inappropriate steps: such as clicking the Back button in their browser and resubmitting the form.

How to Get Started

When you put up a site that is designed to share data, the layout of your database and pages reflects the data involved as well as the people who will be using the site—is it totally public, totally private, public for viewing and limited in who can post to it, or some combination? Still, the basic flow of control is much the same in all such sites. This section describes the basic pages and database design that you will probably use.

Designing the Pages	The six pages shown earlier in this section are usually repeated for each site on which data is shared. Table 18-1 lists the standard pages along with a description of each one.

Page	Description
Home page	Instructions for the site. Static. Links to data entry and retrieval.
Retrieval page	Selection for categories or other criteria of messages to be retrieved. Static. Links to a dynamic Web page via a form with a Submit button. (Note: If categories are dynamic, this is a dynamic page, and it retrieves the categories from the database rather than having them hard-coded in static HTML.)
Summary display page	Several records in summary. If necessary, has links to next and prior sets of records. Dynamic. Links to individual full record pages.
Full record display page	Dynamic. May link to home, retrieval home, or data entry.
Data entry page	Static. Usually a form with a Submit button.
Confirmation page	Static or dynamic. Confirms data entry; may display entered data—or may have a link to full record display for entered data.

TABLE 18-1. Pages for Sharing Data on the Web

Designing the Database	Although the layout of a database for a site like this is fairly standard, there are a number of pitfalls to watch out for. Here are some of them:

- You do not have control over the content of the data that is published to the site, unless you institute some kind of editorial function as described in "Editorial Review" on page 440. For that reason, you should periodically review the site to make certain that no one has posted inappropriate material. (You may want to use a non-Web interface to the database for this, quickly scanning records using whatever tools are available.)

- Since the people who post to the database are responsible for categorizing information, be prepared to recategorize information that is placed in the wrong area.

- Try to keep messages and information short. In the UVME example shown here, it must be a constant struggle to prevent people from posting multiple materials in a single record; nevertheless, a donated chair and a donated computer must be placed in separate entries in order for the retrieval system to work.

The layout of a database for a site like this is shown in Table 18-2. You may not use all of these fields—or you may use other ones; consider them suggestions and use them to jog your imagination.

Field	Description
Title	Each item in the database should be named. You may generate these names automatically (either for the database or just for the Web site's display). Titles can help you create threads of messages. If you add a Reply button to a data display screen, you can use Javascript to bring the title of the retrieved data forward automatically and insert it in the appropriate field of the new item. (For more details, see "Copying Data" on page 289.)
Summary	You may want a summary of each data element. This is particularly valuable if the data elements can be lengthy or if they can consist of graphics or other non-textual information without any textual equivalent. This field (if it is used) should be severely limited in length.
Information (text)	This is the basic information to be shared.

TABLE 18-2. Fields for a Message Database

Field	Description
Information (image)	You may add an image field to most modern databases; it may be used to augment the textual information or to replace it.
Information (blob)	Similarly, you can use a generalized field to store movies, animations, and other dynamic data.
Category	This is the single category in which the data is primarily stored.
Keywords	This field lets users (or an editor) specify a number of keywords to assist in searching. Note that keeping up keywords fields can be time consuming. With the speed of modern computers, it is almost always faster just to search the text of items for wanted words rather than to maintain a separate keyword field.
Author ID	You usually need to keep track of the author of each item. This may be a collection of fields (including address, e-mail, and so forth), or it may be an ID that is expanded in a related file to the full information about an individual.
Posting time stamp	You should keep track of when each item is posted. This time stamp should be calculated automatically by the computer on which the database resides (not inserted into a data entry form by a browser); use the database's computer as the arbiter of time.
Revisor ID	If items are revised or edited, you may want to keep track of who did it.
Last revision time stamp	In some high-security applications, you want to keep track of each revision; in most cases, however, it is sufficient to keep track of the date and time of initial entry and then of the date and time of the latest revision (if any).
Display status	This field allows you to mark an item as being ready to display; a database query that generates a summary display should include only those items with a satisfactory display status. (This allows for editing and approval.)

TABLE 18-2. Fields for a Message Database (Continued)

Field	Description
Content status	You may need a displayable field that describes some status of the data; in the UVME example, the status lets you know if the item is available or not.
Starting time stamp	You can use this time stamp to control a range of dates and times during which the item is displayed. For databases containing calendars and schedules, this allows you to enter data in advance and specify its period of display without having to update the database at specific times.
Ending time stamp	Working with the starting time stamp, this field lets you terminate listings.

TABLE 18-2. Fields for a Message Database (Continued)

Summary

With a two-way interchange such as this, it is only a matter of time before you will start to think about commercial interchanges: e-commerce. The next chapter explores that area.

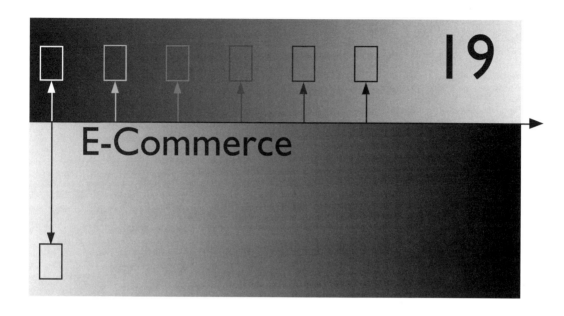

19

E-Commerce

One of the areas attracting the most interest today is e-commerce—
shopping on the Web. E-commerce refers to stores that may sell tangible goods or electronic information; it also includes Web sites that
are like other sites but that charge for admission.

This chapter provides a walk through the Apple Store; it then provides a guide to the pages and databases necessary for you to set up
your own e-commerce site.

The Apple Store

The Apple Store is powered by WebObjects (an Apple Product). It opened for business on November 30, 1997 and within 30 days had done $12 million worth of business. Although this might sound impressive, it pales next to the fact that by May of 1998 it did $1.9 million in a single day.

One of the greatest attractions of online stores is the fact that variations in sales volumes like this can be accommodated relatively easily. Additional computer power may be required, but accommodating more or fewer customers requires little in the way of new facilities or staff—expensive resources, and those with particularly long lead times in terms of construction and training.

In the case of Apple, the goods that are sold in the store are built to order: many of them are assembled only in response to orders. Transforming the company's production facilities to this model was no mean feat, but its savings in stockpiles of inventory that might or might not sell proved significant.

Online stores are like many other Web sites, but certain considerations are of particular importance:

- At some point, security must be provided for transmission of payment information. (For more details, see "Security" on page 355.)

- They must work. This may seem flippant, but there is a big difference between following a link to a nonexistent page on someone's personal Web site and discovering that your shopping cart with 14 items in it has disappeared into an electronic miasma.

- If they sell tangible objects (rather than software or digital books), they must be successfully integrated into standard supply and deliver procedures: you must not sell items that you cannot deliver.

Product Page

The Apple Store starts with a home page that presents the specials of the day. Users then proceed to a page for the type of product in which they are interested. Figure 19-1 shows the product page for Apple servers.

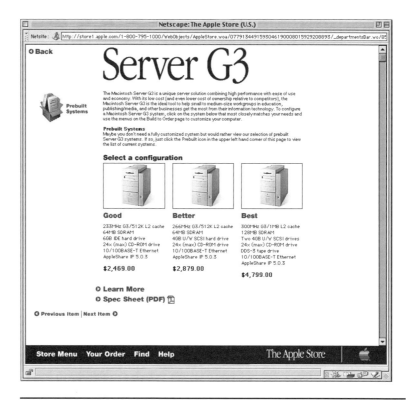

FIGURE 19-1. Apple Store Product Page

Product pages have descriptions of products and often have illustrations, videos, or other graphics. As is the case here ("Learn More" and "Spec Sheet"), additional information on other pages and in other formats is available. These pages are much like print advertisements, and they serve the same purpose. Unlike advertisements, however, they may contain dynamic up-to-the-minute information drawn from a database; such information as price (for volatile items such as commodities) or number of items on hand is commonly displayed on this page.

The Shopping Cart

In an online store, each customer has a shopping cart into which purchases can be put. At each moment, you can check to see what is in your shopping cart, as in Figure 19-2.

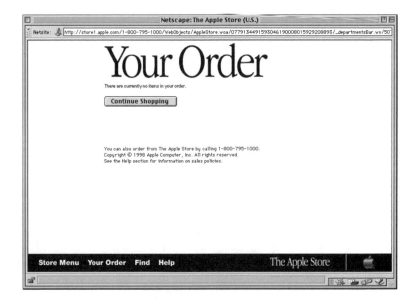

FIGURE 19-2. Shopping Cart at the Apple Store

Implementing a Shopping Cart

In order to maintain the shopping cart, you need to maintain state information—something about who the customer is and what is in the cart. (See "Transaction Processing" on page 227 for more information.) The two standard methods of creating transactions are using cookies on the user's computer and storing intermediate information in the database or elsewhere on the server.

Your choice of which method (or both) to use should be determined by the type of store that you are creating and the kind of shopping that will be done. A store—like the Apple Store—in which people buy single items at a time has needs much different from those of an online bookstore or grocer, where people may have shopping carts with scores of items that need to be stored safely until checkout.

In most cases, it is more likely that the user's computer, Internet connection, or browser will fail than it is that your Web server will fail. That is an argument for preserving the shopping cart in a temporary file or database on your server. However, to do so, you need to store information about the user with that information. One way to do this is to require a user login—but that makes "window shopping" harder for the casual shopper.

Another way is to generate a unique number for each shopper automatically and to store that in a cookie on the user's machine. If someone logs on to your store, you look for a cookie, and if you find one that is no more than 5 minutes old, you match that ID to an in-process shopping cart on your server. Whatever you do, do not automatically carry forward names or credit card information; when someone goes to checkout, they can review the contents of their cart to see if they are familiar. At that time, they should enter identification and credit card information.

Order Options

Once customers have chosen an item to buy, they may choose a variety of options for that item. This is dependent on the items that you sell: if they are books or chairs or pineapples, the options are few and probably nonexistent. Computers and cars usually have many options. However, do not assume that only expensive items have options: shirts have sizes and colors, and many garden statues come in only one style (pecu-liar).

Specifying the Options

If you do let users select options for their purchases, you cre-ate a page such as that shown in Figures 19-3 and 19-4.

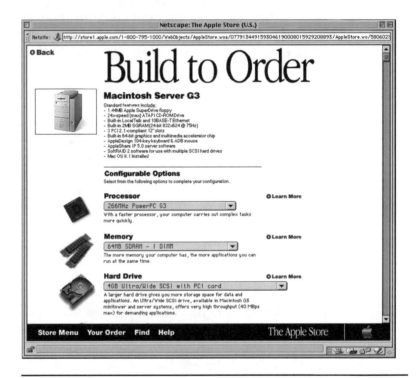

FIGURE 19-3. Order Options Page (Top)

Each option provides the same sort of information as the product page did: price, an image, and a button to click for more information. In some cases (and the Apple Store is a good example of this), this page is built dynamically based on the product selected. Since you have a database, take advan-tage of it and include all information that you have in your shopping cart to build an appropriate options page.

You know, for example, if the customer has ordered a computer monitor. You know, too, if the customer has ordered more than one other computer (in such a case, a wider variety of networking options might be provided).

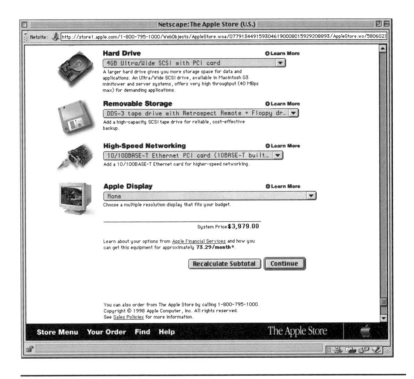

FIGURE 19-4. Order Options Page (Bottom)

Just as on the product page, a price is clearly displayed at the bottom. When the user is satisfied with a configuration, the Continue button goes to the order confirmation page (Figure 19-5).

Confirming the Order

This page is required only if you allow options; it can be dispensed with if the options are trivial and do not affect the price (but it is best to catch problems—including those of size and color—early).

Although it is best to use a dynamically created order options page to present only options that are feasible, the order confirmation page is your opportunity to check for items that are in stock, combinations of options that are illegal, and so forth. Remember that although it takes only a mouse click to move from one page to another, going back four or five pages is not most people's idea of fun.

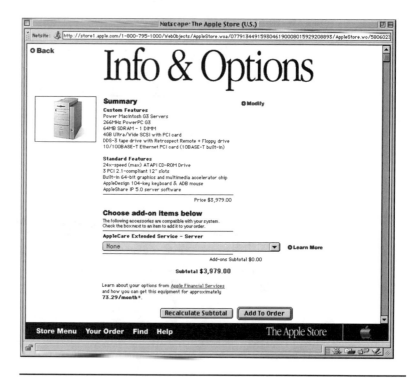

FIGURE 19-5. Order Confirmation Page

The Shopping Cart in Action

At any time, the user can click on a shopping cart icon (here, the words "Your Order" in the banner at the bottom of the page) to review the contents of the shopping cart as shown in Figure 19-6. Obviously, this page must be constructed dynamically. Note that there is a link (the small arrow) next to the item ordered; users may want to go back to review exactly what it is that they have ordered.

This page typically allows only one change—that is to the quantity of an item ordered. (Changing the quantity to zero cancels that item.) Remember that changing the quantity of an item may cause someone to order more than you have: display that message as soon as possible.

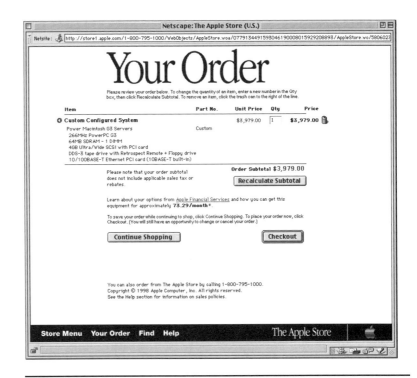

FIGURE 19-6. Shopping Cart Contents

Final Processing

The final processing for an order includes shipping information, payment instructions, and legal information that needs to be provided (warranties, customs declarations, and so forth). Figures 19-7 and 19-8 show the final processing screen from the Apple Store.

FIGURE 19-7. Final Processing (Top)

Although you should have checked for stock availability along the way, this is your last chance to do so (and to commit the transaction). Depending on your resources, you may check the user's credit information on line or you may have to do that later; if you do it later, you should send an e-mail message confirming the approved transaction. (For more information, see "E-Commerce and Secure Servers" on page 89.)

Note in Figure 19-8 that this is the first time that customers have to give their name at the Apple Store. You do not have to log on to the store, so you can browse to your heart's content. The choice of exactly what moment to ask for a user's identity is up to you: it is almost totally a marketing concern. In general, asking users to identify themselves causes a certain number to turn away—the Web-based equivalent of "Just looking" to the importunate sales clerk.

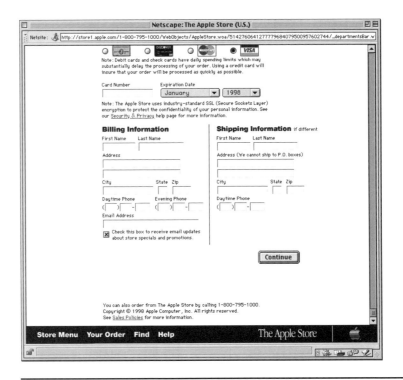

FIGURE 19-8. Final Processing (Bottom)

These are the basic pages that you find in all e-commerce; your pages will reflect your operation and the products that you sell.

How to Get Started

The basic groundwork for setting up a Web-based store is mostly about marketing, sales, and distribution. Visit other Web-based stores and see what you like and do not like about them. Then design your versions of the basic pages and implement your databases.

Designing the Pages

There are four basic types of pages used in e-commerce on the Web. The first two may or may not be dynamic, but the last two always must be.

Page	Description
Product page	Like an advertisement, but if it is dynamically generated it may include current prices (for commodities and other volatile products) as well as on-hand quantities, estimated delivery times, etc. Users can either choose an item to add directly to their shopping cart or customize it with an order options page.
Order options page	This page lets users specify options such as style, color, size, or flavor. Depending on the product, it may be a static or dynamic page. (In some cases—clothing, for instance—the same order options page can be used for many products that share the same options such as size and color.)

TABLE 19-1. Pages for an E-Commerce Database

Page	Description
Shopping cart page	Always dynamically generated, this page reflects all of the current shopper's transactions. Before checkout, it is temporarily stored as "in process" work—either in a cookie, in a database, or in some combination of both.
Final processing page	This page allows the user to complete the transaction. Details about shipping and payment are included here. On completion, the shopping cart is destroyed and converted to an invoice and packing list. In-stock databases are updated, as are accounts. If you use cookies to help you recover incomplete shopping carts (as in the case of communications failure), be certain that you do not recover checked-out shopping carts.

TABLE 19-1. Pages for an E-Commerce Database (Continued)

Designing the Database

It is unlikely that you can develop a Web-based store with a single database table. Table 19-2 lists the tables that you typically use.

Table	Description
Customers	Each record contains name and address details; account information, credit limits, and other such information; a CustomerID uniquely identifies each one.
Products	Each record contains information about a product; a ProductID uniquely identifies each one; this is information that generally does not change. (Note: On-hand information is usually not stored here; prices may or may not be.)
Product status	Each record has a ProductID that matches a record in the Products table. This is the table with current price, on-hand and on-order quantities, and any other information that changes frequently.

TABLE 19-2. Tables for an E-Commerce Database

Table	Description
Shopping carts	Each record contains a CartID, CustomerID, a ProductID, a quantity, and other information needed to support the shopping cart pages. A single shopping cart is retrieved by selecting all records with a given CartID that you generate internally and uniquely. (You cannot use CustomerID, because two people from the same company may be shopping at the same time.)
Order details	Each record here is similar to (or identical to) a shopping cart record, except that CartIDs are transformed to OrderIDs to identify the contents of each order uniquely.
Orders	For each order, a single record in the Order details table with the OrderID uniquely identifying it is generated. This contains information about the order that does not need to be repeated for each item—shipping details, purchase order, etc.

TABLE 19-2. Tables for an E-Commerce Database (Continued)

There are many variations on this design, but most implementations use some combination of these tables. If you are integrating a Web-based store with existing operations, the customers, products, orders, and order details tables may already exist: you may use these tables or you may use copies of them dedicated only to online shopping.

The only difference between databases supporting online stores and those supporting other retail operations is that online stores need to support the in-process shopping cart, correctly keeping it around when needed and correctly emptying and unloading it if the customer decides to leave without checking out.

Summary

E-commerce takes several forms:

- It may consist of sites like all of the others in this section that charge for admission; those sites may be informational, they may be fora in which to share information, or they may be totally database-driven Web sites.

- E-commerce can consist of sites that allow people to buy and receive information over the Web; such sites sell software, digital books, and other electronic information that can be downloaded and sent to the consumer without the need for any special transfer to occur.

- An online store can sell products that are then sent to purchasers using conventional carriers. In the last few years, such stores have proliferated. This chapter has described one of the most successful ones: the Apple Store.

Totally Database-Driven Web Sites

20

This chapter shows you how to build and maintain a Web site that is created with databases. For the most part, it does not appear that a database is involved: the site simply works the way users expect it to.

An actual site, belonging to RNN—The Regional News Network, is examined. You will see the site from the points of view of its two sets of users: the reporters and editors who maintain the site using Web pages and a database, as well as the viewers and Web surfers who see the results of the work of the reporters and editors.

Finally, there is a section on how you might design a database for your own Web site as well as tips on performance issues that relate to database-driven Web sites such as this one.

RNN-TV

RNN—The Regional News Network. RNN serves the Hudson Valley of New York, much of New Jersey, the northern suburbs of New York City (Westchester and Rockland counties), and parts of New York City and Long Island. It is an independent station, and it focuses to a large extent on local news. Its Web site provides continuing information about that news; in addition, it provides a live WebCast of the show, gives background information on the station and its staff, and has links to Web sites that are mentioned on the newscasts. The site is also used to conduct viewer surveys on topics of interest to the community.

In many ways, the site is similar to those of other television stations (as well as many other dynamically produced sites for all sorts of organizations). What is important to note is that the RNN site works the same way the CBS and MSNBC sites do, yet the resources available to RNN are a small fraction of those available to CBS and MSNBC. Up-to-the-minute updates on Web pages are feasible for any site.

RNN Home

Figure 20-1 shows the RNN home page. This page is created dynamically (it uses Tango; the databases used on the site are both Microsoft Access and FileMaker Pro).

Parts of the page are static—the titles and the links at the left and the bottom. Just about everything else is dynamic and is retrieved from a database. Individual reporters enter their stories; the editor reviews and prioritizes them, determining how they will be ordered on the site; finally, the editor releases them.

This is a common process for building a dynamic Web site, but it has some characteristics that may not be duplicated in other cases (see "How to Get Started" on page 446 for some alternatives).

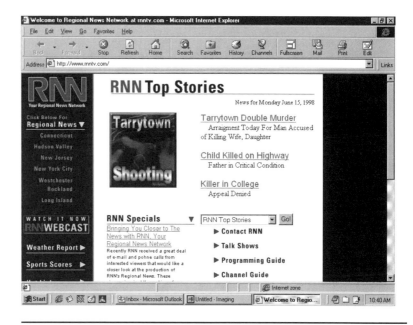

FIGURE 20-1. RNN Home Page

How a Story Gets On to the Site

The process of placing a story on the home page starts with reporters entering the story in the screen shown in Figure 20-2. You can see how the database fields in the figure map to elements of the home page.

Each story is identified with a single region (or the home page for the entire viewing area). The teaser is the brief summary of the story (such as "Arraignment Today for Man Accused of Killing Wife, Daughter"). Note that stories contain only text, but they may be associated with images. Images are stored separately in the database, and they are entered using the screen shown in Figure 20-3.

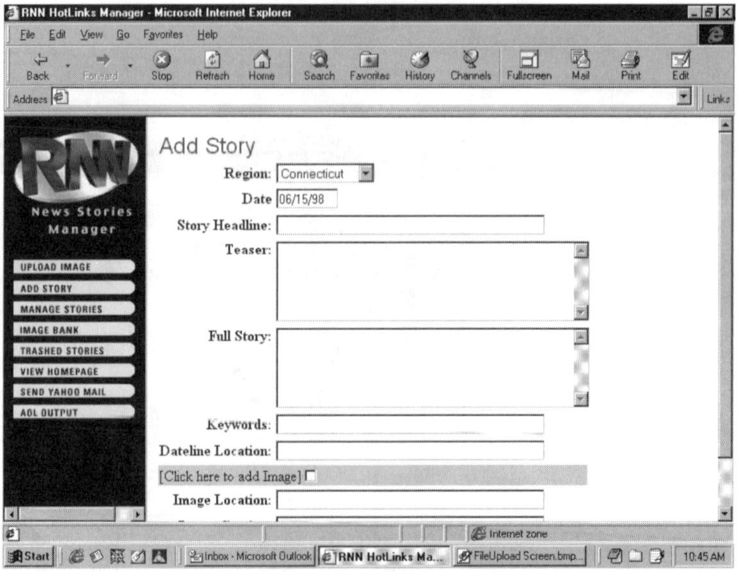

FIGURE 20-2. Add Story

FIGURE 20-3. Image Bank

Remember that all of these entry screens are used to update a database: no one is writing HTML.

Figure 20-4 shows the final component of the data entry process: a screen that allows reporters to upload files to a specific URL on the site. This allows a story—which contains only text—to reference images (uploaded via the Image Bank) as well as files that might contain additional textual information, movies, or other nontextual material.

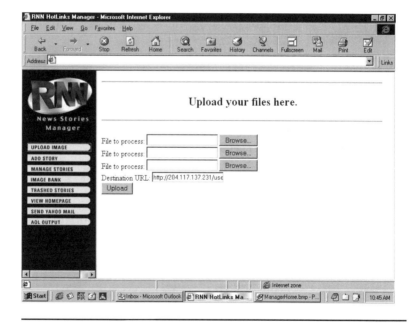

FIGURE 20-4. Uploading Files

If you design a database-driven Web site, you, too, will probably need these basic screens:

• Primary data entry (stories)

- Secondary data entry (images that can be linked to one or more stories)

- Nondatabase upload for material that is to be placed on the site but that is not located inside the database

---

Note that this site uses HTML forms for data input; nothing prevents you from using another input format (such as the database's own data entry screens).

Editorial Review

Stories, images, and files are entered as they are created by reporters. The editor chooses the stories for the newscast and the home page using the screens introduced by the one shown in Figure 20-5.

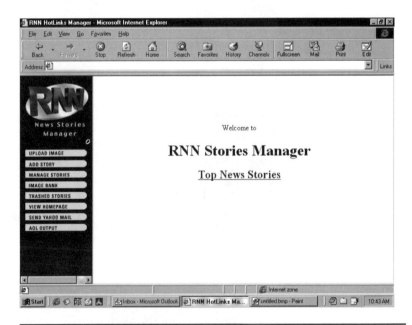

FIGURE 20-5. Stories Manager

The screens that the reporters use are available only over the station's local area network: that security is easily implemented (it is different for each application server and database, so you will need to consult your documentation to see how to set up that security).

The RNN Stories Manager, however, is another situation: its security needs to be restricted to specific individuals who have the authorization to create the pages of the site.

Once authorization is granted, the editor sees the stories that have been entered, as shown in Figure 20-6.

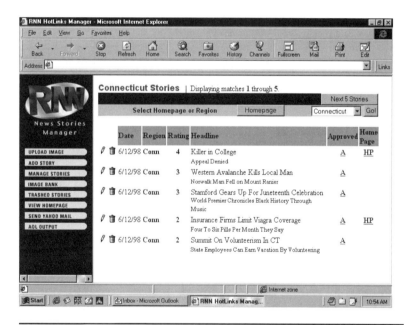

FIGURE 20-6. Stories Manager Detail

By clicking on the pencil icon, the editor can edit a story; the trash can icon lets stories be moved to the trash (Figure 20-7)—but they can still be restored by using the screen shown in Figure 20-6.

FIGURE 20-7. Trash

In addition to editing and approving (or trashing) stories, the editor rates them; when the pages are generated dynamically, the highest rated stories are shown first. As an incentive to reporters to include images with their stories, a story with an image automatically gets the highest rating.

Note that the process described here is familiar to anyone who has worked on a newspaper at any time in history. This uses the latest Internet and database technology, but it is nothing new. No new concepts have been introduced. This makes it easy to explain the system to people who may not be particularly comfortable with technology, and it is almost always a hallmark of a system that is quickly adopted by its users.

Enhancing the Site

Once the infrastructure shown here is in place, it is easy to implement other features on the Web site. At RNN, there are two such public areas, each of which provides a unique benefit to viewers and visitors to the Web site.

HotLinks

As part of its regular broadcasts, RNN covers sites of interest on the Web. This process is formalized on the Web site. A link on the home page goes to a section of URLs. Figure 20-8 shows how reporters enter URLs and descriptions to the HotLinks section.

As with everything else, these are stored in a database. You, too, may want to store URLs in a database together with annotations such as those shown in Figure 20-8. On some sites, this type of data entry screen is available to the public (or at least to all of your users on an intranet). You can quickly develop a very useful set of links for your organization in this way. (You might also want to consider adding an editorial step to review them before they are posted.)

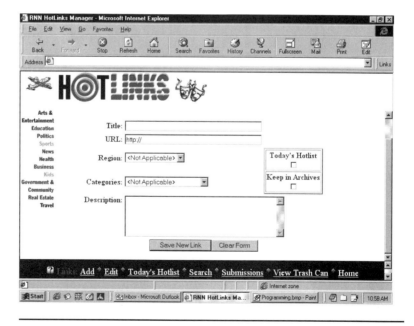

FIGURE 20-8. HotLinks

Voting Booth

Another feature implemented on this site is a voting booth. This serves the dual purposes of providing more interaction of users with the station's site and gathering an unscientific sample of opinion. Figure 20-9 shows the public side of the voting booth.

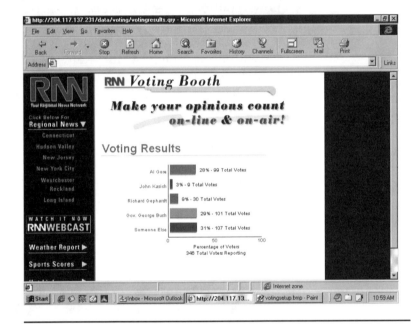

FIGURE 20-9. Voting Results

Setting up the voting booth is no different than setting up anything else on the site: a screen (Figure 20-10) is used to update the database, and then the dynamically produced page shown in Figure 20-9 is automatically generated.

Program Database

It gets easier and easier to add new features to a database and the site. For example, Figure 20-11 shows the internal view of the database containing the programming schedule; it is easy to create a dynamic Web page with this data, too.

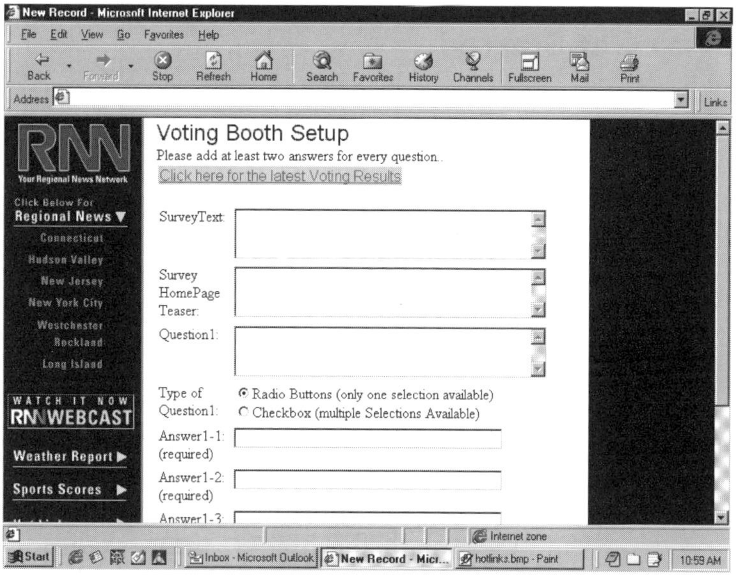

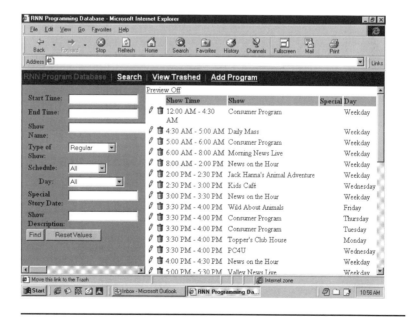

FIGURE 20-10. Voting Setup

FIGURE 20-11. Program Database

How to Get Started

As before, you need to design your Web pages and the database that supports them. In the cases of information sharing and e-commerce, you may give primacy to the database; in this case, the page layout is often the primary design concern. In all cases, though, you need to do both at the same time, modifying pages and database designs as you go.

Designing the Pages

The simplest way to get started is to lay out the page with paper and pencil (and a good eraser). Decide what the characteristics of the items are: are they to be the most recent items, those with the highest priority, those that match predetermined (or ad hoc) keywords, or all items in alphabetical order? Deciding this requires no knowledge of databases or the Web: it requires a knowledge of the information on the site. As soon as you have decided what these characteristics are, you will have made a start at designing the database fields.

Next, look at the information that you want to display: how can you categorize its content? Does each item have an author's name? What about a URL for further reference? Are multiple URLs allowed? What about images? Is it the case (as with RNN) that each item has a title and a summary—the teaser of news stories? As soon as you have figured out what your information is like, you will have more fields for the database.

Finally, go back and look at each field to determine what restrictions you should place on it. Are titles to be limited to 50 characters? Is a priority required—or is a default priority to be assigned if none is entered?

With these ideas in your mind, it should be easy to get started; you can also start from the database layout described in the next section.

Designing the Database

Each type of database-driven Web page will have a different database layout or schema depending on its information. However, the layout described in Table 20-1 handles many of the variables needed to display a Web page with a number of items—each of which may have a title, an author, a reference URL, and a whole host of descriptive information used to help generate the page. This database layout could drive a dynamic page like the news page shown throughout this chapter, or it could be used to generate a corporate newsletter, a Web site for a far-flung advocacy organization—or your site.

Samples of HTML are provided indicating how the variables from the database could be displayed. These are only samples and are designed to get you thinking. Each sample consists of two versions: the first is for Microsoft Access, and the second is for FileMaker Pro.

Remember that these references to database fields must be placed within [FMP-RECORD] and [/FMP-RECORD] tags for FileMaker Pro and within <%BeginDetail%> and <%EndDetail%> tags for Microsoft Access. (These tags bracket all of the references to variables rather than being repeated for each variable.)

The variables at the beginning of the table are those that will be shown on Web pages; those later on are used to help carry out the queries that will retrieve the information for the Web page. Your query will typically implement issues such as security: a WHERE clause will a reference to the security levels to include or exclude.

Field	Description

Title	Heading for the item. This will often be displayed using a header element or in boldface—as in
	
	`<B> <%title%> </B>`
	
	`<B>[FMP-FIELD: title]</B>`

Content	The information. This is normally displayed in a simple paragraph element:
	
	`<P> <%content%> </P>`
	
	`<P>[FMP-FIELD: content]</P>`

URL	If a URL is associated with the item, you often want to display it as a link. You will need to repeat the field: in the first case, it serves as the destination for the HREF attribute (this is the actual link); in the second case, the text of the URL is displayed. The URL will appear only once on the Web page that is generated.
	
	`<A HREF="<%URL%>"> <%URL%> </A>`
	
	`<A HREF="[FMP-FIELD: URL]">[FMP-FIELD: URL] </A>`
	
	This might also be a case in which you want to bracket the code with if statements—if the URL is an optional field in the database. You might also want to add text such as "For further information see." Here is that full-blown example
	
	`<%if>`
	`For further information see`
	`<A HREF="<%URL%>"> <%URL%> </A>`
	`<%endif%>`
	
	`[FMP-IF: URL .neq.]`
	`For further information see`
	`<A HREF="[FMP-FIELD: URL]">[FMP-FIELD: URL] </A>`
	`[/FMP-IF]`

TABLE 20-1. Fields for a Web Page Database

Field	Description

URL name	Instead of displaying the URL for a link, you can create an anchor for the URL and display a name for the link (this is the difference between displaying http://www.ibm.com and IBM Corporation); the underlying link is the same. If you want to do this, add a field to the database for the URL name.
	
	`<A HREF="<%URL%>"> <%URLName%> </A>`
	
	`<A HREF="[FMP-FIELD: URL]">`
	`[FMP-FIELD: URLName] </A>`

Author	You often want to be able to identify the author of each item. A common method is to place the author's name below the item, preceded by a dash, right justified, and in italics. Of course, this field may not be required, and you may not have an author for each item. The following HTML code snippets account for that situation.
	
	`<P>`
	`<%if>`
	`<P ALIGN=right>`
	`<I>-<%author1%></I>`
	`<%endif%>`
	`</P>`
	
	`<P>`
	`[FMP-IF: author .neq.]`
	`<P ALIGN=right>`
	`<I>-[FMP-FIELD: author1]</I>`
	`[/FMP-IF]`
	`</P>`

Priority	This field is likely not to be displayed. You can use it to prioritize the items that are entered (as the editor does for news stories). You can use this in conjunction with user options to allow people to choose whether they want all items displayed or just the most important ones. The values for a priority field are usually few and clearly defined—such as the numbers one through five.

TABLE 20-1. Fields for a Web Page Database (Continued)

Field	Description
Key words	This field is typically used to facilitate searches. You can create a database query from a Web page that looks only in this field for items that may be relevant.
Category	You can categorize items in many ways. At RNN, they are categorized by region, but depending on what your Web page deals with, you might want to categorize items by department, topic, location, or anything else that matters. Categories are usually predefined (an HTML value list is good for this). If there are too many categories, they cease to serve their purpose.
Rating	A rating can provide information about the content of the information. Although most people think of ratings in terms of sex or violence, this type of meta-information can also be used to indicate reading level of the text or even the language of the information.
Security	You may want to be able to mark items with different levels of security; as Web pages are automatically generated, items will be accepted or rejecting based on this value. As with priority, this field should be defined to contain a limited number of values.
Approved	This field is often more than a yes or no; there may be many stages of approval before an item is deemed publishable automatically. Note that a common value for this variable is "expired": that lets you mark an item as no longer retrievable without removing it from the database.
Page	Although you can use a field like the Category field to determine where items should be displayed, you may also want to set items explicitly to appear on various pages.

TABLE 20-1. Fields for a Web Page Database (Continued)

In addition to these fields, you may well have a whole host of time stamp fields that indicate when the item was entered, when it was approved, and so forth. As always, the content of the database and the purpose of your Web page determine the degree of security to which you need to attend.

When it comes to retrieving information from the database, you have two choices:

1. You can retrieve items based on space; in the RNN case, the home page retrieves the three items with the highest ratings (on a slow news day, they might all have a rating of two; on another day, they might be rated four and five).

2. You can retrieve items based on content, keywords, or other fields. In this scenario, you might have one (or no) story for a given day; on another day you might have nine.

Your choice of these two methods of retrieving items influences your database design as well as the design of the Web page.

Some Notes on Performance

Some people are hesitant to use databases to drive Web sites because they think that they are sluggish and inefficient. That is not the case with today's computers; in fact, databases have been optimized for performance for decades, and they may well be the most efficient component of your Web site.

Nevertheless, there are some valid concerns in this area. Here are a few issues to consider.

Static versus Dynamic Home Pages

There is certainly some benefit to having your home page as static HTML rather than dynamically generating it from a database. If your home page contains overview information and is accessed by many people, this could make for significant efficiencies.

However, if your site is about changing information—as is the case for a television station—then a static home page just gets in the way. There is no saving in having users see your logo and then having to click to see the dynamic page with up-to-the-minute data that they wanted to see in the first place.

There is a hybrid solution available in extreme cases: you can generate your home page dynamically and then save the HTML source file that was produced. (Do this by opening it in your browser and then using the Save As command from the File menu to save the source.) Then, post the source code as your home page. If your home page is dynamically generated but changes only once a day, this may be a useful technique.

Before doing anything about performance, verify that you have a problem—and that it is not cheaper to buy your way out of it with faster computers. Implementing features—such as saving HTML of dynamically generated pages—may be far more costly. And in many cases, people have discovered that poor performance comes from sluggish network connections. Databases are always blamed for poor performance, and it is often a bum rap.

Caching

Databases cache information that they have retrieved so that if another request comes along for the same information, it may be retrieved without another full-scale database access. The amount of memory (and disk space) available for caching can be set for each database installation. If your site contains a limited amount of information that is displayed over and over, it may be worth increasing the size of your database cache. (This is sometimes called tuning the database.)

Ramdisk

Databases are usually stored on disk, but nothing prevents you from storing most databases in memory—on ramdisks, which appear to the operating system to be just like hard disks. RAM is more expensive than disk, and storing large databases in RAM is likely to be prohibitively expensive; it can also pose problems if the system crashes. However, for relatively small databases that are not updated on line, memory-based disk may provide significant performance improvements.

Cookies, Options, and Parameters

Web sites driven by databases can be so dynamic that the same page is never generated twice. The combinations quickly become enormous, particularly in the case of pages that are generated based on logical criteria rather than physical layout criteria such as page numbers in the database.

Where to Store Them	The logical criteria can be set by the Web site designer or by users. It makes little difference if the search query that generates the data for a page contains parameters set by users or by Webmasters. These criteria can be entered interactively by users (as you do when you use an Internet search engine like Excite or AltaVista), but they can also be set and stored to reflect an individual's preferences.

As discussed in "Cookies" on page 373, you can store any information that you want in a cookie on a user's machine; this enables that machine to have options set that control what will be displayed on a dynamically generated Web page.

If you want to allow people to customize the pages that they view regardless of what computer they are using, you normally need to have them log in with a user name that you can then use to retrieve preferences from your database. Note that these are not necessarily two mutually exclusive choices: you might enforce user login to determine the content that will be displayed, but you might use a cookie to store preferred types of display so that a user can have different choices for a laptop and a desktop machine.

Implementing Options and Preferences	One way to implement options and preferences is to have a special page with a form that lets people choose what they want to see. This form can be used to set a cookie (see "Creating a Cookie" on page 377 and "Retrieving a Cookie" on page 378).

This page can be linked from your home page—or it may not be linked from anywhere. Users who do not know about the cookie-setting page will get the default displays (since they will not have cookies set). Users who know that they can customize their Web pages by going to a page such as http://www.yourdomain.com/userpreferences/securityopts.html can customize their pages. |
| **Where to Place the Cookie** | If the contents of a cookie are going to be used to determine what data is displayed on a database-driven Web page, the contents must be available when the query is launched: that is, they must be available to the page on which the link to the page is (rather than to the page that has been generated). For this reason, you should assign the cookie to the entire domain or site and not to a specific page. |

If your site involves several servers, you may need to set several duplicate cookies—one for each server's domain name.

Summary

This chapter and the ones before it in this section describe the basic ways in which you can use database-driven Web sites. The following chapter explores how you can combine these techniques into a new type of organization.

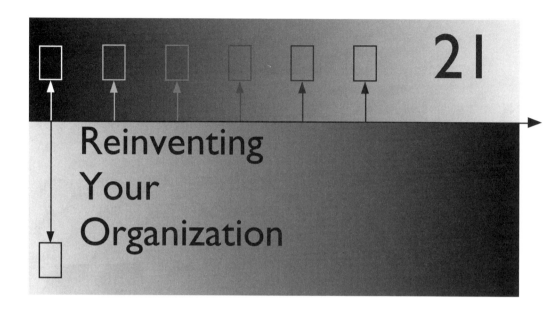

Reinventing Your Organization

21

The previous chapters in this part of the book have outlined real-life examples of the four primary types of database-driven Web sites and have given you some general guidance on the types of pages and databases that you can use to implement them. This chapter is about a different type of topic: changing your organization (or creating a new one) with database-driven Web sites.

The case shown here is precisely that: a company that used the opportunities of technology to open new markets for itself. Their Web site is shown because there are some specific issues (particularly the security features and automated e-mail) that have not been dealt with previously.

TECNON Consulting Group

Parpinelli TECNON srl was established in 1959; it is an international independent consulting organization specializing in energy, petroleum, plastics, and speciality chemicals. In the late 1980s, it joined with DiCesare Sas to bring its consultancy services to the PC market. Then, in 1997, they launched Data-See, a company that creates applications allowing users to query TECNON's databases on the Web.

The databases cover information on plant characteristics, location, processing, and capacities as well as economic and other statistics on the countries of the world. In addition, the databases cover information on over 100 petrochemicals. This information has been gathered over time; it was first placed in a computer database in 1978, and, in the early 1990s, clients were able to access it locally on their personal computers.

In one sense, placing this data on the Web is only an extension of the growth of the company; but in another sense, it is a significant change: the clientele is worldwide to an extent never possible before. There are many companies like this that gather extremely specialized data and publish it at high prices to small customer bases. The development of a global tool like the Web makes it possible to sell small elements of the database at low prices to very large customer bases.

This is more than evolution: it is a very different kind of business. It is also a business that is still evolving. Some companies that produced such industry-specific information started publishing that data electronically at very high prices: prices comparable to those of their paper-based publications. A company that purchases an industry-specific reference each year for a few thousand dollars automatically gets all of the data published in a several-hundred-page book. In the electronic world, a company may want to purchase one page—or one statistic—from the electronic database.

Login

This site is a form of e-commerce: something is being sold. Unlike the computers of the Apple Store, this is electronic information: the transaction is completed on line. As a result, security issues are much greater (and different). After the user has logged off from the Apple Store, there are many opportunities before a computer is physically shipped to stop the transaction if a credit card is rejected or some other problem arises. In this case, there is no such opportunity. Figure 21-1 shows the first login page.

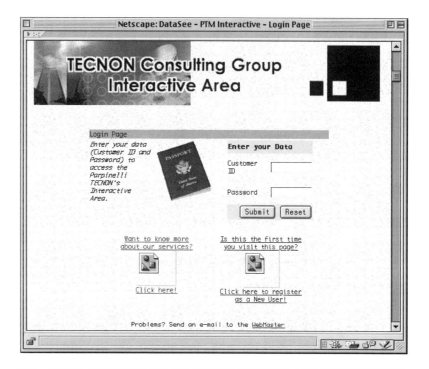

FIGURE 21-1. Login Page

Users who have already visited can enter with their CustomerID; others must register in a new user registration area. (Contrast this with the Apple Store where there is no login and names are required only when the sale is consummated.)

New User
Registration

Users can choose their own ID and password, as shown in Figure 21-2. This is a convenience to users, but it opens some security concerns (see "The Password Issue" on page 360).

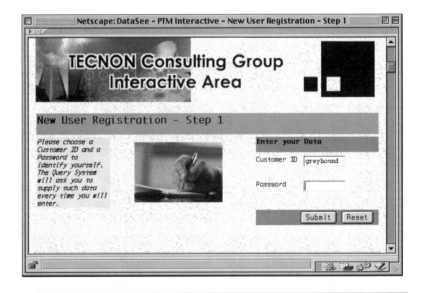

FIGURE 21-2. TECNON New User Registration Page

The registration process takes the user to a standard data entry page. As is usual in such cases, certain fields are required, and they are marked accordingly.

Registration is right at the beginning of the site: as opposed to a consumer-oriented business like the Apple Store, this company is not particularly interested in Web-based window shopping or browsing. Most of their clientele are recommended to them by others, and there is no need to provide samples.

Indeed, after the registration page is submitted, the user receives two acknowledgments. One, shown in Figure 21-3, is a Web-based thank you.

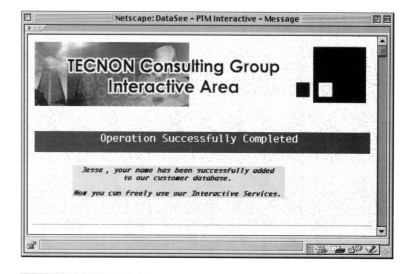

FIGURE 21-3. Registration Confirmation Page

The other confirmation is an e-mail message, which is shown here. (An example of the Perl code to send an e-mail message is provided later in "Automatically Sending E-Mail" on page 468.)

```
From: PTM Consulting Group <webmaster@ttecnon.com>
To: Jesse Feiler <jfeiler@philmontmill.com>
Date: Mon, 27 Jul 1998 21:14:45 "GMT"
Subject:  PTM Interactive - New Registration
Mime-Version: 1.0

Jesse,
Thank you for your registration on PTM's Internet Service!

Please let us know how you feel about the service.
```

```
May we remind you about the following parameters
to allow you to access the system:
   web site:    www.tecnon.com
   User ID:     GREYHOUND
   Password:    xxxx

Please let us know if you would like to buy further credits.
Each credit costs US$2.00, and the minimum purchase is 500
credits. Discounts are available for high volume purchases.

Please find attached an order form in PDF format,
(ADOBE Acrobat reader format - if you do not have it
you can download it at www.adobe.com).
To buy credits please fill in the attached form,
and fax it back to +39 2 4800.xxxx.

For any further information, please do not hesitate
to contact us.

Best regards.

PTM

---------------------------------
/// Parpinelli TECNON Srl (member of the PTM Consulting Group)
\\\ Via Egadi 7 - 20144 Milano - Italy
/// Phone +39.2.43.00.67.1 - Fax +39.2.48.00.81.07
\\\ www.tecnon.com
/// info@tecnon.com
Attachment converted: Tilling:credform.pdf (PDF /CARO)
(0003B469)
```

Home Page

Once users have registered for the site, they can visit the introductory page shown in Figure 21-4.

The products available include online versions of traditional paper-based reports, as well as the database that can be searched interactively over the Web. To search the database, you need to have purchased search credits in advance; if you have done so, you can formulate your searches as you need them.

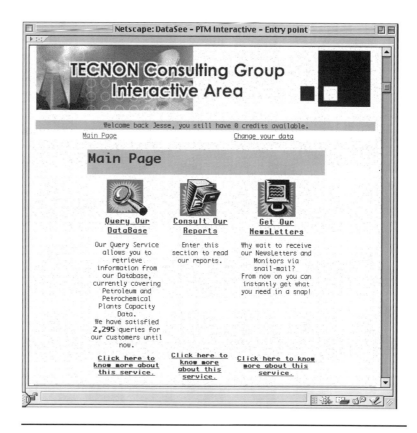

FIGURE 21-4. TECNON Main Page

**Service
Selection**

In Figure 21-5, you see the page that lets you select the table you want to search. (These are Microsoft Access tables, and the site runs on Microsoft Internet Information Servers using ActiveX Server Pages.)

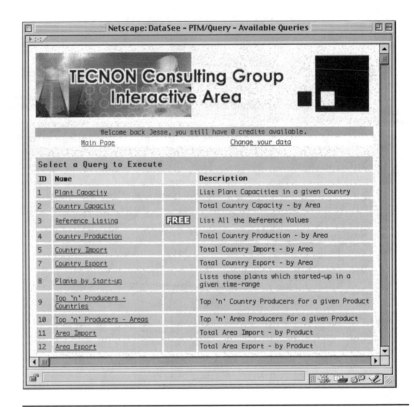

FIGURE 21-5. Table Selection Page

A typical information retrieval system like this may have several pages to select the service required. In this case, Figure 21-5 shows the various tables that can be queried. When you click on each one, you get an appropriate follow-on screen that lets you choose options and values for that table. (This is much like the order options that follow product pages in an online store.) Figure 21-6 shows the follow-on options for the service selected in Figure 21-5.

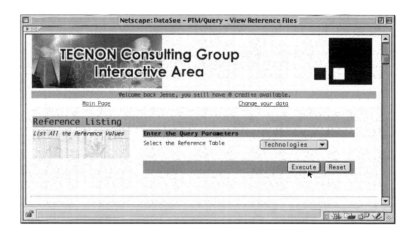

FIGURE 21-6. Options Specification Page

Service Approval	An online information system (particularly one that charges for the information delivered) typically has an approval phase that is missing in other types of sites. Figure 21-7 shows a page that implements this phase.

The purpose of the approval page is to let the user know what the cost of the transaction will be. As here, some preliminary information (the number of records found) is presented; if there are too many (or too few) the user may choose to change the query.

Note that at this point if the user chooses to accept the query, a choice of on-line or file-based output is provided; some systems like this also allow an option to have results sent by e-mail in a text or .pdf file.

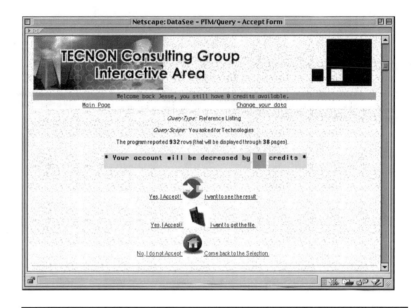

FIGURE 21-7. Approval Confirmation Page

Service Information

The actual data is similar to that retrieved from any database with a Web interface, but there is one important difference: this is not just information, this is the total product that you are providing. The display of information should not just be neat and easy to read, it should also provide every possible feature that you can think of to make it easy to use.

Some of the useful options were shown in Figure 21-7; they include the ability to get the data as a file or in a display. If your HTML and scripting prowess includes the ability to provide resizable columns (or even dynamic rearrangement of columns), that can be very useful to a user.

Whatever you do, make certain that it works, works well, and works quickly. Also, know your users: if they are repeat customers and sophisticated computer users, a spreadsheet or text-delimited file will often be the best choice. If your customers are one-time visitors, you may want to provide a very different interface.

Along those lines, you may even want to provide two types of services: if you are charging for the data, you may be able to charge for the presentation. (For example, if you provide data used by news media, some of them may appreciate your being able to deliver to them automatically camera-ready graphs and charts; others of them may prefer the rawest form of data possible so that they can develop their own graphics.)

How to Get Started

The tools to take advantage of these opportunities are relatively inexpensive and easy to use. Following the ideas in this book, you can quickly install a personal computer–based database such as FileMaker Pro or Microsoft Access and produce a Web interface to your databases using the automated tools that ship with those products. This can provide you with "proof of concept" Web pages and help you to learn about what can be done—and what you personally are interested in doing.

After that, converting the concept to reality may mean no more than moving your database to a public server—or it may mean reimplementing your test site in a database such as Oracle or DB2. In any case, the principles are the same, and you will find vendors competing for your business.

The example used in this chapter automatically sends an e-mail message at one point in the registration process. Most application server products have options to do this; if yours does not, the following section shows you how to write a simple Perl script to send the message.

Automatically Sending E-Mail	Perl is a scripting language that is available on most Web servers. It is used for a variety of purposes and is well suited to tasks such as sending e-mail messages or producing dynamic HTML pages (particularly when they are small).

One way to send e-mail is from the Submit button of a form using a POST method. Such a form could be explicitly filled in by the user, or it could be populated automatically with information on a confirmation screen (such as the one shown in Figure 21-3). Such a form would start with HTML code like this:

```
<FORM ACTION="/cgi-bin/psmform.pl" METHOD=POST
```

In this case, it is assumed that the form contains one field—called "address"—which contains the e-mail address to which to send the message.

You must provide a Perl program (psmform.pl, in this case) to receive the information. That program must do two things:

1. It must generate and send an e-mail message.

2. It must create a Web page to return to the user.

Generating and Sending an E-Mail Message	You do not need to know much about Perl to follow this script; you need know even less to actually use it. Underlined lines need to be customized for your server; the rest can be typed verbatim.

```
#!/usr/bin/perl
```

The file must start with a directive locating the Perl software. Your ISP administrator will tell you what the directory should be. /usr/bin is a common one but not the only one. (It may help to tell your ISP administrator what this line looks like; any modifications will be apparent.)

```
$SENDMAIL = "/usr/sbin/sendmail -t";
```

The script will need access to the server's SENDMAIL program (to actually send the e-mail). Again, your ISP administrator will tell you what this line should look like. In some cases, you will not be allowed to use SENDMAIL. You must talk to your administrator about this; however, most ISPs do let you do this.

You can pass a number of variables in the QUERY_STRING (for GET methods) or STDIN (for POST methods). Parsing QUERY_STRING or reading multiple entries from standard in is beyond the scope of this section but not particularly difficult.

```
read(STDIN,$in,$ENV{'CONTENT_LENGTH'});
```

This line reads the number of characters sent as part of the form.

```
($key, $recipient) = split(/=/,$in);
```

This line of code splits the input into a key (address) and the recipient (something like anaddress@adomain.com) using the required = sign that separates them in the POST method.

```
$filename = "|" . $SENDMAIL;
```

This line names a file for output using the SENDMAIL variable in which you have identified the SENDMAIL program on your server. You do not need to change this line.

```
open (OUT, $filename);
print OUT "To: ", $recipient, "\n";
print OUT "From: ", yourname@yourdomain.com"}, "\n";
print OUT "Subject:", New User Registration, " \n";
print OUT "\n";
```

You generate the e-mail header with the lines shown here; you must substitute your return address and the subject for the message. (Remember that the return address need not be from the domain of the server: it should be the address at which you normally receive mail.)

The message you want to send is then sent using print OUT lines of code, with a new line character (\n) at the end of each line. For example, you might send:

```
print OUT "Thank you for registering with us.\n";
print OUT "\n";
print OUT "We hope to see you in the future.\n";
print OUT "Sincerely,\n";
print OUT "Our Company\n";
```

(Note the blank line between the first and third lines of text.)

```
close (OUT);
```

Finally, you close the file and the e-mail is sent.

Creating a Web Page

Next, your script needs to create a Web page to return to the user. The following code produces an HTML page that says Thank You and has a link to a page called newregistrant.html; that link is an anchor called Return. Any of these items (underlined here) can be changed and customized.

```
print "Content-type: text/html\n\n";
print "<html>\n";
print "<head>\n";
print "Thank you". \n";
print "<CENTER><A HREF="newregistrant.html">Return </A>
    </CENTER> \n";
print "</body></html>\n";
exit 0;
```

Summary

Implementing a Web site like this is not particularly difficult: its elements are not different from those of any of the Web sites discussed previously. The obstacles (if any) are more likely to be organizational than technical.

The opportunities for database-driven Web sites parallel the four types of Web sites described in his book:

1. You can expand your services beyond your existing users, your immediate neighborhood, and the hours that you are open for business (information-based sites such as MoMA's DADABASE are good examples of this).

2. You can create new services that you have not been able to offer before (UVME's sharing data on the Web is one such service).

3. You can develop new ways of working—the Apple Store with its build-to-order business model is a good case in point (implementing it required changes throughout the corporation—including changes within factories that produce the computers).

4. You can compete with—and often surpass—other (and larger) organizations by nimbly using the Web, databases, and your imagination to provide services that heretofore were the province of major enterprises (RNN-TV's Web site is an example).

These are not trivial changes to your organization—greatly enlarged customer or user bases, new services, new ways of working, and competing with much bigger players in your market. They all have in common the possibility of large rewards, and they require imagination and commitment. They do not require enormous investments in equipment or expertise: the point of the Web's rapid growth is that it is basically so simple.

And it is important to remember that these opportunities are open to anyone: including your competitors.

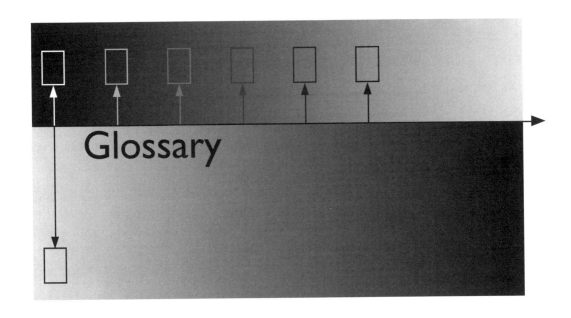

Glossary

24x7 Twenty-four hours a day, seven days a week. Pronounced "twenty-four seven" or "twenty-four by seven." Used in reference to operations that must always be available; 24x7 often connotes attended operation of a system.

applet A small piece of computer code that is typically downloaded from a Web site as part of a Web page. Applets are often written in machine-independent languages (such as Java). They may be used to enhance the user experience with animation; they may also be used for editing and data access. Scripts (written in Visual Basic, JavaScript, and Perl) are similar to applets, but they contain instructions that the browser must fully convert. Applets contain partially generated computer code, and require less work from the browser.

application
A term used to refer to a computer program (as in a "word processing application") or to a process developed for a specific functional purpose (as in "the insurance claim processing application").

application server
Software that typically interacts with a database and template files in order to produce dynamic HTML for database-driven applications. Also called "middleware."

browser
Programs such as Netscape Communicator, Microsoft Internet Explorer, or NCSA Mosaic that let you explore the World Wide Web. Proprietary systems such as America Online and private organizations' software may use their own browsers.

CGI (common gateway interface)
The standard for communication between a Web server application and other programs. CGI files are often stored in the cgi-bin directory on a server.

controls
Parts of Web-based forms that you can manipulate. They include buttons, text areas, and drop-down menus.

CRT screens
Cathode ray tubes. The devices used to view computer data before flat-panel displays were invented.

data element
An entry in a database structure, such as age, address, or price. Each data element has a name; a data element usually has many values in a database—each value corresponds to one observation, record, or individual.

database
A collection of data that is organized for easy storage and retrieval. Databases are managed by database software such as Oracle or Microsoft Access.

database project
A user-created set of database data that includes data entry screens, documentation, assistance, and reports.

database software	Software that manages databases. Some products are Microsoft Access, DB2, Oracle, Sybase, and FileMaker Pro.
DBMS	Database management system. Database software.
DNS	Domain name system tables. The Internet addressing tables that translate domain names to IP addresses. DNS tables are maintained at central Internet sites ("base servers"); their contents are propagated throughout the Internet as routine addressing is carried out.
domain	A named location on the Internet that corresponds to a specific IP address. The connection between the domain name (such as www.philmontmill.com) and an IP address (such as 205.231.144.10) is maintained by DNS tables.
DHCP	Dynamic host configuration protocol. A local networking protocol that assigns variable IP addresses to computers as they attempt to connect to the Internet.
e-commerce	The use of the Internet for commercial purposes such as buying and selling goods and information. E-commerce Web sites are often powered by databases.
fields	A single piece of data within a database record. (Also called a data element.) The contents of a field or data element are data values. A field (such as "age") may have many values (reflecting the ages of individuals whose information is contained in the database).
firmware	Computer instructions that are stored in a hardware device (rather than in memory or on a medium such as disk or CD-ROM). Firmware is normally installed when the computer is assembled. It may be upgraded later, but is generally regarded as fixed and immutable for most purposes.
flat file	A traditional computer file (such as text or graphics) that does not have the indexing and fast retrieval features of database files.

FTP	File transfer protocol. The Internet protocol used to transfer files between computers.
Gopher	The Internet text-based menu system for organizing data. Largely replaced by the World Wide Web.
GIF	Graphical interchange format. A format (including image compression) that is used primarily for computer-generated images on the Internet. Compare to JPEG.
hot	Part of a computer image that responds to a mouse click. Buttons and links on Web pages are hot.
HTML	HyperText Markup Language. The language used to design and format Web pages. If you use a graphical Web page editor, you may rarely see raw HTML.
IDE	Integrated development environment. A graphically based environment that contains a program text editor, compiler, linker, and debugger. IDEs allow programmers to switch between writing and testing code; often, changes can be made to source code while the application is running.
intranet	A network that uses Internet protocols but which is not open to the general public.
IP address	A set of four numbers that identify an Internet node. The numbers are separated by dots as in 205.231.144.10. IP addresses are often associated with domain names which are easier for people to deal with.
JPEG	A format (including image compression) that is typically used for natural images (photographs, for example), on the Internet. JPEG compression is "lossy"—each repeated saving of a JPEG file loses part of the image data.
key	A field that is used to retrieve or identify data. Keys are usually indexed in a database by the database software for fast retrieval.

legacy	Old systems, files, and databases that need to be incorporated into current processes.
LAN	Local area network. A network within a limited area (room, floor, building, airplane, or space station). LANs may be connected to other networks, but themselves are self-contained and are not subject to public regulation.
meta-data	Data about data. Meta-data includes names of fields (as distinct from their values).
middleware	Software that exists between database data and user interface manipulation. Often used as a synonym for "application servers."
MIME	Multipurpose Internet Mail Extension. A format that allows for non-text data to be incorporated into messages.
normalization	A set of rules for structuring database data to avoid duplication, improve efficiency, and minimize operational problems.
ODBC	Open Database Connectivity is a language that lets data sources (databases, flat files, spreadsheets, etc.) communicate with applications. It is based on SQL queries. ODBC is installed on a computer as an extension to the operating system; ODBC drivers for specific types of data sources are available from various vendors. The use of ODBC makes it possible for applications to communicate at a high level with data sources about which they have little knowledge.
plug-in	A section of code that can be added to an application (such as a Web server). It adheres to the application's standards and is called by the application as necessary. Plug-ins may be used to handle database access. They are often developed by third parties (that is, not by the Web server developer). In addition to Web servers, plug-ins are often used to add functionality to graphics programs such as Photoshop and QuarkXPress.
port	The entity on a network node that communicates with other network entities. A given computer typically has a variety of

numbered ports. Each port number is assigned to a specific service (for example, http is typically port 80). The communications link for the computer can support a variety of ports. All messages for a given port are routed to a specific application (such as a Web server for port 80).

program

Also known as an application or application program. The software that performs tasks using hardware and communications devices.

query

A request to a database for information. Queries may also be used to add information to a database. Today, most queries are formulated using SQL.

record

A given data instance—one student, one shopping order, etc. Each data instance consists of the data values for each of the fields in the table.

RFC

Request for Comments. Internet standards are developed collaboratively within the Internet community. Requests for Comments are issued and input accepted until a standard is set. These standards may later be modified or replaced. RFCs are numbered. For the ultimate word on specific Internet concepts, consult the RFCs. You can find them in many places including www.internic.net; you can also search for "RFC" with a search engine.

scalability

The ability of a system (hardware or software) to be enlarged or decreased in size. Scalability often refers to large changes in size such as going from a Web site that supports 50 transactions a day to one that supports 50,000 transactions a day. Typically, such drastic changes have stressed hardware and software. Desktop software often does not scale up; likewise, enterprise software does not scale down.

schema

The structure of a database table.

search engine

A Web site or application that lets you search the Internet using words or combinations of words. Search engines are contrasted with prepared indices in which you must know the identification code for the item you wish to retrieve.

session
For dial-in computer users, the connection that is established over a telephone line and a modem with an Internet service provider. For other users, the connection that is established between log in of a password and user ID and log out.

SGML
Structured Generalized Markup Language. Languages that combine formatting and content in a text-based document. HTML is an example of an SGML.

site
A registered location on the Internet; a site normally has a domain name. Sites may contain subsites that may or may not be located on the same computer.

Standards Information
Excellent glossaries of terms are available on the Internet. One of the best for telecommunications issues is *Federal Standard 1037C: Glossary of Telecommunications Terms*. It is available at http://ntia.its.bldrdoc.gov/fs-1037/dir-001/_0067.htm.

W3C—The World Wide Web Consortium develops standards for Web protocols including HTML. You can access W3C at http://www.w3.org/.

SQL standards can be obtained from the American National Standards Institute at http://web.ansi.org.

Information about standards and terminology can also be obtained from vendors of specific products.

stateless
Usually used in reference to HTML, stateless refers to the fact that the server does not store information about the client between transmissions. As a result, each message sent to the server must contain all of the data that the server will need to process the transaction.

system
A non-specific term that can apply to a specific operation ("payroll system"), hardware (computer system), or application software. A source of confusion in many cases.

table	In HTML, tables are used to organize information into rows and columns. Forms are often used to collect data from users; tables are often used to display results of database queries. In relational databases, tables refer to the organized structure of data. Rows (records) and columns (fields) contain observations for each individual/instance and data element.
teletype	1950s and 1960s data entry and display devices. Teletypes use continuous rolls of paper. They contain mechanisms to advance the paper (but not to reverse it). A number of controls are still part of standard communications protocols (top of page, top of form, etc.).
template file	A file containing part of a Web page. Written in HTML, template files have special elements that enable an application server to merge dynamic information with the prepared HTML in the template.
text document	A document containing only visible text characters (no graphics, no applets, etc.).
transaction	A process that may consist of a number of database accesses (retrievals, entries, and updates), but which is considered as a single unit. Transactions can typically be cancelled or rolled back: in those cases, all parts of the transaction are cancelled or rolled back.
URL	Uniform resource locators. An Internet address.
value	The contents of a field in a given record; alternatively, the contents of a row in a given column.
Web server	A program that provides Web pages on demand to clients. A Web server is assigned a port on a computer; all messages that come to that computer's port go to the Web server. A Web server may also be the computer that runs a Web server. By using several port numbers, a single Web server computer can run a number of Web server programs.
Webmaster	The person responsible for a Web site.

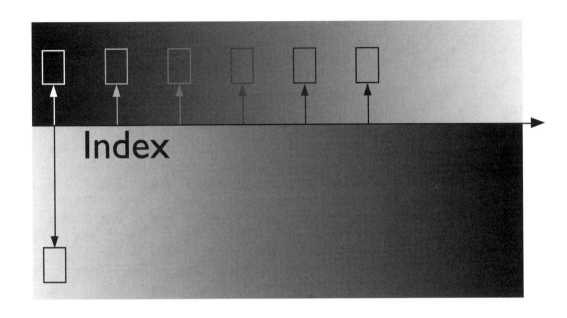

Index

Principal entries and definitions are shown in **bold**.

I

About the Author

JESSE FEILER is Software Director of Philmont Software Mill. He has served as consultant, author, and/or speaker for organizations including the Federal Reserve Bank of New York, Prodigy, Kodak, Young & Rubicam, The Josef and Anni Albers Foundation, and Yale University Press.

His technical credits span mainframes to personal computers including machines from IBM, Apple, Burroughs, and Control Data; databases from IBM, Burroughs, Oracle, Microsoft, and Claris; object-oriented frameworks including MacApp and OpenStep; languages ranging from Fortran, Algol, and Cobol to Pascal, C++, Java, and Objective-C; as well as a host of end user and productivity tools from vendors including Microsoft, Apple, IBM, and Claris.

He is the author of a number of books including *FileMaker Pro and the World Wide Web* (FileMaker Press, 1999); *Programming FileMaker* (Morgan Kaufmann, 1999); *Cyberdog* (AP Professional, 1996); *ClarisWorks 5.0: The Internet, New Media, and Paperless Documents* (Claris Press, 1998); *Rhapsody Developer's Guide* (AP Professional, 1997); *Essential OpenDoc* (with Anthony Meadow, Addison-Wesley, 1996); and *Real World Apple Guide* (M&T Books, 1995). His *Application Servers: Powering the Web-Based Enterprise* (Morgan Kaufmann, 1999) is a companion to this book.

Together with Barbara Butler, he wrote *Finding and Fixing Your Year 2000 Problem: A Guide for Small Businesses and Organizations* (AP Professional, 1998). They have spoken, written, and consulted extensively on the Year 2000 problem.

Jesse Feiler serves on the boards of the HB Playwrights Foundation, the Philmont Public Library, and the Mid-Hudson Library System. He is the 1997 recipient of the Velma K. Moore Award given by the New York State Association of Library Boards for "exemplary service and dedication to libraries."

Philmont Software Mill is located on the Web at www.philmontmill.com.